Michael Hughes is currently a Lecturer in the School of History, University of Liverpool, and from 1990 to 1998 was Lecturer in the Department of Government, Brunel University. He is the author of *Inside the Enigma: British Officials in Russia, 1900–39*.

STUDIES IN DIPLOMACY

General Editor: G. R. Berridge, Professor of International Politics and Director of Research, Centre for the Study of Diplomacy, University of Leicester

The series was launched in 1994. Its chief purpose is to encourage original scholarship on the theory and practice of international diplomacy, including its legal regulation. The interests of the series thus embrace such diplomatic functions as signalling, negotiation and consular work, and methods such as summitry and the multilateral conference. Whilst it has a sharp focus on diplomacy at the expense of foreign policy, therefore, the series has no prejudice as to historical period or approach. It also aims to include manuals on protocol and other aspects of diplomatic practice which will be of immediate, day-to-day relevance to professional diplomats. A final ambition is to reprint inaccessible classic works on diplomacy.

Titles include:

Andrew F. Cooper (*editor*)
NICHE DIPLOMACY
Middle Powers after the Cold War

David H. Dunn (*editor*)
DIPLOMACY AT THE HIGHEST LEVEL
The Evolution of International Summitry

Brian Hocking (*editor*)
FOREIGN MINISTRIES
Change and Adaptation

Michael Hughes
DIPLOMACY BEFORE THE RUSSIAN REVOLUTION
Britain, Russia and the Old Diplomacy, 1894–1917

Donna Lee
MIDDLE POWERS AND COMMERCIAL DIPLOMACY
British Influence at the Kennedy Trade Round

Jan Melissen (*editor*)
INNOVATION IN DIPLOMATIC PRACTICE

Peter Neville
APPEASING HITLER
The Diplomacy of Sir Nevile Henderson, 1937–39

M. J. Peterson
RECOGNITION OF GOVERNMENTS
Legal Doctrine and State Practice, 1815–1995

Gary D. Rawnsley
RADIO DIPLOMACY AND PROPAGANDA
The BBC and VOA in International Politics, 1956–64

TAIWAN'S INFORMAL DIPLOMACY AND PROPAGANDA

Studies in Diplomacy
Series Standing Order ISBN 0–333–71495–4
(*outside North America only*)

You can receive future titles in this series as they are published by placing a standing order. Please contact your bookseller or, in case of difficulty, write to us at the address below with your name and address, the title of the series and the ISBN quoted above.

Customer Services Department, Macmillan Distribution Ltd
Houndmills, Basingstoke, Hampshire RG21 6XS, England

Diplomacy before the Russian Revolution

Britain, Russia and the Old Diplomacy, 1894–1917

Michael Hughes
Lecturer
School of History
University of Liverpool

First published in Great Britain 2000 by
MACMILLAN PRESS LTD
Houndmills, Basingstoke, Hampshire RG21 6XS and London
Companies and representatives throughout the world

A catalogue record for this book is available from the British Library.

ISBN 0-333-65942-2

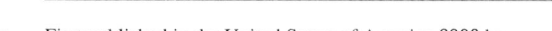

 First published in the United States of America 2000 by
ST. MARTIN'S PRESS, INC.,
Scholarly and Reference Division,
175 Fifth Avenue, New York, N.Y. 10010

ISBN 0-312-22548-2

Library of Congress Cataloging-in-Publication Data
Hughes, Michael, 1961–
Diplomacy before the Russian Revolution : Britain, Russia and the
old diplomacy, 1894–1917 / Michael Hughes.
p. cm. — (Studies in diplomacy)
Includes bibliographical references and index.
ISBN 0-312-22548-2 (cloth)
1. Russia—Foreign relations—Great Britain. 2. Great Britain–
–Foreign relations—Russia. 3. Russia—Foreign
relations—1894–1917. I. Title. II. Series.
JZ1615.A57G7 1999
327.47041'09'041—dc21   99–25939
                                                   CIP

© Michael Hughes 2000

All rights reserved. No reproduction, copy or transmission of this publication may be made without written permission.

No paragraph of this publication may be reproduced, copied or transmitted save with written permission or in accordance with the provisions of the Copyright, Designs and Patents Act 1988, or under the terms of any licence permitting limited copying issued by the Copyright Licensing Agency, 90 Tottenham Court Road, London W1P 0LP.

Any person who does any unauthorised act in relation to this publication may be liable to criminal prosecution and civil claims for damages.

The author has asserted his right to be identified as the author of this work in accordance with the Copyright, Designs and Patents Act 1988.

This book is printed on paper suitable for recycling and made from fully managed and sustained forest sources.

10 9 8 7 6 5 4 3 2 1
09 08 07 06 05 04 03 02 01 00

Printed and bound in Great Britain by
Antony Rowe Ltd, Chippenham, Wiltshire

Contents

List of Tables		vii
Preface		ix
1	The Old Diplomacy and Anglo–Russian Relations	1
2	The British Foreign Office and Russia	20
3	The British Embassy in St Petersburg	62
4	British Consuls in Russia	97
5	The Russian Ministry of Foreign Affairs 1894–1914	124
6	The British and Russian Diplomatic Establishments 1914–17	178
Conclusion		200
Select Bibliography		208
Index		218

List of Tables

2.1	Educational Backgrounds of Individuals Serving as Senior Clerk or Above in the Foreign Office 1894–1918	22
2.2	Educational Backgrounds of Individuals Appointed as Junior Clerk in the Foreign Office 1908–13	22
3.1	British Ambassadors in St Petersburg (1894–1918)	65
3.2	Counsellors and Secretaries at the St Petersburg Embassy (1894–1918)	66
4.1	Value of the Total Exports of the Produce and Manufactures of the United Kingdom 1895–9	99
4.2	Cost of Maintaining British Consular Establishments in Various Countries in 1910	100
4.3	Russian Experience of Consular Officials in Post on 1 July 1913	103

Preface

This is not a book about British policy towards Russia during the last twenty years before the 1917 Revolution. Nor is it a book about Anglo–Russian relations in the same period. It is instead a book about the organisation and operation of the British and Russian diplomatic establishments during the final years of what has conventionally been termed the 'old diplomacy'. The study of diplomats has become a deeply unfashionable pursuit among scholars during the past 20 years. This is to a certain extent justified, a reaction against a time when the study of international affairs was reduced to a scrutiny of official records produced by the men who staffed the embassies and chancelleries of the great powers. As Keith Neilson points out in his recent study of British policy toward Russia in the reign of Tsar Nicholas II, the foreign policy-making process almost always involves a much wider range of actors, each with their own motivations and perceptions. Nevertheless, the institutions and personnel of 'proper' diplomacy did play a pivotal role in the organisation of international life in the years before 1914, with the result that the study of the diplomats and diplomatic institutions of the period must remain a topic of considerable importance.

The present book has two main themes. The first emphasises the extent to which the organisation and operation of the national diplomatic establishments of pre-war Europe were governed by domestic considerations. This is not to deny that there was a strong sense of solidarity between the foreign-policy 'professionals' of the great powers during the years before the First World War, nor that the existence of a strong sense of corporate identity helped in the resolution of conflicts between national governments. It is, however, important to remember that the diplomats of pre-war Europe, like diplomats today, operated in two distinct arenas. They were in the first place members of national bureaucratic institutions, subject to domestic administrative rules and political norms. At the same time, however, they were by the very nature of their work integrated into an international milieu that had its own distinct perspectives and values. One of the major criticisms made by the vociferous opponents of the 'old diplomacy' in the first two decades of the twentieth century was that diplomats and foreign ministry officials had become too detached from the values and constraints of the political and administrative systems to which they belonged. The reality was, however, a good deal more complicated. The study of the British and Russian diplomatic establishments developed in the following chapters shows that the autonomy of the foreign policy 'professionals' varied enormously according to a whole host of circumstances, ranging from changes in the constitutional distribution of power through to the domestic political salience of a particular international issue.

The second theme of the book is closely linked to the first. Critics of the old diplomacy in pre-war Europe and America seemed to imagine that the diplomatic institutions and procedures which existed in 1914 had changed little over the previous decades. Many historians have subsequently given credence to this view by arguing that the First World War marked a fundamental shift from the old to the new diplomacy, characterised by a decline in the status of professional diplomats and the emergence of new diplomatic actors. In reality, major changes were taking place in the organisation and operation of diplomatic life in Europe *before* the outbreak of war. While these were to some extent manifested in developments in the international arena, the biggest changes took place in the way in which particular diplomatic establishments were located within the administrative and political fabric of the nation state. It will be seen in the following chapters that attempts took place during the first decade of the twentieth century to modernise both the British and Russian diplomatic establishments, in an effort to make them more effective at responding to the growing press of international business. While Paul Lauren has rightly shown that this trend was international in its scope, both the initiation and the implementation of reform in practice reflected the dictates of domestic circumstances. Even more importantly, the place of the two diplomatic establishments in the foreign policy making process of their respective countries fluctuated sharply according to a complex configuration of factors, ranging from the state of public opinion through to the determination of other political and administrative actors to involve themselves in international affairs. In short, the changing *modus operandi* and structure of the British and Russian diplomatic establishments were profoundly affected by developments which took place in the domestic environment.

A brief word is also required about the methodology employed in the following pages. There is a tension in any work of this kind between the need to construct an argument while at the same time remaining sensitive to the fact that the complexities and contingencies of empirical evidence seldom lend themselves to neat conclusions. The selection of the British and Russian diplomatic establishments as the focus for this study has been governed by two factors. In the first place they would seem to represent, at least at first glance, two extremes on a kind of continuum. The British Foreign Office and Diplomatic Service operated in a political system governed by the norms of liberal representative government, and formed part of an administrative structure that had undergone major changes since the Northcote–Trevelyan reforms of the mid nineteenth century. The Russian Ministry of Foreign Affairs, by contrast, formed part of a highly-centralised and (at least before 1906) autocratic political system, infamous across Europe for its corruption and inefficiency. In reality, however, the following pages show that changes in the organisation and operation of both the British and Russian diplomatic establishments can be looked at through a similar prism. The influence of diplomats and foreign ministry officials in the two countries was to a large degree governed by administrative and political developments over which they had only limited control. It was for this reason that senior members of the two diplomatic establishments were forced to engage in constant bureaucratic battles, both for resources and – far more importantly – for the right to assert themselves as primary agents in the foreign policy making process. While limitations of space make it impossible to extend the analysis to other diplomatic establishments, a review of the situation in France or Germany would doubtless conclude that a similar situation existed there as well.

A good deal of attention is given in the pages that follow to the developments leading up to the Anglo–Russian convention of 1907. This is not necessarily to argue that the convention was the pivotal moment in Anglo–Russian relations before 1914 (although such a case could certainly be made). It is, rather, a reflection of the fact that the general themes of this book can be illustrated by focusing on a comparatively limited series of events. A study of foreign policy making in Britain and Russia during this period shows how the operation of the two diplomatic establishments could change rapidly in a short period of time, given certain changes elsewhere in the political and administrative systems of the two countries. It is therefore virtually impossible to come to any definite conclusion about such broad questions as the role and influence of the British Foreign Office or the Russian Foreign Ministry during the years before 1914. Such questions can only be assessed by looking at a particular issue at a given moment in time. All that can be usefully done here is to identify in a concrete historical setting some of the factors that influenced the organisation and operation of national diplomatic establishments in a certain period.

I have of course incurred numerous debts in the course of my research. I must therefore confine myself to thanking Geoff Berridge for his support and understanding during this project, and to acknowledge the fact that my previous employer, Brunel University, provided me with a short period of study leave. My numerous intellectual debts will be apparent from the end notes and bibliography. I should also thank the editors of *Diplomacy and Statecraft* and *European History Quarterly* for giving me permission to draw on work I have already published. Material in the Hardinge Papers is reproduced by permission of the Syndics of Cambridge University Library; material in the Royal Archives is reproduced by the gracious permission of Her Majesty Queen Elizabeth II; Crown copyright material in the Public Record Office is reproduced by permission of Her Majesty's Stationery Office.

This book is dedicated to Katie, who has been a constant reminder that all the most important things in life take place outside universities.

Michael Hughes
London

1 The Old Diplomacy and Anglo–Russian Relations

Any bilateral relationship has its own particular character, a texture determined by the complexities of history, geography and culture. These factors can sometimes make for harmony, as with the 'special relationship' between the United States and Great Britain in the years after 1945, when the dictates of the international environment and a common Anglo-Saxon heritage helped to forge an elite consensus on many key international economic and military questions. The Franco–German relationship, by contrast, was characterised by tension and conflict for three generations following the Franco–Prussian War of 1870–1, an international 'fault-line' that created instability across the European continent. This is not of course to argue that there is anything inevitable about the pattern of international friendships and enmities, although there can be little doubt that national stereotypes sometimes acquire a depth and resonance that endure far beyond the circumstances that give them birth. Over the past 100 years, the stereotypical British view of France, at both a popular and governmental level, has remained somewhat less than benign despite the *entente cordiale* and two world wars in which the countries fought a common enemy. Nevertheless, both images and realities can change across time, as witnessed so dramatically by the development of a new Franco–German relationship in the years since 1945.

The Anglo–Russian relationship has for centuries presented something of a paradox. The two countries have fought on the same side in three major conflicts since the closing years of the Napoleonic Wars, while the only significant direct military confrontation took place in the Crimea during the 1850s. At the same time, however, relations between Great Britain and Russia have seldom been warm since the time when the explorer Richard Chancellor arrived at the Court of Ivan the Terrible in the middle of the sixteenth century. Within a few decades, the writings of English adventurers and diplomats routinely portrayed Russia as an alien and barbaric land, where a wild and uncivilised people were governed by an autocratic Tsar untrammelled by considerations of law and humanity.[1] Even though England and Russia seldom came into direct conflict during the sixteenth and seventeenth centuries, by the end of the eighteenth century Anglo–Russian tension was becoming a well-established feature of the international landscape.[2] The real deterioration in the relationship between the two countries was, however, a product of the nineteenth century, when the defeat of Napoleon signalled the start of an era of comparative peace in Europe, which in turn allowed the great powers to concentrate their attention on matters of empire. As Russia moved its frontiers ever southward, while the British continued to strengthen their rule in India, the whole of central Asia became a critical flashpoint between the two countries. The era of the Great Game, characterised by mutual suspicion and complex military and political manoeuvrings of a kind familiar to any student of the Cold War, determined the texture of relations between London and St Petersburg until 1907, when a formal *entente* was established between the two countries, signalling a rapprochement that allowed them to turn their attention to European politics. While numerous disagreements dogged Anglo–Russian relations during the following years, the 1907 agreement, by complementing the existing Franco–Russian alliance and the Anglo–French *entente cordiale*, helped to solidify the division of Europe into the two great blocks that finally went to war in 1914.

The texture of a particular bilateral relationship is not simply determined by a certain configuration of strategic, economic and cultural factors; it is also profoundly influenced by the way in which the relationship is managed by those responsible for the conduct of international relations. During the past 500 years, there has been a general growth in the density and complexity of the interactions between European states and societies, but by far and away the most dramatic changes have taken place in the past 80 years or so.[3] Before the First World War, the formal institutional apparatus of diplomacy, with its panoply of embassies and foreign ministries, was central to the conduct of relations between the various European powers. While the following chapters will suggest that the *domestic* power and influence of national diplomatic establishments varied from country to country in the years before the First World War, European states still primarily dealt with one another through the established mechanisms and institutions of diplomacy. Other political and administrative channels did operate from time to time, but there was nothing that resembled the dense pattern of interactions between politicians and civil servants which characterises the relationship between contemporary European states. During the years between 1894 and 1914, the formal relationship between Russia and Great Britain adhered to this general pattern. No British prime minister or foreign secretary visited Russia in the 20 years between 1894 and 1914; nor did any senior British politician of the period have personal or family links with Russia of a kind that might have served as a basis for informal negotiations or discussions. There were close ties between the Romanov and Windsor dynasties, while King Edward VII played a considerable role in the moves which led up to the 1907 Anglo–Russian convention, but on the whole such episodes as royal visits were important for their symbolic value rather than as a setting for significant negotiations between monarchs. Most communications between the two governments were handled by their respective embassies and foreign ministries. This is not, however, to suggest that professional diplomats were necessarily the architects of foreign policy; nor does it signify that they were able to control the actions of other state employees in matters affecting Britain's relations with Russia. Many of the tensions that erupted between London and St Petersburg before 1907 were either the result of policies with which most members of the two diplomatic establishments disagreed, or a consequence of unauthorised actions by individuals ranging from Russian subalterns in central Asia through to the Viceroy in India. It is true, however, that attempts to manage and resolve these problems were largely conducted by diplomats operating according to the rules and rituals that governed their profession. The study of their mentality and behaviour is therefore a subject of great importance. The pressures that determined the course of the Anglo–Russian relationship in the critical years before 1914 were largely mediated through the institutional prism of the diplomatic establishments of the two countries.

THE ASSAULT ON THE 'OLD DIPLOMACY'

The men who worked in the foreign ministries and embassies of Europe before the First World War have not had a good press. The carnage that followed the outbreak of hostilities in 1914 created an understandable search for scapegoats who could be blamed for failing to prevent the bloodshed of the Somme and Ypres. The horrors of war provoked a searching critique of the institutions and procedures which were widely believed to be the hallmark of international diplomacy in the late nineteenth and early twentieth centuries. Hundreds of books and articles were published attacking the 'old diplomacy'. In the United States, President Wilson launched his crusade for a 'new diplomacy' that would transform the structure of the international system, by creating a new international organisation capable of providing 'mutual guarantees of political independence and territorial integrity to great and small states alike'. Despite a degree of caution on the part of the French and British governments, the President was eventually able to take advantage of his country's new-found international power and influence to promote the cause of the League of Nations at the Versailles Peace Conference.[4] Attacks on the old diplomacy also became increasingly audible in the countries of western Europe as the war progressed at the cost of millions of lives. The breakdown of the coalition of the 'forces of order' and the 'forces of movement' across Europe, from 1916 onwards, signalled the beginning of a widespread rejection of the assumptions of the old diplomacy in countries like Britain, France and Germany.[5] The desire to extend democratic control over the foreign policy process, when combined with a growing reluctance among left-of-centre politicians to endorse expansionist war aims, stimulated a revulsion against 'secret diplomacy' and the supposed machinations of professional diplomats. In Britain, members of organisations such as the Union of Democratic Control campaigned for a peace settlement that would allocate territories according to the wishes of the local population, rather than in line with the dictates of the diplomats and their political masters.[6] In Germany, a significant number of Social Democrat deputies began to question the uncritical 'defencist' position taken by a majority of their party in the summer of 1914, preferring to emphasise once again the essential class character of the war. In France, left-wing deputies in the National Assembly repeatedly attacked the Clemenceau government and its predecessors for refusing to consider any means for concluding the war other than by a complete military surrender by the central powers. By the end of 1916, a growing number of American liberals, German socialists and British radicals were committed to a belief that public opinion in all countries was at all times inherently peace-loving, with the result that the establishment of greater popular control over those responsible for making foreign policy would lead to a reduction in international tension.

While the massive scale of slaughter on the battlefields of Europe provided a catalyst for the growing chorus of attacks on the old diplomacy that developed in almost all the belligerent countries after 1914, anxiety about the organisation and operation of national diplomatic establishments was on the rise from the end of the nineteenth century. Professional diplomats had of course been the target of criticism for many years before this. One of Goethe's characters described the typical ambassador as a 'punctilious fool', while the British radical John Bright famously condemned the nineteenth-century British Diplomatic Service as a source of 'outdoor relief' for the aristocracy. It was only from around 1900, however, that a more concerted assault began to take place on diplomatic institutions and the men who staffed them.

The pattern of this assault varied from country to country, reflecting diverse patterns of political culture and political circumstance. In the United States, for example, diplomats serving abroad attracted widespread opprobium as effete representatives of a snobbish Eastern establishment, unable to comprehend the sentiments of a population supposedly imbued with egalitarian values. There was not, however, any widespread popular concern that American diplomats serving abroad, or bureaucrats working in the State Department in Washington, were able to exercise an undue influence on the foreign policy process. The American public may have believed that its diplomats were incompetent, but they did not generally consider them to be malevolent.[7] In most European countries, by contrast, the pattern of criticism levelled against the various national diplomatic services before 1914 was more complex and wide-ranging. Critics from within the political establishment usually focused on administrative shortcomings and the failure of professional diplomats to defend the national interest with sufficient vigour. Critics on the left of the political spectrum were by contrast more worried about the elitist character of the diplomatic service and the supposed inability of some governments to establish control over the activities of their officials. A brief glance at some of the attacks made on the British, French and Russian diplomatic establishments before 1914 can illustrate the diverse concerns of their critics.

The British Foreign Office became something of a *bête noire* for many British radicals in the years after 1900, viewed as the institutional architect of a foreign policy that was both immoral and dangerous. Writers such as the journalist E.D. Morel attacked the organisation for being 'closed to men of brains, education and intelligence', arguing that it was instead staffed by unimaginative officials who failed to understand the need for a new and more ethical approach to the conduct of international relations.[8] Morel was particularly critical of the secrecy surrounding the formulation and implementation of British foreign policy, which he believed made it impossible for Parliament to ensure effective scrutiny and control.[9] These themes were echoed by many other writers, including H.N. Brailsford and Norman Angell, as well as by a considerable number of MPs belonging to the Labour Party and the radical wing of the Liberal Party. Criticism grew particularly sharply after the appointment of Sir Edward Grey as Foreign Secretary, at the end of 1905, particularly once the burgeoning tension with Germany seemed to make war a real possibility. Many Labour and some Liberal MPs were frustrated by the convention of a bipartisan approach towards major questions of foreign policy, which they believed insulated it from any real public scrutiny. Brailsford was a particularly trenchant critic of the doctrine of continuity which 'so operated as to destroy any possibility of a democratic impulse in foreign affairs',[10] while making foreign policy the preserve of 'a coterie of government experts, colonial officials and self-interested financiers'.[11] While Brailsford's quasi-Marxist analysis meant that he believed radical social and economic change was required in order to transform the character of British policy, his call for a special parliamentary Select Committee for Foreign Affairs was echoed by many more moderate figures, anxious to rein in the supposed independence and arrogance of the country's diplomatic establishment. There was a particular concern, evident both in parliamentary debates and articles in the radical press, that Grey relied too much on the opinion of his officials rather than his Cabinet colleagues during his ten years in office.[12] Many critics also followed Morel and Brailsford in suggesting that the socially elitist character of the Foreign Office and Diplomatic Service hindered public scrutiny of their activities, since the men who worked in them were not instinctively attuned to the values of a modern quasi-democratic age, and consequently failed to pay sufficient attention to public and political opinion.

Concern about the British diplomatic establishment before the outbreak of the First World War was not a monopoly of the political left. The débâcle of the Boer War fostered growing public unease about the decline of British power and strength *vis à vis* its principal international competitors, which in turn provoked a debate about the need to promote greater 'national efficiency' via reform of established political, social and economic institutions.[13] The institutions responsible for supervising Britain's political and commercial relations across the globe could not remain immune to the impact of this new mood, which led to the establishment of various committees and commissions dedicated to reforming major public institutions. The 1903 Walrond Committee proposed reforms to make British consuls more effective at increasing British trade.[14] The Royal Commission on the Reform of the Civil Service, which produced a 1914 report on the organisation of Britain's overseas representation, was also primarily concerned with questions of effectiveness and efficiency.[15] Those commissioners who did express doubts about the privileged composition of the Diplomatic Service were usually most anxious that the scions of aristocratic and wealthy professional families might not be well-suited to reporting on the political and social changes taking place 'in the great democratic governing countries'. While their final report recommended changes to recruitment procedures in order to attract candidates from a wider range of backgrounds, the main impetus for the proposal was to foster efficiency via an improvement in the quality of personnel; it was not to increase accountability or egalitarianism. Nor were members of the British diplomatic establishment themselves unaware of the need for change in the years before 1914; it will be seen in the next chapter that the administrative reforms introduced at the Foreign Office during the period 1903–6 originated *within* the organisation. The importance of creating new institutional structures and operational procedures to enhance the effectiveness of the British diplomatic establishment was widely accepted *before* the outbreak of war in 1914 focused the spotlight more closely than ever on the Foreign Office and Diplomatic Service.

A similar pattern was evident in France before 1914, where public criticism of the country's diplomatic establishment was characterised by an eclectic set of concerns.[16] The Dreyfus affair had undoubtedly helped to shake popular faith in the central pillars of the French establishment, leading to increased demands for change in many areas of public life. As in Britain, parliamentarians concerned about foreign policy focused a good deal of their attention on the institutions charged with managing the country's international relationships. The Budget and Finance commissions of the two houses of the National Assembly produced regular reports highlighting the antiquated and archaic procedures of the Foreign Ministry, as well as criticising recruitment procedures biased in favour of young men from wealthy and well-connected families. Deputies from the Radical Party, in particular, urged the need for administrative reform and the recruitment of new officials with the talent and vigour to perform their duties effectively. As in Britain, the most significant reforms tended to come from within the diplomatic establishment, albeit that they were in large part prompted by the need to respond to growing external criticism. When Stephen Pichon served as Foreign Minister, he established a Commission on Administrative Reforms which included among its members a young Embassy secretary, Philippe Berthelot, who over the following years became the principal architect of change at the *Quai d'Orsay*. While Berthelot was sensitive to the demands for greater public accountability, the reforms he promoted were primarily an organisational response to the growth in business conducted by the Foreign Ministry in Paris. As was the case with the 1903–6 reforms at the British Foreign Office, the main objective of the innovations made at the *Quai d'Orsay* before 1914 was the promotion of a more rational system of internal administration designed to create greater specialisation and more congruence between organisational structure and function. Extra appropriations were in turn

8   *Diplomacy Before the Russian Revolution*

approved by deputies to allow the *Quai d'Orsay* to be brought into the modern age. Change was brought about by a coalition of bureaucrats and politicians committed to the modernisation of an institution they considered to be both inefficient and outdated.

The Russian diplomatic establishment was also subjected to numerous attacks and some organisational changes in the years between the 1905 Revolution and the outbreak of the First World War. The revolutionary parties such as the Bolsheviks and Socialist Revolutionaries were not particularly concerned with such mundane issues as the bureaucratic organisation of the tsarist Foreign Ministry. The relaxation of censorship and the establishment of a new Legislature (Duma) after the 1905 Revolution did, however, provide opportunities for more moderate critics of the Ministry of Foreign Affairs to articulate their concerns. As in Britain and France, attacks on the organisation and operation of the Ministry were frequently bound up with criticism of policy. Many journalists and deputies wrote scathingly about the antiquated procedures and bureaucratic confusion that prevailed in the Ministry's central headquarters, which was situated in the centre of St Petersburg near the Winter Palace. The appointment of A.P. Izvol'skii as Foreign Minister in the spring of 1906, a professional diplomat who had for some time been a fierce critic of the Ministry's internal organisation, provided a catalyst for the beginning of a prolonged battle to implement the kind of 'rationalising' reforms made to the British and French diplomatic establishments around the same time.[17] As was the case in Paris, the changes were planned by a small number of 'enlightened bureaucrats' willing to respond both to public criticism and, more particularly, to their own perception of the Ministry's shortcomings. The various attempts to reform national diplomatic establishments in Britain, France and Russia before 1914 were therefore all prompted by a pervasive sense that the diplomatic institutions and procedures which had existed in the nineteenth century were no longer adequate to the demands of the modern world. The quest for efficiency and the need to respond to public criticism meant that significant changes were already taking place in the old diplomacy some years before the First World War finally signalled its death-knell.

CLASSIFYING THE OLD DIPLOMACY

While the old diplomacy was widely blamed by its critics for allowing war to break out in the summer of 1914, the term itself was seldom defined with much real precision, being used instead as part of a polemic that had as its principal objective the promotion of institutional and political change. The term was for obvious linguistic reasons most widely employed in the United States and Britain, although the ideas and sentiments associated with it were echoed in the other major combatant countries as well. Even in the Anglo–American context, however, there was no agreement about what constituted the old diplomacy. Every journalist or politician who used the phrase had in mind a more or less coherent understanding of its meaning which they assumed, often incorrectly, was shared by their audience. There was, as already noted, something of a distinction between an establishment and a radical critique of the old diplomacy, although the boundary between the two was not always precise. As early as 1912, an editorial in the London *Times*, then the most authoritative of all British newspapers, attacked the chancelleries of Europe for 'playing with human lives as pawns in a game of chess', a sentiment that was heartily endorsed by radicals such as Morel and Brailsford. The differences were, however, usually more striking than the similarities. In the years following the outbreak of the First World War, British advocates of a 'new diplomacy' included such individuals as the Conservative politician Lord Robert Cecil and the Labour MP Ramsay MacDonald, but their views about the shortcomings of the diplomatic *ancien régime* varied considerably. In a similar fashion, while Lloyd George showed himself to be instinctively impatient both of professional diplomats and the rituals of conventional diplomacy after he became Prime Minister at the end of 1916,[18] he displayed little sympathy with demands that foreign policy should be subject to more popular scrutiny and censure. In the United States, President Wilson's dislike of the traditional pattern of international diplomacy owed everything to his liberal idealism and little to the cultural insularity and egalitarianism that was at the root of the typical American's dislike of the 'cookie-pushers' who worked in missions abroad.[19] In France, as has already been seen, Berthelot's modernising reforms were driven by a search for efficiency rather than by a desire to establish the sort of democratic control over the foreign policy making process that was sought by many deputies in the National Assembly. The old diplomacy was a shapeless beast that lacked precise insititutional and operational form. The attacks of its critics varied so greatly because they could not agree about the nature of the animal they wished to slay.

While it is impossible to define precisely the nature of the old diplomacy as seen through the eyes of its multifarious opponents, most of the attacks focused on three of its supposed characteristics. Critics concentrated in the first place on questions of *autonomy* and *control*. Sidney Low's observation in 1912 that anxiety about the lack of parliamentary control over the British Foreign Office had 'become one of the commonplaces of politics' may have been an exaggeration,[20] but it was certainly an issue of considerable controversy. For Low, like many other radical writers and politicians, the problem was not simply one of constitutional mechanics, although his call for a new parliamentary committee to oversee the Foreign Office was a staple of radical pamphlets on the conduct of foreign affairs. He also bitterly criticised the emphasis on secrecy that was widely deemed to be a procedural hallmark of international relations in the years before 1914, arguing that while negotiations might have to be conducted in private, the results should always be made public, so that Parliament could have an opportunity to comment on new agreements and treaties. The diplomatic mystique exuded by members of the Diplomatic Service and Foreign Office in London was also a favourite target for E.D. Morel, who repeatedly insisted that 'in discussing "diplomacy" we must begin by grasping the simple fact that what we are really discussing is not an abstruse science, a complicated chess gambit, a Chinese puzzle, or a problem of higher mathematics',[21] but rather something that could easily be grasped by 'the citizen of education and intelligence'.[22]

The whole question of establishing effective control over the men responsible for making foreign policy was not only a matter of concern in Britain. In Germany, where officials at the *Wilhelmstrasse* in Berlin were not as influential as their British counterparts at affecting the course of policy, radicals in the peace movement and the *Reichstag* focused their criticism less on the diplomatic establishment 'proper' and more on the network of advisers and officials surrounding the Kaiser.[23] In Russia, liberal deputies in the Duma fought hard to establish their influence on the foreign policy making process throughout the years leading up to 1914. Establishing effective control over the individuals who made foreign policy was not, however, only a matter of concern for those on the left of the political spectrum. In France, the direct involvement of government ministers in foreign affairs during the First World War was a direct response to the exigencies of war rather than a sign of unease about the autonomy of the country's diplomatic establishment. In Russia, Tsar Nicholas II faced continuous pressure from many conservative-minded members of his Court both before and after 1914 to push Russian foreign policy towards greater accommodation with Berlin, a move which was opposed by a majority of senior officials in the Foreign Ministry. Questions of the operation and reform of national diplomatic establishments inevitably became intimately bound up with wider considerations of policy.

A second characteristic feature of the old diplomacy according to many of its critics – whether from the left, centre or right – was one that has already been touched on: namely, the *privileged social background* of the vast majority of its practitioners. In Britain, where the organisational distinction between the Foreign Office and Diplomatic Service was comparatively watertight, it was widely believed that diplomats were generally more 'blue-blooded' than their counterparts in Downing Street. A similar pattern was noted by critics of the Russian diplomatic establishment, since obtaining a post abroad usually required better connections and greater wealth than securing a position in St Petersburg. Although politicians and writers on the left were usually the most concerned about the privileged composition of the various national diplomatic establishments, the subject was also of concern to those from 'establishment' circles who were perturbed about the danger of excluding efficient individuals capable of carrying out the work most effectively. The subject was discussed extensively both in the French National Assembly and by the men who served on the Royal Commission on the Reform of the Civil Service that reported in 1914. In Russia, writers on conservative newspapers such as *Novoe Vremia* and liberal publications like *Rech'* fretted about the damage caused by the Foreign Ministry's failure to recruit energetic and intelligent men simply because they did not have the right kind of social and educational background. The potential virtues and benefits of a quasi-meritocracy in the recruitment of diplomats and foreign ministry officials appealed to critics ranging from English liberal politicians through to Russian conservative journalists.

The third feature that defined the old diplomacy according to its array of critics was its practitioners' supposed *incompetence*. Radicals across Europe were concerned both before and after 1914 that members of the various diplomatic establishments were wedded to concepts and procedures that made the outbreak of war almost inevitable. Sidney Low's attack on the continued use of 'the methods which prevailed when wars and alliances were made in the closets of sovereigns' was not an isolated one.[24] The idea of the balance of power attracted particular opprobrium from critics who considered it too dangerous to establish international order on the basis that conflict could only be deterred by the threat of a military response. The agitation for new forms of institutional arrangement to promote international conciliation reflected a widespread belief that alternative mechanisms could be established to create global order. The distinction between the radical and establishment critiques of this feature of the old diplomacy was as ever imprecise. Many radical writers in Britain and France, in particular, could never quite decide whether they believed that members of their countries' national diplomatic establishments were straightforwardly incompetent, unable to deal effectively with the kind of misunderstandings and tensions that led to war, or whether they were simply pig-headedly unwilling to abandon principles which had guided diplomatic practice for so many decades. Politicians and writers from the centre and right were usually more concerned, particularly before 1914, about the ability of diplomats to defend national interests in a changing economic and political environment. The horrors that followed the outbreak of war did, however, place the management of conflict at the centre of the political agenda in virtually every major power. While the League of Nations would almost certainly never have been created if President Wilson had not been in a position to use America's new-found international power to promote his vision of a 'league to defend peace', the willingness of important sections of the governing classes in Britain and France to accept major reforms to the structure of the global order was a prerequisite for change. By the time the Versailles Treaty was signed in 1919, the notion that the old diplomacy was characterised by too much reliance on secret alliances and the balance of power had entered the political mainstream in all the victor powers and was no longer the preserve of those on the left of the political spectrum.

The attacks on the old diplomacy before and during the First World War inevitably provoked a response from those who had been involved in diplomatic life before 1914. Sir James Rennell Rodd, who was British Ambassador in Rome during the pre-war years, wrote later in his memoirs that even though foreign affairs had not always been 'handled with consumate knowledge or ability.... I do consider that an unnecessary amount of facile and unreflecting criticism has been passed on what is called the old diplomacy'. He staunchly defended the notion that diplomacy was a craft which required a particular skill and 'special training' that provided knowledge of 'what to do, and especially when not to do it'.[25] Sir George Buchanan, who was British Ambassador in St Petersburg from 1910 to 1918, also reflected bitterly on the loss of power and influence suffered by professional diplomats with the passing of the old order. The memoirs published after the end of the First World War by men who had played a part in the diplomatic life of the continent before 1914 – be they British, Russian, German or French – were all inevitably tainted to a greater or lesser degree by the usual problems of bias and parochialism. Nor was it an easy task to defend a system of international diplomacy which had, at least on the face of it, failed to prevent the most devastating war in human history. When men like Rennell Rodd and George Buchanan attempted to defend the old diplomacy during the 1920s, the very language they used was dictated by their detractors, since they were forced to engage with a term that had originated as a critical epithet before becoming widely accepted as a shorthand description of the system of pre-war diplomacy. The variegated assumptions that underpinned the assault on the old diplomacy during the first two decades of the century continued to inform much of the discussion about the subject until the start of the Second World War.

Harold Nicolson's celebrated Chichele lectures delivered at Oxford University in 1953, which were subsequently published under the title *The Evolution of Diplomatic Method*, provided their audience with an interesting attempt to analyse the old diplomacy at a time when much of the polemical sting had begun to fade from the subject, overtaken in both academic and popular discourse by a concern with the tensions that led Europe to war in 1939. Nicolson's own diplomatic life had begun before 1914, and he made little secret either in his Chichele lectures or in his other writings that he believed the old diplomacy had been seriously maligned by its detractors. At the same time, however, his attempt to define the features of the old diplomacy had both the patina and the substance of a quasi-academic neutrality. Nicolson used the term 'old diplomacy' as a virtual synonym for the so-called 'French' system of diplomacy, 'originated by Richlieu...and adopted by all European countries during the three centuries that preceeded the change of 1919'.[26] He argued that the diplomatic system which existed before 1914 was defined by a hotchpotch of institutional and procedural elements. The system of diplomacy on the eve of the First World War was, according to Nicolson, characterised by its eurocentricity, its assumption that great powers provided the pivot of the system, the existence of 'a professional diplomatic service on a more or less identical model' in every major country, and a general acceptance that 'sound negotiation must be continuous and confidential'. Nicolson also argued that the individuals who served in the principal national diplomatic establishments on the eve of the First World War were men of considerable integrity, who shared a common identity and a strong conviction that 'the purpose of diplomacy was the preservation of peace'.[27] There are in reality many problems with Nicolson's attempt to define the nature of the old diplomacy, but the shortcomings of his treatment do have the virtue of highlighting the difficulties involved in trying to grasp such a heterogenous and fluid phenomenon. Some features identified by Nicolson are concerned with operational procedures ('continuous negotiation'); others are effectively institutional characteristics ('a professional diplomatic service'); still others are little more than general characterisations ('eurocentric'). Diplomacy is by its very nature a complex and multifaceted phenomenon, the character of which is determined at any given time by a range of shifting institutional and procedural attributes. Any attempt to characterise a particular diplomatic system therefore needs to recognise this diversity and acknowledge the impossibility of applying simple labels and descriptions.

THE DIVERSITY OF NATIONAL DIPLOMATIC ESTABLISHMENTS

It is difficult to identify the precise contours and boundaries of a particular diplomatic establishment. The term is certainly not used here as a synonym for 'foreign policy making elite'. While some senior diplomats and foreign ministry officials played an important role in the formulation of policy in the years before 1914, the situation varied from country to country; indeed, weighing the contribution of the British and Russian diplomatic establishments in the policy making process is one of the central concerns of this book. The phrase 'diplomatic establishment' is used here to refer to those individuals who carried out diplomatic work in foreign ministries at home and at diplomatic missions abroad; it is not used to refer to the whole array of politicians, businessmen and journalists who played an important part in influencing the relationship between governments.[28] It is also used, perhaps more unusually, to include full-time members of the various national consular services, since it will be seen in later chapters that some consuls carried out important quasi-diplomatic work. Even this definition is, however, still subject to the charge of imprecision, not least because the definition of 'diplomatic work' is itself elusive. It will be seen in the next two chapters, for example, that many British Foreign Office clerks and diplomatic secretaries spent much of their time carrying out routine administrative duties which were little more than clerical drudgery; the same was even more true of officials at the Foreign Ministry in St Petersburg. At the other end of the scale, Satow argued that the British foreign secretary should be considered a diplomat even though he was a political appointee whose tenure depended on the fate of the government to which he belonged.[29] The problem of comparing different national diplomatic establishments is therefore compounded by the diversity in their structure and organisation. Nevertheless, by concentrating on the men who worked in foreign ministries, diplomatic missions and consulates, it is possible to achieve a precise enough focus for the purposes of this book.

In the years before the First World War, all European diplomats in post abroad and foreign ministry officials working at home had to be cognisant of two distinct sets of relationships affecting the operation of the organisations in which they worked, the first determined by particular international norms and conventions and the second by domestic political and administrative factors. The structure and *modus operandi* of international diplomacy before 1914 were governed by a complex array of customs and treaties, which had evolved over hundreds of years in an effort to facilitate effective and safe communication between sovereign states. As a result, as Harold Nicolson noted in his Chichele lectures, the formal structure of embassies and other diplomatic missions of the various powers closely resembled one another; the same was true, although to a lesser degree, of the structure of the major foreign ministries. The relationship between a particular embassy and the foreign ministry of its host country naturally fluctuated according to the personalities and circumstances involved, but elaborate (if only half-articulated) conventions helped to facilitate communication. The weak boundary between the professional and social element of a diplomat's duties was one of the defining characteristics of the old diplomacy, allowing the development at *soirées* and dinner parties of a private network of relationships and friendships. The elaborate social life characteristic of European diplomacy before 1914 – which was the object of such sharp attacks from many of its critics – helped to cement a network of social and professional ties that cut across the boundaries of national identity and forged what Nicolson termed a 'corporate identity' among its practitioners.[30] The diplomatic world was in any case very small before 1914, and the peripatetic lifestyle enjoyed by many members of national diplomatic establishments meant that they frequently came across the same individuals at different stages of their career. Officials who met as young *attachés* in Paris might later meet as counsellors or ambassadors in Berlin. Even the briefest glance at the records of the British Foreign Office and the Russian Foreign Ministry shows that staff in the two organisations usually had a formidable stock of private intelligence on the character and views of senior members of the diplomatic establishments of other countries.

The sense of common identity that bound together members of the various national diplomatic establishments before 1914 was bolstered by shared values and experiences. Most of them were, as their critics knew only too well, drawn from the privileged classes of their respective countries. It is, however, important not to overstate the extent to which European diplomats formed a kind of international class bound together by shared values and interests. The character and operation of the different diplomatic establishments varied according to the dictates of domestic circumstances. There were, for example, certain straightforward differences in institutional structure. In Britain, there was until 1919 a formal division between the Foreign Office and the Diplomatic Service (although transfers between the two were sometimes possible); as a result, the outlook of a man who had spent his career 'in the field' was likely to be different from that of a colleague who had spent his working life in London. In Russia, by contrast, there was no such clearcut division, although a host of informal conventions and practices did create a rather similar distinction between centre and periphery. The relationship between consuls and diplomats also varied from country to country; the comparatively rigid boundary between the Diplomatic and Consular Services found in Britain was less pronounced in the Russian case. Comparisons between the different national diplomatic establishments should not however be confined to a study of their formal institutional structure, since the mode of their day-to-day operation was determined by a wide range of constitutional, political and administrative factors. The degree to which senior officials in a particular foreign ministry could exert influence on the policy making process, either directly or by asserting their status as 'gatekeepers' purveying authoritative information and advice to decision makers, was governed by the extent to which other individual and institutional actors possessed the authority and resources to challenge them. It will be seen in Chapter 2 that in Britain, where foreign policy making was the constitutional preserve of the Cabinet and the monarch, the influence of permanent officials in the Foreign Office and Diplomatic Service fluctuated sharply according to circumstances. The same pattern existed in Russia, although the situation there was made even more complicated by a shift in the constitutional location of decision making power in the wake of the 1905 Revolution. The administrative and political environment set a broad framework within which there was considerable scope for diversity and change.

The chapters that follow are designed to amplify the argument sketched out above. The focus is not on the foreign policy making process *per se*, except in so far as it illuminates the operation of the British and Russian diplomatic establishments in the years between 1894 and 1917.[31] It is of course quite impossible to provide a detailed review of such a complex topic as the management of Anglo–Russian relations during almost a quarter of a century. For this reason, most attention is given to the period leading up to the Anglo–Russian convention of 1907, which can in retrospect be seen as a pivotal moment in the evolution of European politics as well as in the development of relations between London and St Petersburg. The years between 1903 and 1907, conventionally if somewhat erroneously seen as the key period for tracing the origins of the Anglo–Russian *entente*, were a turbulent period in the history of relations between the two countries. The traditional enmity of the Great Game gave way to a cautious friendship, but only after the Dogger Bank incident of October 1904 had almost led to war between the two countries. While the rapprochement was in part governed by the logic of changes in the international environment, ranging from fear of Germany through to a mutual desire to reduce the burdens of imperial engagement in Asia, it was also partly rooted in developments that took place *inside* each country during the period. The 1905 Revolution in Russia and the launch of the Constitutional Experiment that followed it changed both the political and administrative context in which foreign policy was formulated and executed. The replacement of a floundering Conservative administration in London by a new Liberal government, when combined with simultaneous changes in the organisation and administrative culture of the Foreign Office, similarly transformed the domestic environment in which foreign policy was made and implemented in Britain. Understanding the response of the two diplomatic establishments to this complex interplay of international and domestic change can tell us a great deal about their organisation and operation.

The following chapters also attempt to evaluate the fairness of the charges made against the old diplomacy by its critics in the early years of the twentieth century. It was seen earlier that diplomats and foreign ministry officials across Europe were widely believed to be privileged scions of upper class families, lacking the skills needed to operate in an international environment that was becoming more complex and threatening with every passing year. There was also a widespread belief that officials responsible for foreign affairs were unresponsive to the normal mechanisms of political scrutiny. The diversity of the attacks made on the old diplomacy makes it impossible to present a simple defence of its practitioners. And, in any case, some of the charges – most notably that of social elitism – were without doubt largely true. Nevertheless, one of the central themes in the following pages is the difficulty of generalising about such a complex phenomenon as the old diplomacy. While there may have been a certain amount of continuity in the international organisation of diplomatic life in Europe in the years before 1914, there were also important changes in the structure and operation of national diplomatic establishments which themselves had ramifications for the way in which the wider diplomatic system operated. The old diplomacy was a dynamic and complex phenomenon which cannot be easily captured by neat definitions or static conceptual frameworks.

NOTES

1. See, for example, Giles Fletcher, *Of the Russe Commonwealth*.
2. For further details, see D.B. Horn, *Great Britain and Europe in the Eighteenth Century*, Chapter 8.
3. For a valuable overview, see Keith Hamilton and Richard Langhorne, *The Practice of Diplomacy*, pp. 136–245.
4. There is a large secondary literature on the origins of the League of Nations, of which the following are particularly helpful: Elmer Bendiner, *A Time for Angels*; F.S. Northedge, *The League of Nations: Its Life and Times, 1920–1946*.
5. For a detailed discussion on this theme, see Arno Mayer, *Political Origins of the New Diplomacy, 1917–1918, passim*.
6. On the Union of Democratic Control, see H.M. Swanick, *Builders of Peace*.
7. Useful material about the American diplomatic establishment in the early twentieth century can be found in Henry E. Mattox, *The Twilight of Amateur Diplomacy*; Robert D. Schulzinger, *The Making of the Diplomatic Mind*; Waldo H. Heinrichs, 'Bureaucracy and Professionalism in the Development of American Career Diplomacy', in John Braeman, Robert H. Bremner and David Brody (eds), *Twentieth Century American Foreign Policy*, pp. 119–206.
8. Quoted in Catherine Ann Cline, 'E.D. Morel and the Crusade Against the Foreign Office', *Journal of Modern History*, 39, 2 (1967), p. 131. Also on Morel, see Catherine Ann Cline, 'E.D. Morel: From the Congo to the Rhine', in A.J. Anthony Morris (ed), *Edwardian Radicalism, 1900–1914*, pp. 234–45.
9. See, for example, E.D. Morel, *Morocco in Diplomacy*, pp. 72–3.

10. Henry Noel Brailsford, *The War of Steel and Gold*, p. 131.
11. Quoted in F.M. Leventhal, 'H.N. Brailsford and the Search for a New International Order', in Morris, *Edwardian Radicalism*, p. 214.
12. For a useful discussion of this theme, see John A. Murray, 'Foreign Policy Debated: Sir Edward Grey and his Critics, 1911–1912', in Lillian Parker Wallace and Willam C. Askew (eds), *Power, Public Opinion and Diplomacy*, pp. 141–71.
13. On the national efficiency movement, see G.R. Searle, *The Quest for National Efficiency*.
14. See, for example, the 'Report of the Committee appointed to Inquire into the Constitution of the Consular Service', *British Parliamentary Papers (henceforth BPP), 1903*, 55 (cd 1634).
15. 'Royal Commission on the Civil Service. Fifth Report', *BPP, 1914–16*, 11 (cd 7748).
16. The following paragraph is partly drawn from Paul Gordon Lauren, *Diplomats and Bureaucrats*, pp. 79–117.
17. On the Izvol'skii-Gubastov reforms, see G.H. Bolsover, 'Izvolsky and Reform of the Russian Ministry of Foreign Affairs', *Slavonic and East European Review*, 63, 1 (1985), pp. 21–40.
18. For details of Lloyd George's views about the failings of the old diplomacy, see his *War Memoirs*, Vol. 1, p. 46ff. Lloyd George's contempt for professional diplomats was heartily reciprocated; see Hardinge of Penshurst, *Old Diplomacy*, p. 205.
19. On Wilson's approach to foreign affairs, see Lloyd C. Ambrosius, *Woodrow Wilson and the American Diplomatic Tradition*; Arthur S. Link, *Wilson the Diplomatist*; Thomas J. Knock, *To End All Wars: Woodrow Wilson and the Quest for a New World Order*.
20. Sidney Low, 'The Foreign Office Autocracy', *Fortnightly Review*, January 1912, p. 1.
21. E.D. Morel, *Truth and the War*, p. 107.
22. E.D. Morel, *Morocco in Diplomacy*, p. 72.
23. On the peace movement in Germany, see Roger Chickering, *Imperial Germany and a World Without War. The Peace Movement and German Society 1892–1914*; on the organisation and operation of the German Diplomatic Service in this period, see Lamar Cecil, *The German Diplomatic Service, 1871–1914*.
24. Low, *Foreign Office Autocracy*, p. 10.
25. Sir James Rennell Rodd, *Social and Diplomatic Memoirs*, Vol. 1, p. vi.
26. Harold Nicolson, *The Evolution of Diplomatic Method*, p. 72.
27. Nicolson, *Evolution*, pp. 73–9.
28. For a rather similar definition see Sir Ernest Satow, *A Guide to Diplomatic Practice*, Vol. 1, p. 4.
29. Satow, *Guide to Diplomatic Practice* Vol. 1, p. 4.
30. Nicolson, *Evolution*, p. 75.
31. For an excellent study of British policy towards Russia during this period, see Keith Neilson, *Britain and the last Tsar*; for a recent valuable study of the Russian foreign policy making process, see David Maclaren McDonald, *United Government and Foreign Policy in Russia, 1900–1914*.

2 The British Foreign Office and Russia

The previous chapter suggested that the term 'old diplomacy' was forged in a shifting historical and polemical environment, with the result that it never acquired a single well-defined meaning. There was, however, considerable agreement among critics of the old diplomacy about the nature and extent of its shortcomings. This chapter aims to examine the validity of some of these charges by focusing on the organisation of the British Foreign Office in the first decade of the twentieth century, along with its role in determining policy towards Russia during the years leading up to the Anglo–Russian convention of 1907. It is of course impossible to make too many generalisations about the role and influence of the Foreign Office on the basis of particular case-studies. What emerges is, however, that most critics of the Foreign Office only managed to capture a single aspect of a complex and changing picture. While the officials who worked there were certainly drawn from a narrow range of social backgrounds, many of them were intelligent individuals committed to carrying out their duties in a dedicated and professional manner. Nor is it true that senior Foreign Office officials were necessarily able to dictate the course of British foreign policy. Their influence at any one time depended on a huge number of factors ranging from the political sensitivity of the policy under review through to the determination of other administrative and political actors to assert their own authority and influence.

THE BACKGROUND OF THE FOREIGN OFFICE PROFESSIONALS

The Foreign Office was a very small organisation before 1914. In 1905 its staff included just one permanent under-secretary, three assistant under-secretaries, eight senior clerks, nine assistant clerks and 28 junior clerks. There were also some 30 Second Division clerks, who dealt with routine clerical and administrative matters, along with 15 other officials working in such sections as the Financial Department and the Library. Around 40 individuals worked as secretaries, office keepers and messengers. The total number of people working in the cramped Foreign Office building in Downing Street was therefore probably less than 150, a tiny number given the extent of Britain's global interests and responsibilities.[1]

It is not hard to prove that the men who occupied the diplomatic posts at the Foreign Office in the years before 1914 came from privileged social backgrounds; the more interesting question concerns the nature and significance of the fact. The definition of 'privilege' is itself a vexed exercise, perhaps never more so than when dealing with late Victorian and Edwardian Britain, since the British class system was a good deal more fluid in the late nineteenth and early twentieth centuries than is sometimes realised. Birth, education, wealth and profession were combined in various ways to create complex patterns of status. Money might not buy an aristocratic or gentry lineage, but it could sometimes buy entry to the educational institutions that provided access to the more desirable professions. Zara Steiner has suggested that the diplomatic clerks at the Foreign Office were drawn almost exclusively from families securely located within the confines of the British establishment,[2] a milieu that can probably be defined no more precisely than as 'a secure, conservative, socially-dominant group' whose members were imbued with a powerful sense of their 'right to rule'.[3] Nevertheless, only a minority of officials at the Foreign Office, such as Francis Bertie, who served as an Assistant Secretary before being appointed Ambassador to Rome in 1903, came from a genuinely 'aristocratic' background.[4] Most were brought up in families that can more usefully be labelled as 'upper middle class' or 'professional'. Among the handful of men recruited as junior clerks between 1908 and 1913, for example, none came from mercantile or trade backgrounds, while a majority were the sons of city bankers or military officers. The same pattern largely held true for individuals entering the Foreign Office throughout the previous few decades, although some allowance does have to be made for the shifting occupational pattern evident in the second half of the nineteenth century.[5] While senior members of the British diplomatic establishment insisted on the eve of the First World War that 'the net was thrown very widely for recruits',[6] there seems to have been a considerable degree of 'self-selection' among applicants; few candidates came from backgrounds strikingly different from those characteristic of officials already in post.

Most conventional treatments of the subject assume that members of a particular class are bound together by a collective mentality as well as by certain shared social and economic characteristics. One of the most effective ways to examine the foundations of privilege is therefore to focus on education, in order to see how the process inculcates a particular

Table 2.1 Educational Backgrounds of Individuals Serving as Senior Clerk or Above in the Foreign Office 1894–1918

Number of Officials	at Public School	at Eton	Educated at Oxbridge *	at other university *
37	31	16	14	2

*Does not necessarily imply graduation.

Table 2.2 Educational Backgrounds of Individuals Appointed as Junior Clerk in the Foreign Office 1908–13

Number of Officials	at Public School	at Eton	Educated at Oxbridge *	at other university *
16	15	9	15	1

*Does not necessarily imply graduation. Figures exclude brief periods of study.

set of values as well as providing an institutional framework that limits access to positions commanding high power and status. The whole question does, however, need to be handled with some care when looking at the background of officials who worked in the Foreign Office before 1914. A senior official in post at the turn of the century would probably have received most of his education in the 1850s or 1860s, half a century before a junior official recruited in 1910. The presence of different age cohorts therefore makes generalisation difficult, particularly since the role of education in the creation and perpetuation of social status changed sharply in the second half of the nineteenth century. The raw data set down in Tables 2.1 and 2.2 suggests that attendance at public school (particularly Eton) and university (almost always Oxford or Cambridge) became increasingly *de rigueur* for recruits to the Foreign Office in the decades before the First World War.[7]

Recruits who entered the Foreign Office immediately before 1914 had on average received more formal education, at public school and university, than the cohort of officials who joined (typically) between 1880 and 1900. The shift was in part a consequence of reforms made while Lord Lansdowne was Foreign Secretary, which effectively made a university education a requirement for new recruits. It was also, however, rooted in a wider pattern of social change characterised by a decline of the private tutor and home-based learning in favour of formal education at specialised institutions. After the educational reforms proposed by the Clarendon Commission in the 1860s, entry to the most desirable professions became increasingly dependent on education at public school and university.[8] Because attendance at the leading institutions – whose graduates dominated recruitment to prestigious organisations like the Foreign Office – was for the most part limited to young men from families boasting considerable financial and social status, education helped to preserve and transmit privilege across the generations. The potential tension between a society based on knowledge and a society based on birth was resolved in late Victorian and Edwardian Britain by ensuring that access to the leading educational institutions was for the most part limited to those from 'appropriate' backgrounds.

The growing emphasis on formal education also reflected the value placed by the Foreign Office on intellectual ability when selecting new recruits. By the beginning of the twentieth century, successful candidates achieved on average considerably higher marks than those obtained by candidates who secured a place in the Diplomatic Service. Success in the wide-ranging examinations demanded intelligence and a certain amount of specialised knowledge – certainly more than was usually acquired through study at school and university. Most aspiring Foreign Office clerks had to travel abroad for a considerable period of time in order to bring their languages up to the desired standard, before attending Scoones's Academy in the Strand where they were 'crammed' in subjects ranging from geography through to orthography. Not surprisingly, then, successful candidates were usually men of considerable intellectual calibre, even if the conventional British distrust of 'cleverness' meant that their intelligence was articulated in a restrained and pragmatic fashion. In 1902, when J.D. Gregory and E.H.J. Leslie gained the two available places, the unsuccessful candidates included such a distinguished figure as Picton Bagge, who later played an important role as a British consular official in Russia during the 1917 Revolution and its aftermath.[9] Although the number of applicants for Foreign Office clerkships was not particularly large, the high calibre of candidates meant that the selection process had become genuinely competitive by the end of the nineteenth century. A considerable degree of intellectual ability was a *sine qua non* for any young man aspiring to become an established clerk in the Foreign Office.

The fusion of social privilege and intellectual ability helped to define the culture of the Foreign Office in the years before 1914. The clerks who formed the diplomatic establishment were not only drawn from a social background whose members imbibed from their earliest years the notion that they belonged to the 'governing class' of the British

Empire; they were also part of a milieu in which intellectual ability was both expected and valued. Education at a small handful of schools and universities helped to encourage still further a certain *esprit de corps*. The ideal of 'professionalism' was becoming an increasingly pronounced feature of British culture from the late Victorian age onwards, as new occupational groups both inside and outside the state administration sought to enhance their social and economic status by proclaiming the specialised nature of their work.[10] The attacks on 'amateurism', which were a pronounced theme of political discourse in Edwardian England, particularly from those associated with the so-called National Efficiency movement, helped to foster a climate in which prestige was increasingly associated with specialised knowledge and skills. While it would be misleading to locate the early twentieth-century Foreign Office within this framework, given that an established post there had commanded social prestige for many centuries, it may still help to explain why some members of the British diplomatic establishment were increasingly inclined to the view before 1914 that the conduct of foreign affairs required a particular expertise. Although the ideal of the dedicated amateur continued to hold considerable sway among Foreign Office officials, even this most prestigious of occupations was not immune to the demands of the *zeitgeist*.

The idea that the foreign policy 'professionals' were best-placed to understand the intricacies of international affairs was only really articulated *in public* following the barrage of criticism of the old diplomacy that exploded during the First World War – an example, perhaps, of how 'unspoken assumptions' are seldom examined except when faced by a direct challenge. The nature of the requisite expertise was, however, seldom spelt out in explicit terms. When J.D. Gregory retired from the Foreign Office in 1928, he noted in his memoirs that a successful diplomat or Foreign Office official required a 'long training' to perform his work effectively, while at the same time acknowledging that there was 'no such thing as an "expert" in diplomacy'.[11] His sentiments echoed the views of his colleagues who worked with him in Downing Street before the First World War, where the conventional wisdom held that an ideal diplomat or Foreign Office clerk combined an instinctive *nous* with a wisdom that could only be acquired after a long period in the job. Expertise in the conduct of foreign affairs was seen as an art and not a science, dependent on a particular skill and intuition rather than possession of highly specialised and formal knowledge, as in the more conventional professions.

It is not easy to determine whether critics of the old diplomacy were justified in accusing officials at the pre-war Foreign Office of deliberately clothing foreign affairs in a veil of mystery that could only be penetrated by those with the requisite knowledge and experience.[12] It is even harder to define something so nebulous as 'expertise' in the conduct of foreign affairs, or to determine whether the typical career structure and training of an official working in the Foreign Office before 1914 provided opportunities to develop it. While certain changes were made to the entrance requirements during the 25 years before 1914, general intellectual ability was almost always prized above knowledge of particular subjects. Languages formed a central part of the entrance examination, but the typical diplomatic clerk was seldom a true polyglot. Nor was he likely to be recruited on the strength of his expert knowledge about a particular country or region. Despite important administrative reforms between 1903 and 1906, which are discussed further below, there was no real attempt to encourage officials to develop specialist knowledge of a particular geographical area. The Eastern Department, which was responsible, among other things, for the official correspondence relating to Russian affairs, never became an 'in-house' centre of expertise on the countries which came within its purview. Most junior clerks only stayed there for two or three years before moving on to another department, which gave them little time or opportunity to master the complexities of Russian affairs. R.P. Maxwell acquired a considerable knowledge of the domestic and foreign affairs of the Tsarist Empire during his time as acting Senior Clerk and Senior Clerk in the Department, from 1901 to 1913, although his input into discussions of policy was always quite limited. Herman Norman also spent a long period in the Eastern Department following his return from a posting at the Embassy in St Petersburg, but his undoubted expertise did not always translate into great influence on policy, particularly in the period between 1906 and 1910 when Sir Charles Hardinge served as permanent secretary. While the situation changed somewhat when Hardinge left to become Viceroy of India, the ethos of the generalist continued to dominate the Foreign Office. The notion of expertise that prevailed there before 1914 always rested on a less tangible foundation than the acquisition of specialist regional knowledge.

THE CHANGING CULTURE AND ORGANISATION OF THE FOREIGN OFFICE IN THE EARLY TWENTIETH CENTURY

During the final years of the nineteenth century, permanent officials at the Foreign Office rarely exercised much real influence on British foreign policy. When Lord Salisbury served as Foreign Secretary, he dictated much of his correspondence in his house at Hatfield and rarely discussed issues of policy with his staff.[13] Ten years after the start of the new century, however, the situation was quite different. Sir Charles Hardinge worked closely with the Foreign Secretary, Sir Edward Grey, on virtually every important question of policy. The transformation was a consequence of a complex set of factors ranging from changes in political circumstances and administrative culture through to the personalities involved.

While Lord Salisbury's preferred style of working helped to shape the Foreign Office in the years before 1900, it was not the only factor constraining the influence on policy of permanent officials. The administrative procedures employed in the Foreign Office were extraordinarily antiquated, requiring even senior officials to spend much of their time checking that routine clerical tasks had been performed properly.[14] At the beginning of the twentieth century, most documents were still copied by hand rather than typed; since Second Division clerks were not allowed to carry out work deemed to be diplomatically sensitive, the task normally fell to the junior diplomatic clerks. When the future ambassador to Italy, Rennell Rodd, was first posted to the Foreign Office as a young *attaché* in the 1880s, prior to taking up a post abroad, both he and the resident clerks spent their time in the 'not particularly thrilling' work of copying correspondence and making up the diplomatic bag.[15] H.J. Bruce recalled that when he served as a junior official in the Foreign Office at the end of the nineteenth century he was not 'expected, certainly not encouraged, to have any views of our own on the problems our elders and betters were dealing with'.[16] This regime of red-tape became indelibly and perhaps unfairly associated with the name of Sir Thomas Sanderson, who served as Permanent Secretary from 1894 to 1906. Sanderson was a man of considerable intelligence and administrative ability, but he perceived both his own role, and the role of his colleagues, in an essentially passive manner that dovetailed neatly with the attitudes displayed by Lord Salisbury when he was at the Foreign Office. While the Permanent Secretary possessed a reasonably acute understanding of international politics, he conceived of his role in essentially administrative terms, managing the flow of dispatches into the department and ensuring that the Foreign Secretary's instructions were executed with precision.

The administrative regime in place at the Foreign Office at the end of the nineteenth century was already outmoded by normal Whitehall standards. The Northcote – Trevelyan report of 1854 had advocated the creation of a new breed of permanent officials 'occupying a position duly subordinate to that of Ministers...yet possessing sufficient independence, character, ability and experience to be able to advise, assist, and, to some extent, influence those who are from time to time set over them'.[17] In other words, the report's authors tacitly accepted that senior officials should be concerned with important questions of policy, and by the end of the nineteenth century some senior civil servants in departments such as the Home Office were becoming accustomed to such a role. This change in the wider administrative culture largely bypassed the Foreign Office, however, a pattern that was strikingly apparent in the last few years of the nineteenth century when the Salisbury-Sanderson combination was instrumental in maintaining old patterns of behaviour long after they had started to fade elsewhere in Whitehall. The problems were compounded by Sanderson's determination to maintain control even over comparatively trivial administrative matters, which led to a high degree of centralisation and inefficiency. Nevertheless, by the time Lord Lansdowne replaced Salisbury as Foreign Secretary, in 1900, there was growing pressure from *within* the Foreign Office to modernise the system of administration, despite Sanderson's continued tenure as Permanent Secretary.

The impetus for change had a number of different sources.[18] It is perhaps too easy for historians to forget the critical role that personalities play in any historical drama, particularly when dealing with such a small organisation as the pre-1914 Foreign Office. No study of the Foreign Office in this period can ignore the impact on its development of a man like Charles Hardinge, who took over as Permanent Secretary at the beginning of 1906 determined to set his stamp on British policy in Europe and beyond.[19] Nor is it possible to discount the importance of officials like Francis Bertie or Eyre Crowe, both of whom, like Hardinge, were convinced by the early years of the century that British policy should be predicated on the assumption that Germany was the primary threat to Britain's global interests.[20] In the years after 1900, the traditional culture of Foreign Office passivity associated with Sanderson also faced increasing criticism from a younger cohort of officials impatient with the narrow definition of their role prescribed by the Permanent Secretary. However, while it is tempting to treat the Foreign Office reforms of 1903–6 as an attempt by certain officials to obtain more influence over foreign policy making, such an interpretation would almost certainly be too simplistic. Even though the implementation of the reforms probably had the effect of allowing some Foreign Office officials greater input into the policy making process, the changes were essentially incremental in character, driven by a need to avoid the breakdown of an increasingly sclerotic and inefficient administrative regime. The number of documents handled by the Foreign Office increased enormously in the late nineteenth and early twentieth centuries, with the result that some kind of reform was desperately needed to create a more streamlined bureaucracy capable of managing the increased flow of business.

The conservative character of the first wave of Foreign Office reforms, which began in 1903, would seem to be confirmed by the fact that their principal architect was Francis Villiers, an Assistant Secretary who was by temperament and instinct inclined to Sanderson's views on administrative matters. In a lengthy memorandum written in April 1903 Villiers acknowledged that there was serious discontent among the younger clerks, who felt that they were expected to spend too great a proportion of their time on mundane work that failed to make proper use of their abilities. He also argued that senior officials should spend less time on minor administrative matters so as to 'leave time for attention to more important matters'.[21] Villiers went on to suggest various remedies, the most important being that senior officials should delegate a greater proportion of their work, a move which would provide them with extra time to deal with serious matters as well as allowing their juniors to become more used to taking greater responsibility and interest in matters of policy. Over the next few months, a number of more detailed proposals were made about the best method of promoting decentralisation. Lord Lansdowne, who served as Foreign Secretary between 1900 and 1905, was from the beginning an enthusiastic proponent of change, battling assiduously with the Treasury to obtain extra funds for more Second Division clerks to relieve the diplomatic clerks of their most tedious duties. Even so, while the significance of this first round of reforms should not be underestimated, the changes relied too much on simple exhortation to overhaul the prevailing administrative culture. A truly effective reform required more drastic innovations, along with the allocation of sufficient resources to make them work more effectively. This was achieved to a greater extent in the second round of Foreign Office reforms that took place in 1905–6 which established a General Registry charged with managing the organisation and distribution of incoming and outgoing documents. Lord Lansdowne once again enthusiastically supported the changes, battling for the substantial increase in appropriations required to pay for the extra staff needed to make the new system work.

The reforms of 1905–6 certainly helped to free senior officials from some of their more tedious administrative duties. The changes also coincided with the appointment of Charles Hardinge as Permanent Secretary in place of Sanderson. While Hardinge's part in promoting the Foreign Office reforms was smaller than sometimes believed, the new Permanent Secretary certainly conceived of his role in a very different manner from his predecessor. Not only was he determined to exercise an influence on the foreign policy making process; he also encouraged the rapid promotion of officials in an apparent attempt to shake up the Foreign Office's traditional culture. During Hardinge's first period as Permanent Secretary, the age of those in more senior positions fell sharply. The average age of those appointed senior clerk between 1894 and 1906 was 48; the average age of those appointed between 1906 and 1910 was 41. Hardinge also tried to make sure that men promoted to the more sensitive posts shared his general views on important international questions. Nevertheless, the institutional significance of these changes should perhaps not be exaggerated. The principle of promotion by seniority was still respected in the Hardinge Foreign Office, while the Permanent Secretary himself was instinctively reluctant to delegate any of the more important decisions to his colleagues. The organisation and culture of the Foreign Office changed in the first decade of the twentieth century, but they were not transformed.

THE FOREIGN OFFICE, THE CABINET, AND THE CHANGING ARCHITECTURE OF DECISION MAKING IN THE EARLY TWENTIETH CENTURY

An examination of British policy towards Russia between 1903 and 1908 can help to illuminate the role and influence of the country's diplomatic establishment on foreign policy making in a critical five year period, when the Tsarist Empire moved from being the traditional rival of Britain in central Asia and the Far East to become something of an uneasy partner.[22] During these years, the Foreign Office increasingly replaced the Cabinet as the primary institutional location for determining the course of Britain's Russian policy. The change was in part due to the withdrawal of other potentially influential actors from the policy making process, as well as a consequence of the skill displayed by senior Foreign Office members in establishing administrative and bureaucratic coalitions to support their chosen policy of establishing some form of Anglo–Russian *entente*. It was to a greater extent, however, a consequence of the Foreign Office's success at insulating the policy formulation and implementation process from wider political pressures. The Hardinge–Grey regime that came into existence at the start of 1906 succeeded in establishing a considerable latitude of action for the foreign office professionals in the making of Britain's policy toward Russia. At the same time, however, their primacy was never complete or unchallenged.

The pattern of British foreign policy making toward Russia was of course too complex to be analysed simply in terms of a shift of power and influence within the core executive. Changes in the international environment, most notably the Russo–Japanese War of 1904–5, altered the balance of power between the two countries, making an accommodation with London seem a sensible policy to a growing section of the political elite in St Petersburg. The weakness of Russia also encouraged the advocates of an *entente* in London, who recognised that the Tsarist Empire's vulnerabilities were likely to make its rulers more flexible in negotiations to resolve outstanding issues in central Asia. The possibility of an *entente* had in any case first been seriously entertained by Lansdowne and the Balfour Cabinet before the administrative reforms at the Foreign Office, and the election of a Liberal government, transformed the political and administrative context in which foreign policy was made.[23] Nevertheless, Sir Edward Grey's appointment as Foreign Secretary, along with the almost simultaneous appointment of Charles Hardinge as Permanent Secretary at the Foreign Office, were important factors in facilitating the cause of an *entente* in London.[24] The arrival of two men who were by instinct anxious to reduce imperial tensions in order to focus on the growing crisis in Europe helped to place the improvement of Anglo–Russian relations firmly at the heart of the foreign policy agenda.

It was seen earlier that Lord Salisbury often chose to bypass his officials in dealing with important questions of policy when he served as both Prime Minister and Foreign Secretary between 1894 and 1900 (although there is a danger of exaggerating the eclipse of the Foreign Office during these years). Salisbury was, however, willing to bow to his Cabinet on important matters of policy. In 1895, for example, he deferred to his colleagues on the question of sending the fleet to defend Constantinople against a possible Russian advance, reluctantly accepting the majority view that dispatching ships to the region was too dangerous a move to be justified under the circumstances.[25] A committed 'realist' in all things political, the Prime Minister doubted the wisdom of pursuing any course of action abroad that did not command both public and political support. When Balfour took over as Prime Minister in 1902, two years after Lansdowne had replaced the increasingly weary Salisbury at the Foreign Office, the Cabinet continued to be closely involved in discussions about foreign policy. This was in part because the Balfour Cabinet contained such men as Joseph Chamberlain at the Colonial Office, who displayed an enduring interest in all foreign policy matters, even when they did not directly impinge on his departmental remit.[26] International affairs also attracted the attention of other ministers such as Lord Selborne at the Admiralty.[27] Above all, though, the Prime Minister was himself deeply interested in foreign affairs, particularly as they affected questions of empire. Balfour's obssession with imperial defence naturally focused a good deal of his attention on tsarist Russia, since the country presented the most potent challenge to the British position in central Asia, particularly once the construction of new railways in the region seemed to provide St Petersburg with secure lines of communication.[28] The Prime Minister himself composed a number of memoranda on the subject, most of them presenting a rather gloomy view of Britain's position *vis à vis* Russia in central Asia. It was for this reason that the defence of India became a central focus for the Committee of Imperial Defence (CID), set up by Balfour shortly after he became Prime Minister as a forum for achieving greater coordination between the relevant government departments.[29] During the years Balfour was in office, countering the Russian threat to India became a matter of great concern to a large number of government departments, ranging from the Foreign Office and the Treasury through to the India Office and the War Office. This distinctive combination of personal and institutional interest in Britain's relations with Russia made it difficult for the Foreign Office to assert itself as the principal source of authoritative information and advice about policy towards the Tsarist Empire.

The absence of formal records makes it difficult to identify the nature of the Cabinet's deliberations on matters of foreign policy during the Balfour administration, although the Prime Minister's lengthy letters to Edward VII, along with the surviving Cabinet papers, provide some insight into the discussions. Lord Curzon noted in a 1918 speech to the House of Lords that pre-war cabinets had been organised in such an *ad hoc* manner that ministers 'often only had the haziest notion as to what its decisions were'.[30] While the Balfour Cabinet seems to have been run in a more organised fashion than some of its successors, business was certainly brought before it in a rather haphazard manner. Any minister could request that an item be placed on the agenda even when it concerned a subject that was beyond their departmental remit, but members of the Cabinet usually had a degree of independence when deciding which issues relating to their own department should be brought before their colleagues. The Foreign Office under Lansdowne produced a large number of papers for circulation to the Cabinet, but few of them were concerned with major questions of policy *per se*.[31] If the letters sent by Balfour to the King were an accurate summary of business transacted by ministers, it seems that although the Cabinet spent a good deal of time discussing overseas affairs in the broad sense of the term – that is including such 'imperial' questions as the administration of colonies – consideration of core Foreign Office business was less frequent.[32] Much of the discussion about foreign affairs *proper* in the Balfour Cabinet seems to have been concerned either with comparatively minor 'incremental' questions or, more frequently, with major international crises. Above all, the Cabinet's attention was focused on issues of immediate salience. The Anglo–French *entente* was extensively discussed at the end of 1903 and early 1904, once it was up and running as an important issue of current policy, but there does not seem to have been much prior collective discussion about the wisdom of embarking on such a course of action. The same pattern was evident when British policy towards Russia was under review by the Balfour Cabinet. The subject was apparently seldom discussed in much detail by the full Cabinet in 1903 – not even towards the end of the year when tentative negotiations began about improving the relationship between St Petersburg and London. Nor does the Foreign Office seem to have circulated many papers on the whole question. By contrast, in 1904, when the Russo-Japanese War created enormous tension between the two countries, relations with St Petersburg dominated the Cabinet agenda. At least 16 of the 21 extant letters sent by Balfour to Edward VII in the second half of the year reporting on Cabinet discussions referred to one aspect or another of the Anglo–Russian relationship. While a good deal of foreign policy is by its very nature reactive in character, the Balfour Cabinet seems to have been particularly ineffective at dealing with long-term 'strategic' issues that transcended the management of day-to-day problems. The CID filled this gap to some extent in the military arena, but it could not provide direction across the whole sphere of international relations – although its members did on occasion consider general matters of foreign policy that were more properly the concern of the Foreign Office.

Since the Balfour Cabinet's focus was usually on questions of immediate import, the Foreign Secretary undoubtedly had the chance to exercise considerable influence on the development of British foreign policy, but Lansdowne's instincts and consensual style of working meant that he seldom exploited these opportunities to the full.[33] He developed a perfectly reasonable working relationship with most of his senior officials, who treated him in turn with a good deal of respect, but his natural reserve and somewhat glacial manner meant that relations were seldom particularly warm.[34] The Foreign Secretary was certainly more inclined than Salisbury to seek the advice of his staff on matters of policy, although the system of record-keeping used in the Foreign Office before 1906 makes it difficult to reconstruct in detail deliberations about any particular issue. Nevertheless, Lansdowne was still inclined to the view that critical discussions about policy should take place between himself and his ministerial colleagues, either in the formal setting of Cabinet or in private meetings and correspondence. There is little evidence that most matters of policy were extensively discussed between Lansdowne and his officials before being submitted for approval by the Foreign Secretary's ministerial colleagues. Policy-initiation, to the extent that this concept can be invoked in an inherently reactive process such as the formulation of foreign policy, usually rested with the political rather than the administrative members of the core executive.

While Lansdowne's first instinct was to rely on his own counsel or look to his ministerial colleagues for advice, there is no doubt that a number of senior Foreign Office officials displayed a growing interest in foreign policy questions in the first few years of the twentieth century, convinced, as a previous section suggested, that they possessed both the aptitude and knowledge required to direct the development of Britain's international relations. Charles Hardinge, who served as an Assistant Secretary during 1903–4, before becoming British Ambassador in St Petersburg, had already developed decided views on the virtues of establishing a better relationship with Russia by the time the first tentative moves towards an *entente* took place in the autumn of 1903.[35] Francis Bertie, who also served as an Assistant Secretary before being appointed Ambassador to Rome in 1903, shared many of Hardinge's views on policy, particularly the distrust of Germany, as well as his decided distaste for the bureaucratic 'old guard' grouped around Sanderson.[36] Since Hardinge in particular was able to rely on the support and patronage of Edward VII, the Hardinge–Bertie 'axis' had the potential to exercise a good deal of influence within the Foreign Office, especially since it became a natural focus for some of the younger and more ambitious clerks. Nevertheless, Bertie's departure for the Rome

Embassy in 1903, followed by Hardinge's departure for St Petersburg in the middle of 1904, reined in the scope of their influence. In any case, Sanderson's continued presence as Permanent Secretary until early in 1906, when combined with Lansdowne's instinctive belief that the Foreign Secretary and his ministerial colleagues should be the primary agents in the policy making process, placed limits on the scope of officials for determining policy. As Ambassador in St Petersburg, Hardinge played a vital role in preserving the Anglo–Russian relationship from the worst vagaries of the tense international climate that developed in the Russo–Japanese War, but his absence from London during these critical years almost certainly made it harder for him to influence Lansdowne. The Cabinet continued to exercise an important collective influence on British Policy toward Russia until the collapse of the Balfour Government at the end of 1905.

It has already been seen that the winter of 1905–6 was a turning point in the history of the Anglo–Russian relationship, in large part as a result of the major political and administrative changes that took place in *both* countries during the period. The new Campbell-Bannerman Cabinet was much more concerned with domestic affairs than its predecessor, despite the presence of so-called liberal imperialists such as Asquith and Haldane. Unlike his predecessor, the new Prime Minister had no great knowledge of foreign affairs, and was for the most part willing to leave them to the handful of ministers who did have a strong interest in the subject.[37] The social welfare reforms propounded by Lloyd George at the Treasury were of much greater concern to most of the Cabinet than the intricacies of Britain's overseas relations. As the 'imperialists' were for the most part on close personal or political terms with Grey, they too were inclined to allow the Foreign Secretary a good deal of autonomy.[38] Lloyd George recalled in his memoirs that 'During the eight years that preceeded the war, the Cabinet devoted a ridiculously small percentage of its time to a consideration of foreign affairs', a view confirmed by a number of other ministers who served with him including Haldane.[39] Grey himself wrote in his memoirs that 'Members of the Cabinet are kept in touch with the current work of the Foreign Office to a far greater extent than with the work of any other department',[40] but his claim cannot be accepted uncritically, at least as far as policy towards Russia is concerned. Grey was far less inclined than Lansdowne to identify the Cabinet as the natural focus for foreign policy making.[41] While he kept the Prime Minister informed about most matters of importance, such as the decision to authorise military discussions between French and

British military officers at the start of 1906, the Foreign Secretary felt no need to keep the Cabinet as a whole abreast of such developments. The contemporary records bear out the idea that the Cabinet's collective control of foreign policy was weaker under Campbell-Bannerman than Balfour.[42] Of the 46 extant letters sent by Campbell-Bannerman to Edward VII in 1906 discussing the conduct of Cabinet business, only a quarter mention foreign affairs. The negotiations with Russia that took place during the year barely received any mention, even though they were of such vital concern for Britain's future place in the European order. The talks only figured in detail a couple of times in the letters sent by the Prime Minister to the King during 1907, the year in which an agreement was actually signed. Since Campbell-Bannerman's letters to the monarch were far less detailed than the ones written by his predecessor, the absence of references to foreign affairs in general, and negotiations with Russia in particular, may in part have reflected the different epistolary styles of the two prime ministers. Nevertheless, the small number of papers circulated to the Cabinet on *policy* towards Russia during 1906 and 1907 tends to support the idea that Grey was determined to keep the whole business as free from Cabinet scrutiny as possible (although a surprisingly large number of papers were circulated describing the development of Russia's internal situation). The Committee of Imperial Defence also declined as a possible source of influence on foreign policy during the period, since a rise in membership and a decline in the number of full meetings meant that it became increasingly unwieldy and faction-ridden. In any case, Grey always attended the full meetings of the CID, unlike Lansdowne, while senior Foreign Office officials were present at many of the most important sub-committees.[43] In his first few years in power, Grey therefore managed to secure considerable autonomy for himself in the conduct of foreign affairs, one of the factors which made him a particular target for the more radical critics of the old diplomacy, who deplored the extent to which foreign policy making had supposedly passed beyond the suzerainty of Cabinet and Parliament. The impact of these changes on the Foreign Office *qua* institution was, however, also critically dependent on the relationship that Grey forged with his officials.

While Grey was instinctively reluctant to provide most of his Cabinet colleagues with much information about his Department's business, he was far more ready than Lansdowne to involve permanent staff at the Foreign Office in policy matters. Charles Hardinge recalled in his memoirs that while Lansdowne had not been 'an easy chief to serve owing to his very reserved nature', with Grey he was 'able to discuss everything with the utmost freedom'.[44] The close working relationship that developed between the two men was partly rooted in their shared views about many important questions of policy. Hardinge and Grey were both inclined to identify Germany as the principal threat to British interests both in Europe and beyond, while the Foreign Secretary signalled his desire to establish a closer relationship with St Petersburg from the moment he took office – something which Hardinge had of course advocated for several years.[45] The two men also had a good personal relationship. The death of Grey's wife a few weeks after he became Foreign Secretary, with the associated emotional trauma, undoubtedly meant that he was forced to rely on the professional judgement of his Permanent Secretary to a greater extent than might otherwise have been the case, a pattern that continued until Hardinge's departure from the Foreign Office to take over as Viceroy of India in 1910. Hardinge's well-developed belief that the Foreign Office should serve as a major focus for policy making dovetailed neatly with Grey's instincts and preferred method of working (not least the Foreign Secretary's desire to periodically escape from London to indulge his passion for country sports). Nor was Hardinge the only member of the diplomatic establishment in whom Grey confided, although the Permanent Secretary was without doubt the principal conduit for information and advice. It will be seen later that Sir Arthur Nicolson, who succeeded Hardinge as Ambassador in St Petersburg, played a vital part in the 'triumvirate' that determined the course of Britain's Russian policy in the year leading up the Anglo–Russian *entente*. Hardinge's penchant for promoting men who shared his views and instincts to positions of authority also meant that Grey increasingly found himself surrounded with officials anxious to involve themselves closely in questions of policy. As a result of all these developments, the potential influence of senior officials in the Foreign Office on the policy making process undoubtedly grew sharply in the years after 1906.

THE LIMITS ON FOREIGN OFFICE AUTONOMY: THE MAKING OF BRITAIN'S RUSSIAN POLICY DURING THE BALFOUR ADMINISTRATION

The much vaunted 'end of isolation' of Great Britain in the early years of the twentieth century, which took place via agreements with Japan (1902), France (1904) and Russia (1907), was not the result of a coherent and calculated strategy. Nevertheless, the Foreign Office did serve as an important institutional focus for a series of incremental decisions that, in the course of five years, transformed the pattern of the country's international relations. Lansdowne was himself a strong supporter of the Japanese treaty, designed to provide Britain with a valuable ally should the country become involved in a war with Russia and France, a treaty which he secured in the face of scepticism on the part of many of his Cabinet colleagues (including Balfour). The Foreign Secretary had been struck, like so many of his compatriots, by the danger of Britain's diplomatic isolation which had been revealed so starkly during the early defeats in the Boer War. Lansdowne himself, however, had a decidedly *realpolitik* attitude to the problem of securing allies; like many of his ministerial colleagues, he was for much of his time at the Foreign Office quite open to the idea of forging a closer relationship with Germany in the hope that it would provide a useful counterweight to the challenge posed by France and Russia to British interests. It has already been seen that the same was not true of all his officials.

The editors of the *British Documents on the Origins of the War* chose to begin the volume dealing with the negotiations leading up to the Anglo–Russian convention in 1903, since a series of diplomatic exchanges at the end of that year centred on the possibility of establishing some kind of *detente* between London and St Petersburg. In reality, however, these exchanges, which were soon overtaken by the political furore created by the Russo–Japanese War, were conceived of by both parties as part of an on-going diplomatic dialogue rather than as a potential turning point in the history of the relationship between the two countries. Lansdowne was initially unimpressed by the conversations he had with the Russian Ambassador in London, Count A.K. Benckendorff, about the possibility of establishing some kind of agreement to settle the differences between London and St Petersburg in central Asia, believing that any 'discussions [were] not likely to have much result'.[47] Benckendorff nevertheless broached the subject during a visit to Windsor Castle, knowing that Edward VII had for many years been in favour of establishing better relations between Britain and Russia. Charles Hardinge at the Foreign Office was also more inclined than Lansdowne to look favourably on the value of pursuing negotiations, particularly after a meeting with Benckendorff at which the two men sketched out a possible agreement over Afghanistan, Persia and Tibet.[48] Lansdowne's views started to become more positive, in part as a result of the promptings of Hardinge, with the result that by the end of November the possibility of continuing the talks was considered seriously by the Foreign Secretary.[49]

During November 1903, discussions about the possibility of a rapprochement with Russia mainly involved King Edward, Lansdowne and Hardinge, although Balfour was kept abreast of developments. There is little evidence that the wisdom of such a course of action was widely discussed, at least formally, inside the Foreign Office or among other members of the British diplomatic establishment. The views of the Ambassador in St Petersburg, Sir Charles Scott, were certainly not given much weight in London. Nor does the Cabinet seem to have been kept collectively informed of the discussions that were taking place with Benckendorff at this time; the subject was not mentioned in Balfour's letters to the monarch or in papers circulated to Cabinet by the Foreign Office. By December, however, this pattern began to change, when the looming possibility of a Russo–Japanese War held out the prospect that Britain might be required to come to the aid of its ally. The whole question of a possible agreement between Britain and Russia over their differences in central Asia quickly became caught up in the more immediate crisis in the Far East. As the political sensitivity of Anglo–Russian relations increased, so the ability of the Foreign Office to determine the course of policy started to decline.

The support of Hardinge and Lansdowne for a rapprochement with Russia was not shared by many Cabinet ministers, particularly once the crisis in the Far East started to take a threatening turn. Balfour himself was not opposed to an agreement in principle, since he was convinced that Britain lacked the military resources to prevent a determined Russian expansion in central Asia; he wrote in a December 1903 memorandum that 'There is, I believe, no British government that would not gladly make a permanent arrangement with Russia in Central Asia and the Far East'.[50] The Prime Minister was, however, inclined to think that a Russo–Japanese conflict might have some favourable consequences for Britain, since it would weaken Russia and make its government 'much easier to deal with'.[51] His position attracted support from other senior ministers, including Austen Chamberlain at the Treasury, who told Lansdowne in a private letter that he believed Britain should not fight shy of taking 'advantage of [Russia's] preoccupations and embarassments'.[52] Lansdowne was by contrast convinced that Britain should exercise a moderating influence on its Japanese ally. He argued that while Japanese forces might thrive in the early stages of any conflict, they would soon encounter setbacks that would lead to calls both at home and abroad for Britain to offer military support – something that would of course inevitably destroy the prospects for any Anglo–Russian rapprochement as well as drag the country into war. His position was supported by a number of ministers including Selborne at the Admiralty, but the Foreign Secretary struggled to win Balfour round to his position. In a letter written towards the end of December he told the Prime Minister that 'I attach, I think, more importance to averting war than you do', and urged the need to help Japan 'get out of the impasse in which she finds herself'.[53] The Foreign Secretary continued to promote the cause of an agreement with St Petersburg, circulating a possible draft to the Cabinet on the first day of 1904 with a characteristic request for 'observations' from his colleagues.[54] In reality, however, a combination of international circumstances and Cabinet divisions meant that the time was hardly propitious for such a far-reaching move, despite the attempts by senior members of the Foreign Office to pursue their chosen policy. A few days later, Lansdowne told the British Ambassador in St Petersburg that Benckendorff himself now 'felt some doubt whether the present moment was an opportune one for commencing general discussion with the Russian government'.[55] While Hardinge and Lansdowne were both committed to improving relations with Russia, they were stymied both by opposition from leading ministers and by the vagaries of an increasingly unfavourable international environment. Even though the early discussions with Benckendorff were largely carried out under the auspices of the Foreign Office, Lansdowne's commitment to consulting his colleagues – along with the growing political sensitivity of the Anglo–Russian relationship during a time of international tension – meant that the issue spilled over to become a subject for general Cabinet review. The views of the Foreign Office were as a result of less importance in determining policy at the end of December than they had been a few weeks earlier.

The Balfour government's increasing unpopularity during 1904 and 1905 made it difficult to launch any major changes in domestic or foreign policy, while the tension caused by the Russo–Japanese War reduced the prospects of any significant change in the texture of the Anglo–Russian relationship. The main objective of the Cabinet was to prevent an immediate outbreak of hostilities between London and St Petersburg rather than to secure an agreement between the two governments about central Asia. Charles Hardinge's departure for St Petersburg in the spring of 1904 removed the staunchest advocate of an improved Anglo–Russian relationship from the Foreign Office, although his presence in the Russian capital allowed him to defend the Anglo–Russian relationship during a turbulent period and pave the way for the eventual renewal of negotiations once hostilities had ended. The tentative moves towards an Anglo–Russian *entente* that began in the autumn of 1903 were not simply stymied by an unfavourable international environment; they were instead undermined by a change in the pattern and location of decision-making in London that was itself a consequence of the rise in international tension.

While Lansdowne and Hardinge at the Foreign Office were unable to assert their primacy in the making of Britain's policy towards Russia at the end of 1903 and the beginning of 1904, the Cabinet's putative constitutional status as the location for authoritative decisions about policy towards Russia faced other challenges during the final years of the Balfour administration. The most important of these came from the Indian government, headed from 1900 to 1905 by the impetuously brilliant Lord Curzon.[56] Curzon combined a detailed knowledge of central Asia, garnered during his extensive travels in the region during the 1880s,[57] with a wide network of relationships with senior political figures back in Britain. The Viceroy was by instinct contemptuous of the foreign policy professionals employed by the Foreign Office and Diplomatic Service. Arthur Hardinge, the Minister in Tehran, noted early in 1904, following a meeting with Curzon, that the Viceroy believed the Foreign Office was too craven in its dealings with Russia; he also wrote to Lord Lansdowne telling him that Curzon also 'blames me for being too courteous and diplomatic with the Persians, and treating mendacious Asiatics as if they were European statesmen'.[58] Curzon's views about Anglo–Russian relations were decidedly at odds with those held by a majority of the Cabinet. He failed to understand the extent to which the 'Balfour doctrine' on Russia commanded widespread support in London – namely, that geography gave Russia a huge advantage in central Asia that could only be countered by a combination of cautious diplomacy and careful military planning. Although Curzon was not in principle opposed to establishing some kind of understanding with Russia, he tended in practice to react negatively to any concrete proposals.[59] Since the Viceroy's forthright views were at odds with most of the Cabinet, there was always a danger of a conflict developing between the British and Indian governments over policy towards Russia.

Curzon made strenuous efforts to influence British policy towards Russia by 'lobbying' senior ministers, including Balfour and Lansdowne, with a deluge of private correspondence and formal dispatches. In 1902, for example, the Viceroy demanded that the government in London should make a substantial loan to Persia in order to counter Russia's growing influence in the country. Most of his proposals were in practice quietly ignored, a response which predictably caused profound irritation to Curzon, who believed that he was best-placed to identify ways of defending British interests in central Asia. By 1903, the Viceroy was using 'a quite surprising number of pungent adjectives' to describe the cautious policy of the British government towards Russia.[60] It was this tension that provided the background to the celebrated Younghusband Affair of 1903–4, when the eponymous Indian Army Colonel led a detachment of troops to the Tibetan capital of Lhasa, apparently in direct contravention of orders from London, where there was widespread concern that such an action would provoke a hostile response from Russia.[61] The whole affair, including the role of Curzon, is still surrounded in a good deal of mystery, but there was certainly widespread suspicion in London that the Viceroy had provided tacit support for a forward policy designed to extend British influence in a critical area. While the immediate crisis was smoothed over, in large part by accepting the probable fiction that Younghusband was himself directly responsible for exceeding his instructions, the tension between Curzon and the Cabinet continued to linger.[62] His eventual resignation on the question of army reorganisation came on top of a long-standing feud about the constitutional role of the Viceroy *vis à vis* London. Curzon made no secret that he believed his recommendations about matters of foreign policy that concerned India should be decisive in influencing the decisions of the Cabinet: 'The Viceroy of India is not an agent whom you send out merely to execute your orders or to act as the instrument of a policy conceived at home'.[63] The Prime Minister and his colleagues predictably disagreed, although Balfour made many attempts to flatter Curzon that his opinion was given great attention in London. Just as the Balfour Cabinet took precedence over the Foreign Office when critical decisions about policy towards Russia were under discussion, so in the last analysis ministers proved willing to fend off the challenge of Curzon and the Indian government on important questions of foreign policy.

THE GROWTH IN FOREIGN OFFICE AUTONOMY: THE MAKING OF BRITAIN'S RUSSIAN POLICY DURING THE CAMPBELL-BANNERMAN ADMINISTRATION

It was seen earlier that many members of the Campbell-Bannerman administration which came to office at the end of 1905 were less interested in foreign affairs than their predecessors, while the so-called liberal imperialists were normally willing to allow Grey considerable freedom to exercise his judgement in making important decisions.

When combined with Grey's readiness to consult closely on matters of policy with senior officials at the Foreign Office – where Hardinge was newly-installed as Permanent Secretary – the net result of the political and administrative changes which took place late in 1905 and early in 1906 was to increase the influence of the diplomatic establishment on the foreign policy making process. Throughout much of 1906 and 1907, both the formulation and execution of Britain's Russian policy was in the hands of a 'critical triangle' of men consisting of Grey, Charles Hardinge and Arthur Nicolson (who replaced Hardinge as British Ambassador in St Petersburg in the spring of 1906).[64] Before Nicolson's departure for the Russian capital, the three men discussed at length the strategy to be pursued by the new Ambassador on arrival at his post, conferring on occasion with Morley and Asquith as well.[65] When negotiations finally began in earnest in the final months of 1906, a dense formal and private correspondence between members of the triumvirate helped them to formulate an agreed position on the most important issues that arose during the talks. While Nicolson was careful to seek approval for any particular proposal, he interpreted his ambassadorial role in an essentially proactive manner, making numerous suggestions and raising objections to the directions sent to him by London. Even though the Ambassador received formal instructions about how to handle the negotiations with the Russian government – which in practice focused on resolving the differences between the two countries over Persia, Afghanistan and Tibet – the complexity and dynamism of the talks meant that private letters and daily telegrams provided the principal communications infrastructure governing Nicolson's day-to-day actions. The British position on any particular aspect of the negotiations was therefore to a great extent determined in an *ad hoc* manner by the Foreign Secretary, his Permanent Secretary in London and his Ambassador 'in the field' in St Petersburg.

The growing ability of senior members of the British diplomatic establishment to set the course of Britain's Russian policy depended on the cultivation, or the marginalisation, of individuals who might be in a position to promote or hinder the cause of an Anglo–Russian rapprochement. Grey subsequently observed that the task of securing the Anglo–Russian *entente* would have been much harder without the support of John Morley, the radically-minded Secretary of State for India, who played an important role in reining in the influence of the Indian government on the negotiations.[66] Morley also played a significant role in influencing the course of negotiations, amending Foreign Office proposals and making further suggestions of his own.[67] Both the Indian government and, to a lesser extent, the India Office in London, were always likely to act as an institutional focus for opposition to an *entente*, given the strong tradition of russophobia among those who dealt with Indian affairs. The resignation of Curzon had, however, removed one of the most determined advocates of a forward policy in central Asia from the political landscape. His successor, Lord Minto, quickly came to share Curzon's scepticism about the possibility of placing any trust in declarations of good intent made by the Russian government, but he lacked both the acerbity and the political contacts of his illustrious predecessor.[68] Morley himself was determined to emphasise the supremacy of the India Office over the Indian government, a constitutional relationship that Curzon had always been inclined to challenge. Although the Secretary of State acknowledged in his memoirs that the anxieties of the Indian government were understandable,[69] his correspondence with Minto bordered at times on the brutal. He swept aside the various objections and concerns raised by the Viceroy, arguing that 'this country cannot have two foreign policies.... You have set out your views with signal force. They do not convert us – and so, like other Ministers who cannot carry their colleagues, you will make the best of it'.[70] Hardinge, in particular, continued to look with suspicion at the activities of the India Office during the course of the negotiations of 1906–7, particularly given the delays that occured there in responding to questions put by the Foreign Office.[71] Nevertheless, he too appreciated the role of Morley in steamrollering the critics of an *entente* among the Indian lobby, writing to Nicolson at the end of 1906 that 'since Morley's accession to the India Office the decisions of the Viceroy have not the same formality as formerly'.[72] The reasons for Morley's support for an *entente* with Russia are still unclear, given that his political instincts and values were very different from those of Grey, while the autocratic values of the tsarist regime were an anathema to his liberal instincts. An agreement with Russia certainly held out the prospect of lower defence expenditure, a cause that was close to Morley's heart, which might perhaps have accounted for his willingness to work so closely with the Foreign Office on Russian affairs.[73] Whatever the cause, the good working relationship that developed between senior members of the Foreign Office and the Indian Office during the negotiations for the Anglo–Russian *entente* certainly helped to neutralise one of the most important potential sources of institutional opposition in Whitehall.

The relevant Foreign Office documents suggest that few ministers were consulted with much frequency about the detailed negotiations that took place with Russia during 1906 and 1907. In addition to

Campbell-Bannerman and Morley, the Lord Privy Seal, Lord Ripon, routinely received copies of the most important dispatches and memoranda, although he does not seem to have had any significant influence on the deliberations. Ministers with direct responsibility for defence matters were not consulted extensively either in the preliminary discussions or during the course of the negotiations proper. The Minister of War, Haldane, was on close personal terms with Grey. He did not, however, play a large role in the formulation of Britain's Russian policy during 1906–7, perhaps because his instinctive support for building closer relations with Berlin meant that he was treated with suspicion by the advocates of an *entente* with St Petersburg.[74] The same was largely true of senior army and naval officers, despite the fact that the negotiations often revolved around questions that were strategic in import and technical in character. Even though the whole question of an Anglo–Russian rapprochement was intimately bound up with questions of imperial defence, the subject was seldom discussed in any coherent and sustained manner in the Committee for Imperial Defence – a sharp contrast with the years before 1906. Some copies of key dispatches and telegrams were sent to King Edward VII, who had of course for many years been a staunch proponent of developing better relations with St Petersburg, as well as serving as a powerful patron to Hardinge as he furthered his meteoric career. It appears, however, that Grey and his Permanent Secretary did not put complete trust in Edward's discretion on highly confidential matters; Hardinge told Nicolson on one occasion that while he forwarded most of the Ambassador's private letters to the King, 'some caution has to be observed'.[75] Given the degree of care shown by Grey and Hardinge, it is not surprising that they were for the most part successful in ensuring that the negotiations with Russia remained firmly within the province of the Foreign Office. The British view on the critical question of the boundary between the British and Russian spheres of influence in Persia, for example, was apparently formulated largely within the triumvirate of Grey, Hardinge and Nicolson, following consultation with the India Office in an effort to find out the views of senior officials there.[76] In a similar way, the economic aspects of the negotiations, ranging from questions of trade with Tibet through to the commercial potential of Persia, do not seem to have been referred in any great detail to the Treasury or the Board of Trade. The documentary evidence strongly suggests that the Foreign Office under Grey was the 'engine' of policy making during the lead-up to the Anglo–Russian *entente*.

While the 1903–6 reforms of the Foreign Office were intended to provide junior officials with more opportunities to involve themselves in policy matters, policy towards Russia during 1906–7 was in practice firmly determined 'at the top' – a pattern that was by no means so true several years later, when men like Herman Norman and William Tyrrell exercised a greater influence. The change in the record-keeping system that began with the introduction of the General Registry in 1906 makes it a little easier for the historian to trace debates about policy inside the Foreign Office, although the 'paper trail' can never give a precise record of discussions and opinions. The Senior Clerk in charge of the Eastern Department, R.P. Maxwell, received copies of the most important documents and occasionally added a minute commenting on some aspect of policy, but there is little sign that he was extensively involved in substantial decisions about the negotiations, even though his expertise in dealing with Russian affairs was generally acknowledged at the Foreign Office. Nor is there much evidence that other senior officials in the Foreign Office participated to any great extent in the making of Britain's Russian policy in 1906–7, although Eldon Gorst as Superintending Secretary of the Eastern Department wrote a number of characteristically pithy minutes on various aspects of the negotiations. Diplomats in post abroad were well-aware of the negotiations taking place with Russia, and provided a flood of information about the likely response of other governments to any rapprochement, but none of them except Nicolson were routinely kept abreast about the detailed progress of the talks. Cecil Spring Rice in Tehran waged a solitary and bitter campaign against an agreement with Russia, but he was angrily forced to acknowledge that his views on the agreement were 'neither invited nor desired' by Hardinge and Grey in London.[77] Most other senior members of the diplomatic establishment were apparently in favour of a rapprochement with Russia, but none of them had a decisive influence on establishing the form which it eventually took.

While the political and administrative changes of 1905–6 increased the influence of the most senior members of the British diplomatic establishment *vis à vis* other members of the core executive, they were never able to ignore the wider political environment altogether. Public opinion, as Lord Salisbury had fervently argued during his long political career, imposed a powerful constraint on the freedom of manoeuvre of those who made British foreign policy. Opinion could manifest itself in a variety of different forms: in newspaper editorials; in speeches by Members of Parliament; in the activities of what would today be called 'pressure groups'. Even the most determined Foreign Office official could not expect policy to be made in a complete vacuum, if only because public concern was likely to raise the political salience of a particular controversy and encourage the Cabinet to take a more direct interest in the outcome. The whole question of Britain's relationship with Russia was of considerable public sensitivity in the months and years following the election of a Liberal government, particularly among politicians and journalists on the left of the political spectrum, many of whom were bitterly critical of any attempt to establish a better relationship with an autocratic regime that consistently used force to crush its opponents. Writers like Lucien Wolf waged a long campaign to draw the attention of the British public to some of the atrocities taking place in Russia.[78] Nor was this criticism confined to the political fringes. Campbell-Bannerman himself instinctively identified with the aims of the reform movement in Russia, a sentiment that was shared by several members of his Cabinet. *The Times* was also often critical of the tsarist regime, following the expulsion of its correspondent in 1903 for reporting on the pogroms that regularly erupted across the country.[79] Any successful attempt to promote the cause of an *entente* in Britain therefore required its advocates either to wage a battle for public sentiment or to marginalise the impact of popular opposition on the decision-making process.

The Foreign Office made few concerted attempts to influence public opinion in the years before 1914; the Press Bureau was only established after the outbreak of the First World War, charged among other tasks with managing the Department's relations with the major newspapers.[80] Nevertheless, some senior officials did work hard to cultivate contacts with influential journalists and writers even before this time. Charles Hardinge was particularly assiduous in cultivating Valentine Chirol of *The Times*, calculating that the support of such an influential newspaper for a closer relationship with Russia would have a considerable impact on political opinion. Hardinge also used his extensive contacts among the denizens of the British Establishment, most notably at Court, in an effort to attract support for the cause of the Anglo-Russian rapprochement. For the most part, however, the *de facto* strategy employed by senior members of the Foreign Office was to insulate, as far as possible, the foreign policy making process from the pressure of public opinion. Grey and Hardinge certainly followed the evolution of public opinion towards Russia with great care, particularly when the outbreak of pogroms there in the spring of 1906 sent a wave of repulsion through British society, since they recognised that such developments would make it harder to justify the start of serious negotiations.[81] At the same time, however, they were determined to promote their chosen policy of rapprochement with St Petersburg, marginalising whenever possible the influence of those whom Hardinge scathingly referred to as 'enthusiasts and idealists'.[82]

The biggest crisis faced by the advocates of an Anglo–Russian *entente* in London took place in the spring and early summer of 1906, shortly after Arthur Nicolson arrived in the country to take up his duties. The government in St Petersburg had already made moves to build a closer relationship with London at the beginning of the year, when the then Prime Minister, Sergei Witte, asked the *Daily Telegraph* correspondent in Russia to go to London to sound out the possibility of securing a British loan in return for some kind of agreement to resolve outstanding differences between the two countries.[83] Even though Grey and Hardinge were firmly committed to developing a closer relationship with St Petersburg, they responded cooly to these initial overtures. Hardinge distrusted the instinctively germanophile Witte, and suspected that the Prime Minister was not in a position to deliver on his promise of improved relations, even though the Embassy in St Petersburg informed London that the Foreign Minister, Count V.N. Lamsdorff, was also in favour of an agreement.[84] It was only in the course of the next few months that Grey and Hardinge, in consultation with Nicolson, began to believe that the political situation in Russia might be conducive to the start of meaningful negotiations as opposed to somewhat ritualistic declarations of goodwill. In the event, though, Nicolson's arrival at the St Petersburg Embassy in May coincided with two developments that seemed to threaten the prospects for any agreement. The resignation of Lamsdorff as Foreign Minister, and his replacement by A.P. Izvol'skii, was at first interpreted in London as a triumph for a 'German Party' in St Petersburg.[85] More importantly, Nicolson's arrival coincided with a sudden upsurge in violence against Russia's Jewish population, a development which threatened to alienate public opinion in Britain and weaken the position of the supporters of a rapprochement with St Petersburg. Throughout June and July 1906, Hardinge and Grey had to work hard to prevent public outrage at home from undermining their chosen policy even before they had begun to put it into effect.

In June 1906 one of the worst pogroms in recent Russian history took place in Belostock, the culmination of a whole series of atrocities which had been reported to the British Embassy in St Petersburg by consular officials living in the worst affected areas. The Foreign Office in London had little doubt that at least some local officials were implicated in these outrages. Nevertheless, senior staff at the Foreign Office remained deeply committed to the principle of diplomatic non-interference.

During 1905, when Lansdowne was still in office, both Foreign Office officials and diplomats at the St Petersburg Embassy endorsed Witte's somewhat doubtful claim that violence against Russian Jews was a reflection of popular frustration with the revolutionaries who had fomented the chaos that swept across Russia during the 1905 Revolution, many of whom were of Jewish origin.[86] The protests made to the Foreign Office in the course of the year by representatives of various Jewish groups in Britain were routinely ignored. A similar pattern continued in the late spring and summer of 1906, following the Belostock massacre, which served as a catalyst for an even more fervent crescendo of public outrage. A goodwill visit by the British fleet to Russia had already been in prospect for some weeks, which quickly became a target of criticism for those who feared that such a visit might be seen as an endorsement of the behaviour of the tsarist government. In Parliament, the Labour MP Ramsay MacDonald demanded a reconsideration of the decision to go ahead with the visit given 'the outbreak of Jewish massacres in Western Russia'. Stuart Samuel MP demanded that Grey should 'inform the government of Russia, prior to any steps being taken to establish closer ties of friendship with this country, of the views held by the British people concerning the massacre of Jews in Russia'.[87] The Foreign Office was bombarded with letters demanding the cancellation of the visit of the fleet which might be seen as honouring 'the murderers of so many innocent people'.[88] Jewish groups were particularly assiduous in their efforts to urge the Foreign Office to take a harder line towards the Russians. Members of the Anglo-Jewish society held a series of difficult meetings with Charles Hardinge, culminating in a bad-tempered exchange of letters about a supposed promise by the Permanent Secretary to make 'unofficial' representations to the Russian government about the pogroms.[89] Lord Nathaniel Rothschild also worked hard to encourage the government to pursue a firmer policy in its dealings with St Petersburg.[90] Other non-Jewish groups such as the Russian Freedom Society were similarly active in their attempts to rally British public opinion against the tsarist regime. Detailed coverage of developments inside Russia in such newspapers as *The Times* and the *Daily Telegraph* provided considerable ammunition for critics of the Russian government. Even though senior members of the Foreign Office had gained experience the previous year in fending off pressure from individuals and groups anxious about developments in Russia, the crisis of June and July 1906 provided a stern test of their determination to pursue their chosen policy of rapprochement with the government in St Petersburg.

Grey, Hardinge and Nicolson were all instinctively irritated by the growing chorus of public criticism of Russia. Grey told the House of Commons on 5 July that 'the less comment in this House on Russian affairs the better', since it would only serve to complicate relations with St Petersburg. Hardinge angrily told Nicolson at the end of June that 'The Jews over here are showing great activity' in demanding a less friendly policy towards Russia.[91] Both men knew that any attempt to raise the matter either formally or informally with the Russian government would simply damage relations between Britain and Russia. When Nicolson did briefly refer to the issue in a meeting with Izvol'skii on 20 June, the Foreign Minister predictably reacted with an 'exceeding stiffness' which made it clear that no comment would be tolerated on the subject of pogroms.[92] Nevertheless, the advocates of an *entente* inside the Foreign Office still found it difficult to neutralise the attacks made on the Russian government in Britain. While it was possible for them to ignore tacitly many of the representations made to the Foreign Office about Russia, there was a danger that the growing political salience of the issue would encourage the Cabinet to take a more direct interest. Many Foreign Office papers on internal affairs in Russia were circulated to Cabinet throughout 1906, although it seems that Grey was still largely successful in avoiding many prolonged discussions of Anglo–Russian relations *per se*; indeed, the apparent paucity of discussion on the issue raises the question of why the papers were circulated in the first place. In the event, the problem of the proposed visit of the fleet was effectively resolved in St Petersburg, when the Emperor himself tactfully asked that it be cancelled, prompting Nicolson to write thankfully to Grey about the 'escape from an exceedingly difficult position'.[93]

The cancellation of the visit of the fleet did not end the crisis in Anglo–Russian relations. When Nicholas II prorogued the newly-established Duma (Parliament) in July 1906, just a few weeks after its first meeting, his action was greeted with indignation by many British Liberals for whom the establishment of the new legislature had symbolised the potential for fundamental political reform in Russia. Both Nicolson in St Petersburg and Hardinge in London had originally been hopeful that the new Duma would promote the cause of Anglo–Russian relations, since many of the deputies there were instinctive anglophiles. They were not, however, willing to allow the whole question of the dissolution of the Duma to complicate their cherished project of an Anglo–Russian rapprochement. The two men strongly supported the British loan made to Russia in 1906, even though it gave the government in St Petersburg the financial wherewithal to establish its independence from the Duma. The international significance of the dissolution of the Duma was, however, sharply increased by an astonishing speech made by Campbell-Bannerman to a group of Russian deputies who happened to be visiting Britain at the time, in which the Prime Minister departed from his prepared text with an extempore cry of 'Vive la Douma'.[94] The unscripted outburst was almost certainly a reflection of the Prime Minister's instinctive liberal sentiments, rather than any calculated desire to influence the course of relations with Russia; it has already been seen that Campbell-Bannerman did not greatly involve himself in foreign affairs during his short premiership. The potential consequences for Anglo–Russian relations were, however, clearly baneful. Charles Hardinge was at first surprisingly relaxed about the speech, despite the fact that Benckendorff quickly lodged a protest with the Foreign Office. Nevertheless, the whole affair soon introduced a new note of discord into Anglo–Russian relations, just a few weeks after the whole débacle of the visit of the fleet had been resolved. By the middle of August, Nicolson despairingly wrote from St Petersburg that the Prime Minister 'seems to have destroyed at one blow the edifice which we have been building up with so much care'.[95] The Ambassador was, however, too pessimistic. The crisis caused by Campbell-Bannerman's outburst eventually faded away, in large part because Izvol'skii in St Petersburg was adept at preventing it from giving ammunition to the opponents of an *entente* in the Russian capital. Just as the crisis created by the proposed visit of the fleet to Russia was largely resolved by the Russian government's decision to cancel it, so the crisis caused by the Prime Minister's speech subsided because supporters of an Anglo–Russian rapprochement in St Petersburg gained the upper hand over its opponents. The management of the crisis in Anglo–Russian relations in the early summer of 1906 owed something to the skilful strategy of Grey and Hardinge in London and Nicolson in St Petersburg, but it may have owed even more to circumstances that were largely beyond their control.

The details of negotiations for the Anglo–Russian convention, which was eventually signed at the end of August 1907, can be dealt with quite briefly here. Nicolson first raised the subject with the Russian authorities at the time of his arrival in St Petersburg in May 1906, quickly securing a positive response both from the Emperor and Izvol'skii,[96] before the crisis of June and July erupted to prevent the start of any substantive talks. The Ambassador himself believed that negotiations should start quickly despite the crisis caused by the prospective visit of the fleet and the continuing unrest inside the Tsarist Empire, but his enthusiasm was not shared by Hardinge and Grey, who were reluctant to start serious talks until it was clear that the Russian government was reasonably stable.[97] When discussions finally got underway in the autumn of 1906, the details were kept as secret as possible. Nicolson conducted the talks with Izvol'skii in person; he also had meetings with other officials from the Ministry, such as S.A. Poklevskii-Kozell, who were particularly involved in the whole question of Anglo–Russian relations. The British Military Attaché occasionally reported on the views of senior members of the General Staff,[98] but there were few substantial talks between British officials and representatives of ministries other than the Foreign Ministry. Izvol'skii was under enormous pressure from other ministers and senior army officers in his conduct of the negotiations, but his own Ministry retained a formal 'gatekeeping' role when dealing with the British Embassy. While Nicolson's staff at the Embassy were kept aware of developments – if only because they were responsible for copying and cyphering a vast number of dispatches and telegrams – their formal involvement was limited. Both Nicolson and his officials apparently viewed the negotiating role as a quintessential *ambassadorial* function. It has already been seen that this pattern of secrecy was repeated back in London, where Hardinge and Grey seldom consulted in very much detail either with Foreign Office officials or members of the Cabinet, with the notable exception of Morley at the India Office. There were no British diplomatic missions either in Tibet or Afghanistan, while the strident opposition of Spring Rice in Persia to an agreement with Russia meant that the views of his Mission commanded limited attention in London. The opinion of the British Mission in Peking was routinely sought when the subject of Tibet was under discussion, since the country was nominally under Chinese rule, while the embassies in Paris and Berlin provided frequent reports about the reaction of the French and German governments to the prospect of an agreement between London and St Petersburg.[99] British diplomats in such posts were seldom, however, in a position to make any substantial recommendations about the best way to proceed in the talks since they were not familiar with the details of the negotiations.

The triumvirate of Grey, Hardinge and Nicolson also worked hard to prevent details of the negotiations from leaking out to the public, something which was made a good deal easier by the fact that so few people were actually involved in the talks. Most leaks appear to have come from the Russian side, where many more individuals were privy to the content of the discussions between Izvol'skii and Nicolson, including a considerable number who were deeply suspicious of the whole idea of an Anglo–Russian *entente*. The British press carried rumours about the existence of negotiations to secure an understanding with Russia more or less from the time Nicolson arrived in St Petersburg,[100] but few newspapers were well informed about the talks that followed. Valentine Chirol of *The Times* was informed about the texture of the British proposals by the late autumn of 1906, in an effort to guarantee the newspaper's future support for any agreement, but few others were treated with such confidence.[101] E.J. Dillon of the *Daily Telegraph* published one report derived from a well-informed official source – almost certainly Russian – but this proved to be the exception rather than the rule. Sir Edward Grey studiously refused to comment in the House of Commons on the state of any talks, despite numerous questions from MPs on the subject, particularly in the summer of 1907 when negotiations were drawing to a close.[102] The secrecy surrounding the negotiations for an Anglo–Russian rapprochement helped its proponents to reduce any criticism both from inside or outside government. The agreement finally signed at the end of August was in many ways a typical product of the era of 'old diplomacy', with its emphasis on 'spheres of influence' and *de facto* interference in the internal affairs of nominally sovereign countries.[103] If the more controversial elements of the agreement had become public at a time when they were still under discussion, it would almost certainly have made it harder for Grey and his senior officials to reach agreement with St Petersburg. Liberal and radical opinion would have been repelled by the *realpolitik* aspects of the agreement, while many conservatives might have disputed the need to make any major concessions to Britain's traditional imperial adversary in Persia. Izvol'skii frequently told Nicolson that his freedom of movement was constrained by a need to secure a consensus among ministers and senior army officers in St Petersburg before making proposals or agreeing to suggestions put forward by the British. The Ambassador and his colleagues back in London faced far fewer problems in this regard.

The detailed pattern of the talks between Nicolson and Izvol'skii was also typical of the old diplomacy, characterised by the two men's ability to shift effortlessly between different forms of diplomatic discourse according to the subject in hand. It was seen in Chapter 1 that there was a strong sense of solidarity between members of the various national diplomatic services, based on a subtle mixture of shared social background and personal familiarity, which helped to facilitate communication between the representatives of different countries. Izvol'skii was at first treated with some suspicion by senior members of the British diplomatic establishment,[104] but he quickly won the trust of Nicolson, although the Ambassador was initially irritated by the Foreign Minister's caution and reluctance to make any decisions on his own authority.[105] The Foreign Minister was determined that the talks should be held in St Petersburg, since he wanted to handle them in person, a move that was supported by Grey and Hardinge, who seem to have had some doubts about the ability of Count Benckendorff at the Russian Embassy in London to deal effectively with such a complicated business. Izvol'skii and Nicolson were both adept at using 'informal' discussions to sound out each other about possible patterns of agreement on such problematic issues as the boundary of the 'spheres of influence' in Persia or the development of trade concessions in Afghanistan. The two men also communicated frankly about the political constraints they faced in coming to terms on any particular point, although Izvol'skii in particular was tactically astute at doing this to persuade the Ambassador to make extra concessions.[106]

The talks about Persia, Afghanistan and Tibet were strictly delineated and sequenced, at the insistence of the British,[107] although Izvol'skii tried on a number of occasions to break down the boundary in order to win certain concessions in other areas of Asia. Each series of talks began with a formal set of proposals, but the subsequent negotiations usually developed on a very *ad hoc* basis. Izvol'skii had to fight a difficult set of bureaucratic and political battles to win support for the cause of the Anglo–Russian *entente*, which meant that the Russian side was often very dilatory both in making proposals and in responding to suggestions made by the British. Nicolson's situation was rather different. The sheer density of the telegraphic traffic between London and St Petersburg during the talks provides signal evidence that the technical developments of the previous few decades had already created potential limits on the independence of an ambassador in the final years of 'old diplomacy'; the age of rapid communication had begun to chip away at the principle of ambassadorial autonomy well before 1914. At the same time, however, Nicolson was determined to play an active role in determining the course of the negotiations, rather than simply acting passively on instructions received from London. The Ambassador repeatedly tried to explain to the Foreign Office the constraints faced by Izvol'skii, in an effort to encourage Hardinge and Grey to take a more positive line. It has already been seen that the Ambassador was much keener than Grey and Hardinge to push ahead with negotiations in the summer of 1906, despite the apparent instability of the Russian government at the time. When Morley demanded in the spring of 1907 that the Russians should limit scientific expeditions to Tibet, for fear that they might provide a cover for intelligence and military operations, Nicolson went to great lengths to emphasise in his reports to London that the Russian Foreign Minister would find himself in 'a very difficult position' and 'be sharply attacked by his critics' should he agree to such a proposal.[108] A few months earlier, he had already felt impelled to tell Grey that the Foreign Secretary should not think that 'I am coming under the influence of my local atmosphere', but was instead simply being realistic when 'endeavouring... to regard our negotiations from the standpoint of those who have a [major influence] on the decisions of the Emperor'.[109] While Nicolson seldom made any concrete proposals to Izvol'skii without having first sounded out his colleagues at the Foreign Office, he made repeated suggestions to Hardinge and Grey about the best strategy to follow on any particular question. Hardinge in London normally drafted the more important documents in person, but he was usually quite open to suggestions made by the Ambassador in St Petersburg; Nicolson was only directly over-ruled on a small number of occasions. The complexity of the negotiations sometimes makes it difficult to identify with any precision the author of a particular proposal. The British position on any point usually evolved out of an exchange of views between Grey, Hardinge and Nicolson, with the India Office being asked to provide information or comment on specific documents rather than providing its own drafts.

In the event, the agreement signed at the end of August 1907 commanded a good deal of support in Britain, perhaps surprisingly, given the scale of public disquiet evident over the previous year. As late as June 1907, Hardinge was still fretting that radical opponents of the proposed convention would 'find ready allies amongst many of the Conservatives in picking holes in the Agreement'; he also attacked radicals on the left for supporting 'a foreign policy based on sentimentalism [that] must end in ruin'.[110] Despite these concerns, the agreement received a favourable response in both Houses of Parliament. Balfour was concerned that British trading interests in Persia had not been sufficiently defended, but in general agreed with Lansdowne that 'We on this side are certainly predisposed in favour of a convention'.[111] Lord Curzon predictably launched a fierce assault on the agreement in the House of Lords, decrying a 'bargain which I hold to be unequal and unfair',[112] but his sentiments were not widely supported by his fellow peers. There was a surprising lack of dissent from MPs belonging to the Labour Party or the radical wing of the Liberal Party. Most newspapers also broadly welcomed the agreement, although Chirol at *The Times* made it clear in his private correspondence that he had some doubts about its value. The more germanophobic publications, like the *National Review*, also predictably responded warmly to news of the convention.[113] Ironically, while the handful of men responsible for preparing and negotiating the Anglo–Russian *entente* had taken great pains to protect their independence in the face of possible political and public pressure, the fruits of their labours eventually commanded a high level of bipartisan support.

The previous pages have shown how difficult it is to evaluate the justice of the attacks made on the Foreign Office by critics of old diplomacy in the early years of the twentieth century. The men who worked there before 1914 were certainly drawn from a socially-privileged background, but a privileged background was not necessarily incompatible with the virtues of competence and hard work. By the time the First World War broke out in 1914, the days had long since gone when a post at the Foreign Office was little more than a sinecure for a young man of good family. The organisational culture of the institution had for some time been coalescing around a sentiment that the management of foreign affairs, while an art rather than a science, was an art that required both a particular aptitude and considerable experience if it was to be carried out properly. The previous pages have also cast doubt on the charge that the Foreign Office was in some way able to evade the normal channels of accountability that operated in other spheres of policy formulation and execution during these years. It is certainly true that from the beginning of the century some Foreign Office officials, particularly among the younger generation, were inclined to the view that as 'experts' in the subtleties of foreign affairs they should have a major input into the foreign policy making process. The appointment of Charles Hardinge as Permanent Secretary in place of Thomas Sanderson at the beginning of 1906 was important in this regard as both a symbolic and a practical change. At the same time, however, the role of officials in the policy making process was always governed by a wide array of factors. The Foreign Office's role in initiating and negotiating the Anglo–Russian convention of 1907 was jealously guarded by Grey and Hardinge, while the Foreign Secretary broke sharply with his predecessor in identifying the Foreign Office as the natural location for decisions about foreign policy. At the same time, however, Grey was only able to make this shift because a majority of his Cabinet colleagues were willing to accept it.

While the previous pages have shown that the Foreign Office played a larger role in the formulation of Britain's policy towards Russia during 1906–7 than in the preceding period this does *not* mean that the Grey Foreign Office was in some sense always the pivotal institution in the British foreign policy making process. Indeed, in the years following the establishment of the Anglo–Russian *entente*, the policy of rapprochement with Russia once again became far more controversial, making it harder for the Foreign Secretary and his senior officials to defend their right to be the principal architects of policy. After Charles Hardinge's departure for India, there was in any case a growing division among officials at the Foreign Office itself about the value of maintaining close relations with St Petersburg. William Tyrrell, in particular, echoed Cecil Spring Rice's earlier doubts about the danger of depending on Russian protestations of goodwill, and was instinctively sceptical about the russophilism of Sir Arthur Nicolson, who replaced Hardinge as Permanent Secretary in 1910. During the winter of 1911–12, Grey faced a storm of public protest about the whole thrust of his policy, which was condemned for being too hostile towards Berlin and too craven towards St Petersburg.[114] Numerous critical articles appeared in publications such as the *Nation* and the *Manchester Guardian* demanding that the Foreign Secretary should resign from office. L.T. Hobhouse formed his short-lived Foreign Policy Committee which called for greater publicity in the conduct of foreign affairs, while Arthur Ponsonby and Noel Buxton formed a Foreign Affairs Committee within the parliamentary Liberal party designed to secure greater influence for MPs in determining foreign policy. Anxiety about Grey's supposed russophile orientation, most notably his meek response to Russian assertiveness in Persia, played a significant role in fostering this rise in attacks on the procedures and institutions associated with old diplomacy. While Grey's position was never in serious doubt, public opposition combined with Cabinet divisions to push British foreign policy temporarily towards a short-lived attempt to improve relations with Germany, culminating in Haldane's celebrated mission to Berlin. The whole affair revealed, once again, that the power of the Foreign Secretary and his officials to determine the course of British policy on any particular issue was governed by many different considerations. Even though they commanded considerable resources when trying to assert themselves as the principal actors in the foreign policy decision-making process, they were never able to ignore the dicates of the political and administrative environment in which they operated. The Foreign Office's role in the formulation and execution of Britain's policy toward Russia in the early years of the twentieth century was always governed as much by the dictates of international developments and domestic politics as by the ambitions and aspirations of the men who worked there.

NOTES

1. The biographical information in this paragraph has been compiled from the relevant issues of the *Foreign Office List*.
2. Zara Steiner, 'Elitism and Foreign Policy: the Foreign Office before the Great War', in B.J.C. McKercher and D.J. Moss, *Shadow and Substance in British Foreign Policy, 1895–1939*, pp. 20–1.
3. Samuel Hynes, *The Edwardian Turn of Mind*, p. 11.
4. On Bertie, see Keith Hamilton, *Bertie of Thame: Edwardian Ambassador*.
5. Biographical information compiled from *Dictionary of National Biography*; *The Foreign Office List*; *Who's Who?*; and data published by the MacDonnell Commission.
6. *BPP, 1914–1916*, 11 (cd 7748), Qu. 36,546.
7. Data compiled from *The Dictionary of National Biography*; the *Foreign Office List*; *Who's Who?*; Robert T. Nightingale, *The Personnel of the British Foreign Office and Diplomatic Service, 1851–1929*; and data published by the MacDonnell Commission.
8. For a brilliant treatment of the adaptation of Britain's educational system to the demands of the civil service and the new professions during the third quarter of the nineteenth century, see Bernard S. Silberman, *Cages of Reason*, Chapter 12.
9. Public Record Office, CSC 10/2075, results of the examinations to enter the Foreign Office.
10. For a discussion of the growth of the concept of professionalism in late Victorian and Edwardian Britain, see Harold Perkin, *The Rise of Professional Society*.
11. J.D. Gregory, *On the Edge of Diplomacy*, p. 14.
12. See, for example, E.D. Morel, *Truth and the War*, p. 107.
13. For a somewhat different view of Salisbury's time at the Foreign Office and his relations with officials there, see J.A.S. Grenville, *Lord Salisbury and Foreign Policy at the Close of the Nineteenth Century*, pp. 3–23.
14. See, for example, Hamilton, *Bertie*, p. 5ff; Valerie Cromwell and Zara Steiner, 'The Foreign Office before 1914: A Study in Resistance', in Gillian Sutherland (ed.), *Studies in the Growth of Nineteenth-Century Government*, pp. 167–94.
15. Rennell Rodd, *Memoirs*, Vol. 1, p. 40.
16. H.J. Bruce, *Silken Dalliance*, p. 81.

58   Diplomacy Before the Russian Revolution

17. Quoted in Richard A. Chapman and J.R. Greenaway, *The Dynamics of Administrative Reform*, p. 27.
18. The following paragraphs are based on a study of the original documents as well as the considerable, and by no means unanimous, literature on the Foreign Office reforms of 1903–6. See, for example, E.T. Corp, *The Transformation of the Foreign Office, 1900–1907*; Sibyl Crowe and Edward Corp, *Our Ablest Public Servant: Sir Eyre Crowe*, pp. 88–109; Ray Jones, *The Nineteenth Century Foreign Office*, esp. pp. 111–35; Zara Steiner, 'The Last Years of the Old Foreign Office', pp. 77–82.
19. For a general view of Hardinge's career, see his autobiography *Old Diplomacy*; for a useful biography, see Briton Cooper Busch, *Hardinge of Penshurst: A Study in the Old Diplomacy*.
20. On Bertie, see Hamilton, *Bertie*; on Crowe, see Crowe and Corp, *Eyre Crowe*.
21. E.T. Corp, *Transformation of the Foreign Office*, pp. 176–9.
22. For an excellent general account of British policy towards Russia, see Neilson, *Britain and the Last Tsar*. George Monger, *The End of Isolation: Britain's Foreign Policy, 1900–1907*, still provides a valuable account of the changes in British policy early in the twentieth century.
23. The relevant documents are printed in G.P. Gooch and Harold Temperley (eds), *British Documents on the Origins of the War* (henceforth *BD*), Vol. 4 (docs 181–2).
24. On the Grey-Hardinge relationship, see Zara Steiner, 'Grey, Hardinge and the Foreign Office, 1906–1910', in *The Historical Journal*, 10, 4 (1967), pp. 415–39.
25. Grenville, *Salisbury*, pp. 50–1.
26. Among the large literature on Chamberlain, the mammoth biography by A.L. Garvin contains a wealth of information and insights. Other useful works include Peter Fraser, *Joseph Chamberlain: Radicalism and Empire 1868–1914*; Denis Judd, *Radical Joe: a Life of Joseph Chamberlain*.
27. For a selection from Selborne's papers, see *The Crisis of British Power: The Imperial and Naval Papers of the Second Earl of Selborne, 1895–1910*, ed. D. George Boyce.
28. Many primary documents about Balfour's views can be found in Blanche E.C. Dugdale, *Arthur James Balfour* (2 vols); a useful account can also be found in Denis Judd, *Balfour and the British Empire: A Study in Imperial Revolution, 1874–1932*. For useful accounts of British policy in this period, see Monger, *End of Isolation*; Aaron L. Friedberg, *The Weary Titan: Britain and the Experience of Relative Decline, 1895–1905*; Sneh Mahajan, 'The Defence of India and the End of Isolation. A study in the Foreign Policy of the Conservative Government, 1900–1905', *Journal of Imperial and Commonwealth History*, 10, 2 (1982), pp. 168–93.
29. On the history and operation of the CID, see Nicholas D'Ombrain, *War Machinery and High Policy*. On defence planning towards Russia during the Balfour Administration, see Neilson, *Last Tsar*, pp. 110–43.
30. Lord Hankey, *Diplomacy by Conference*, p. 53.
31. Copies of the extant Cabinet papers circulated by the Foreign Office are contained in Public Record Office, class CAB 37. Papers circulated by

the Foreign Office have been preserved far more systematically than those generated by many other government departments.
32. Balfour's letters to Edward VII are contained in Public Record Office, CAB 41.
33. Steiner, 'Elitism and Foreign Policy', p. 23.
34. Hardinge, *Old Diplomacy*, p. 122.
35. Hardinge, *Old Diplomacy*, p. 97.
36. Hamilton, *Bertie*, p. 16.
37. For a rather different view, although not one really borne out by the documents, see John Wilson, *A Life of Sir Henry Campbell-Bannerman*, p. 522.
38. On the Liberal Imperialists, see H.C.G. Matthew, *The Liberal Imperialists: Ideas and Politics of a post-Gladstonian Elite*.
39. *War Memoirs of David Lloyd George*, Vol. 1, p. 46; Richard Burdon Haldane, *An Autobiography*, p. 217.
40. Grey, *Twenty Five Years*, Vol. 2, p. 259.
41. Zara Steiner, 'Grey, Hardinge and the Foreign Office', *passim*.
42. The relevant letters can be found in class CAB 41 in the Public Record Office.
43. The records of the CID can be found in class CAB 2 at the Public Record Office; also see D'Ombrain, *War Machinery*, *passim*, on the changing influence of the CID.
44. Hardinge, *Old Diplomacy*, p. 122.
45. Grey had in fact signalled an interest in building a closer relationship with Russia even during his years in opposition; see Rogers Platt Churchill, *The Anglo–Russian Convention of 1907*, p. 107.
46. Sir Charles Petrie, *The Life and Letters of the Right Honourable Sir Austen Chamberlain*, Vol. 1, p. 159.
47. BD, Vol. 4, Lansdowne to Spring Rice, 17 November 1903 (doc. 181a).
48. BD, Vol. 4, Hardinge to Lansdowne, 22 November 1903 (doc. 181b).
49. BD. Vol. 4, Lansdowne to Spring Rice, 25 November 1903 (doc. 182).
50. British Museum, Add. Mss 49728, untitled and undated memorandum by Balfour.
51. Dugdale, *Balfour*, Vol. 1, p. 378.
52. BM, Add. Mss 49728, Chamberlain to Lansdowne, 21 December 1903.
53. Dugdale, *Balfour*, Vol. 1, p. 378.
54. Cab 37/68, 'Proposed Agreement With Russia'.
55. FO 65/1677, Lansdowne to Scott, 6 January 1904.
56. Among the extensive literature on Curzon, see David Dilks, *Curzon in India* (2 vols); David Gilmour, *Curzon*; Earl of Ronaldshay, *The Life of Lord Curzon* (3 vols).
57. George N. Curzon, *Russia in Central Asia in 1889, and the Anglo–Russian Question*.
58. Newton, *Lansdowne*, p. 243.
59. See, for example, Dilks, *Curzon in India*, Vol. 1, p. 180.
60. BM, Add. Mss 49732, Balfour to Curzon, March 1903.
61. On the Younghusband Affair, see Anthony Verrier, *Francis Younghusband and the Great Game*; Peter Fleming, *Bayonets to Lhasa*. Selected

60 Diplomacy Before the Russian Revolution

documents relating to the affair were published; see *BPP, 1904*, 57 (cd 1920); *BPP, 1905*, 58 (cd 2370).
62. For Balfour's anger about the whole Younghusband Affair, see BM, Add. Mss 49729, Balfour to Lansdowne, 4 October 1904.
63. BM, Add. Mss 49733, Curzon to Balfour, 19 July 1905.
64. Nicolson's appointment to St Petersburg was, however, first approved by Lansdowne. BM, Add. Mss 49729, Lansdowne to Balfour, 28 September 1905.
65. FO 800/338, Grey to Nicolson, 19 April 1906.
66. BM, Add. Mss 52514, Grey to Campbell-Bannerman, 31 August 1907.
67. The Foreign Office's initial proposals for the negotiations over Afghanistan were, for example, modified by Morley before the final transmission to Nicolson. The relevant documents can be found in FO 371/126 (various).
68. On Minto's time as Viceroy, see Mary, Countess of Minto, *India, Minto and Morley, 1905–1910*.
69. John, Viscount Morley, *Recollections*, Vol. 2, p. 151.
70. Morley, *Recollections*, p. 179; for a specific instance of Morley over-ruling the Indian Government (on the question of scientific expeditions in Tibet), see FO 371/176/26556, India Office to Foreign Office, 2 August 1906 (with enclosures).
71. FO 800/339, Hardinge to Nicolson, 6 February 1907.
72. FO 800/338, Hardinge to Nicolson, 24 December 1906.
73. For a useful analysis of Morley's attitudes while at the India Office, see Stanley A. Wolpert, *Morley and India, 1906–1910*.
74. Haldane, *Autobiography*, p. 215.
75. FO 800/338, Hardinge to Nicolson, 16 October 1906.
76. See, for example, FO 371/369 (various docs) on the question of delineating the boundary between the Russian and British spheres of influence in Persia.
77. FO 371/370/15429, Spring Rice to Grey, 11 April 1907.
78. See, for example, Max Beloff, *Lucien Wolf and the Russian Entente, 1907–1914*.
79. For details see *The History of the Times*, Vol. 3, pp. 382–8.
80. Philip Taylor, 'Publicity and Diplomacy: The Impact of the First World War upon Foreign Office Attitudes towards the Press', in David Dilks (ed.), *Retreat from Power*, Vol. 1, pp. 42–63.
81. See, for example, the various letters on this subject between Hardinge and Nicolson contained in Hardinge Papers, 8.
82. FO 800/339, Hardinge to Nicolson, 10 March 1907.
83. FO 800/72, Spring Rice to Grey, 3 January 1906.
84. FO 800/72, Spring Rice to Grey, 26 January 1906.
85. FO 800/72, Spring Rice to Grey, 24 May 1906.
86. A good deal of useful information on this theme can be found in Eliyahu Feldman, 'British Diplomats and British Diplomacy and the 1905 Pogroms in Russia', *Slavonic and East European Review*, 65, 4 (1987), pp. 579–608.
87. Extracts from the relevant documents and parliamentary debates are contained in FO 371/125/21259, 21353.

88. FO 371/125/21655, Nathan Lazarus to Grey, 24 June 1906.
89. The relevant documents about the meeting between Hardinge and members of the society are contained in FO 371/125.
90. See, for example, BM, Add. Mss 49729, Lansdowne to Balfour, 14 April 1905.
91. FO 800/338, Hardinge to Nicolson, 27 June 1906.
92. FO 371/125/21455, Nicolson to Grey, 20 June 1906.
93. FO 371/126/24880, Nicolson to Grey, 12 July 1906.
94. A brief description of the affair can be found in Wilson, *Campbell-Bannerman*, p. 535ff.
95. FO 800/338, Nicolson to Hardinge, 21 August 1906. Compare, however, his views a week later, contained in Hardinge Papers, 8, Nicolson to Hardinge, 29 August 1906.
96. FO 371/125/19079, Nicolson to Grey, 4 June 1906.
97. Hardinge Papers, 8, Nicolson to Hardinge, 29 July 1906; FO 800/338, Hardinge to Nicolson, 7 August 1906.
98. See FO 371/320/15468, Napier to Nicolson, 27 April 1907, encl. with Nicolson to Grey, 29 April 1907.
99. Bertie took a particular interest in the course of the negotiations. See, for example, FO 800/177, Bertie to Grey, 22 October 1906; Bertie to Mallet, 23 October 1906.
100. *The Times*, 24 May 1906, carried an article on the subject, erroneously suggesting that rumours of Anglo-Russian negotiations were inspired by the *Wilhelmstrasse*. The *Standard* also carried rumours about possible negotiations; see Churchill, *Anglo-Russian Convention*, pp. 121–2.
101. FO 800/338, Chirol to Nicolson, 2 October 1906.
102. See, for example, the response of Grey to various questions on Anglo-Russian affairs contained in *Parliamentary Debates* (1907), no. 177.
103. The final agreement is reprinted in *BD*, Vol. 4, Appendix 1.
104. FO 800/72, Spring Rice to Grey, 10 May 1906.
105. Hardinge Papers, 8, Nicolson to Hardinge, 11 October 1906.
106. See, for example, FO 800/72, Nicolson to Grey, 7 November 1906. Also see FO 371/320/16393, Nicolson to Grey, 15 May 1907 (in which Izvol'skii refers to having had a 'really hard fight' with some of his colleagues to defend the cause of the convention).
107. FO 371/176/20583, Nicolson to Grey, 8 June 1906.
108. FO 371/382/5665, Nicolson to Grey, 19 February 1907. Nicolson returned to the subject in a dispatch found in FO 371/382/18609, Nicolson to Grey, 13 March 1907.
109. FO 800/72, Nicolson to Grey, 7 November 1906.
110. FO 800/339, Hardinge to Nicolson, 26 June 1906.
111. *Parliamentary Debates* (1908), Vol. 183, col. 15.
112. *Parliamentary Debates* (1908), Vol. 183, col. 1023.
113. *Germany on the Brain*, p. 229.
114. John A. Murray, 'Foreign Policy Debated: Sir Edward Grey and his Critics, 1911–1913', in Lillian Parker Wallace and William C. Askew (eds), *Power, Public Opinion and Diplomacy*, pp. 141–71.

3 The British Embassy in St Petersburg

By the beginning of the twentieth century, the British Embassy in St Petersburg ranked third or fourth in status among British embassies behind Paris, Berlin and perhaps Vienna. While the prospect of the harsh climate and the high cost of living worried some British diplomats, most of them treated a posting to the Tsarist Empire as an opportunity to gain valuable experience. This had not always been the case. In Elizabethan and Stuart times, English ambassadors sent to Muscovy often felt they were being exiled to a 'rude and barbarous' kingdom, where a boorish and uncivilised people were ruled over by a savage despot.[1] During the eighteenth century, the heroic attempts by Peter the Great and his successors to westernise Russia were viewed with admiration and awe by British diplomats posted to St Petersburg, but most of them remained convinced that little was changing beneath the ornate surface of life. When Catherine the Great ruled the country, one British ambassador derided the idea that the Russian aristocracy had really imbibed the Enlightenment culture so extravagantly propounded by the Empress, noting caustically that 'a slight though brilliant varnish' could not conceal 'illiterate and unformed minds'.[2] British diplomats who served in Russia in the nineteenth century were usually more generous, especially during the 1860s, when the era of the great reforms suggested that fundamental changes might be about to take place in Russian society. Such hopes were, however, short-lived, particularly once the assassination of Tsar Alexander II in 1881 ushered in an era of reaction. By the end of the century, Russia was still viewed from the British Embassy in St Petersburg as a country that was fundamentally different from its western neighbours.

The St Petersburg Embassy was housed at the end of the nineteenth century in an ornate palace overlooking the Troitskii Bridge across the River Neva. The elaborate lobby and entrance hall gave visitors a suitably grand first impression of the building, while a large dining room and ballroom on the first floor provided the accommodation needed for large receptions and parties.[3] The building also contained lavish living accommodation for the ambassador and his wife. The Embassy was, though, less suited for the conduct of more routine business, since there was little office space for the more junior staff, while the building itself was in such a dreadful state of repair that a good deal of time and energy had to be spent in a fruitless search for a cheaper and more convenient alternative.

The design of the Embassy building, with its emphasis on the ceremonial at the expense of the prosaic, could have served as a metaphor for the failings attributed to the old diplomacy by many of its critics. The idea that diplomats placed too much emphasis on the social round seemed to be embedded in the very bricks and mortar of the St Petersburg Embassy. The real position was, however, more complex. The British diplomatic establishment in the Russian capital was very small. During the years between 1894 and 1914, there were usually just five or six diplomats serving at the St Petersburg Embassy. Nor were these men able to draw on extensive clerical and secretarial help when carrying out their work. While there were plenty of servants to deal with the domestic side of the Embassy, diplomatic staff were expected to carry out in person such routine jobs as copying dispatches and deciphering telegrams. There was even a shortage of typewriters, a subject which filled an inordinate amount of correspondence with the Foreign Office back in London.[4] None of this would have mattered if the workload of the Embassy had been light, but by the early years of the twentieth century this was certainly no longer the case. In 1894, the British Ambassador in Russia felt able to tell the Foreign Office that he was taking a vacation in Finland because there was so little work to do at the Embassy,[5] but such a state of affairs would have been almost unimaginable just ten years later. The handful of diplomats posted to St Petersburg were expected to carry out a wide range of duties extending from the conduct of complex negotiations through to the compilation of reports about the social and political upheavals which swept across the Tsarist Empire during its final 20 years of life. They were also expected to perform many more mundane duties, ranging from reporting on commercial developments through to entertaining visiting British dignatories. When Charles Hardinge left the city to return to London at the beginning of 1906, he made a point of writing to Sir Edward Grey to praise the diligence and ability of his staff.[6] While the Diplomatic Service did not experience the kind of organisational reforms that took place at the Foreign Office early in the twentieth century, it too was experiencing something of a cultural revolution. A successful diplomat was increasingly required to work hard and effectively in order to fulfil his duties properly.

THE EMBASSY STAFF

The British Diplomatic Service was still very small in 1900, comprising around 125 posts. Its members had a reputation for being less intellectually gifted and more blue-blooded than their colleagues in the Foreign Office, a perception which probably contained a degree of truth. The average mark obtained in the entrance exam by new recruits to the Diplomatic Service early in the twentieth century was consistently lower than the one gained by successful applicants for the Foreign Office. Nevertheless, the importance of the bald figures should not be exaggerated. Aspiring recruits to the Diplomatic Service prepared for the entrance exam with the same diligence and nervousness as their counterparts seeking entry to the Foreign Office. Young men who chose a diplomatic career because they could not think of anything else to do with their life were the exception rather than the rule. Most young hopefuls went on long trips abroad to study languages before attending Scoones's Academy in the Strand for 'cramming' in subjects required for the entrance examination. A career in the Diplomatic Service conferred a great deal of status in late Victorian and Edwardian England, with the result that there was real competition for the handful of available places.[7]

Any analysis of the social composition of the Diplomatic Service faces the same problems encountered when looking at the Foreign Office: the shortage of reliable data, the ambiguity inherent in such terms as 'privileged', and so on. More diplomats than Foreign Office clerks came from families that can properly be termed 'aristocratic'. Formal education was also becoming increasingly important in the years before 1914 for young men hoping to join the Diplomatic Service. By the end of the first decade of the twentieth century, attendance at a major public school and one of the ancient universities had become virtually *de rigueur* for an aspiring diplomat.[8] Despite Arthur Nicolson's best efforts to persuade the MacDonnell Commission that the Diplomatic Service was open to anyone who wished to apply, it was in reality even more selective in ethos than the Foreign Office. Not only did a young man who wanted to become a diplomat have to acquire an expensive education and a nomination from the foreign secretary, he was also expected to have a private income of £400 *per annum* so that he could work without pay for his first two years. It is true that senior diplomats were drawn from social backgrounds which were in practice not very different from those of Cabinet ministers or judges,[9] but this simply illustrates how the Diplomatic Service formed part of a complex network of private and public institutions that provided the institutional foundation of the British Establishment before 1914.

A more detailed look at the profile of diplomats who worked at the St Petersburg Embassy between 1894 and 1917 can illustrate some of these points. During these years, half a dozen individuals served as British ambassador in the Russian capital: Sir Frank Lascelles, Sir Nicholas O'Conor, Sir Charles Scott, Sir Charles Hardinge, Sir Arthur Nicolson and Sir George Buchanan. The six men differed greatly in their aptitudes and interests, a matter of considerable importance given the small size of the Embassy. An ambassador could profoundly affect every aspect of the life of his mission, ranging from the organisation of its political reporting through to the living arrangements of the staff. British ambassadors in St Petersburg, like their counterparts in other cities such as Paris and Berlin, were closely involved in the day-to-day work of the Embassy; they composed dispatches and important telegrams in person or, at the very least, carefully scrutinised the drafts handed to them by their staff. They were also the primary conduit through which relations were conducted with the Russian Ministry of Foreign Affairs, routinely attending formal receptions and meetings to discuss Anglo–Russian affairs. While other senior diplomats did on occasion play an important role in liaising with senior tsarist officials, the ambassador was central to the conduct of Embassy business in a way that would be unthinkable today, when the larger embassies are vast and complex bureaucratic structures employing large numbers of specialist staff.

Table 3.1 provides information about the background of the six ambassadors at the time of their appointment to Russia. The St Petersburg Embassy was the first full ambassadorial appointment for five of the men, although all of them had previously been in charge of a

Table 3.1 British Ambassadors in St Petersburg (1894–1918)

Name	Date of appointment	Age at appointment	Months in post	Previous experience at St Petersburg Embassy (months)
Lascelles	1894	53	19	0
O'Conor	1895	52	33	0
Scott	1898	60	69	26
Hardinge	1904	46	22	55
Nicolson	1906	57	57	0
Buchanan	1910	56	87	0

smaller diplomatic mission; only Sir Arthur Nicolson had already served as a full Ambassador (in Madrid). The average age at the time of appointment to St Petersburg was around 55; Charles Hardinge was exceptional in being appointed when just 46. The length of time spent *en poste* varied a good deal, according to personal and political circumstances. Hardinge's short tenure was a result of his early appointment as Permanent Secretary at the Foreign Office, while Buchanan's marathon tour of duty was largely a consequence of the vagaries of war and revolution. Only Hardinge and Scott had served in St Petersburg at an earlier stage in their careers, although Nicolson had spent a good deal of time in countries bordering the Tsarist Empire with the result that he too was fairly well-informed about Russian policy when he took up his post. Lascelles, O'Conor and Buchanan, by contrast, knew comparatively little about Russia at the time of their appointment to St Petersburg. The careers of the six ambassadors were therefore generally characteristic of senior British diplomats. They had spent most of their working life in the Diplomatic Service, serving in a wide variety of posts rather than building up a specialist knowledge of any particular region.

A large gulf in prestige and influence separated the ambassador from the counsellor or secretary of the Embassy, a difference symbolised by the dramatic differences in their salary and expenses. At the beginning of the twentieth century, the British ambassador in St Petersburg received £7800 in salary and expenses; his deputy received around £1050. The counsellor or secretary of the British Embassy in St Petersburg was still a considerable figure among the foreign diplomatic corps in the city, but his profile was much lower than the ambassador's. Table 3.2 gives details of the six men who served in the number two spot during the years between 1894 and 1918.

Table 3.2 Counsellors and Secretaries at the St Petersburg Embassy (1894–1918)

Name	Date of appointment	Age at appointment	Months in post	Previous experience at St Petersburg Embassy (months)
Howard	1890	47	45	0
Goschen	1894	47	46	0
Hardinge	1898	40	55	0
Spring Rice	1903	44	40	0
O'Beirne	1906	39	104	29
Lindley	1915	43	33	0

The small size of the group again makes it difficult to generalise about the distinctive characteristics of the cohort. All six men came from typical Diplomatic Service backgrounds, in most cases receiving appointments as attachés in their early 20s following education at public school and university. The average age at appointment to St Petersburg fell slightly as time went by (a change mirrored at other major posts). Hugh O'Beirne was the only individual who had previous experience of service in Russia. The role of a particular deputy depended a good deal on his own aptitudes and inclinations, as well as those of the ambassador under whom he served. When the ambassador returned home on leave, his deputy was required to carry out the whole gamut of ambassadorial duties. When the ambassador was in residence, however, his deputy played a much more limited role. There was a tendency during the years before 1914 for the number two at the Embassy to specialise in monitoring the internal affairs of the Tsarist Empire. When Charles Hardinge served as Secretary, he devoted much of his time to a diligent study of Russia's domestic politics and administration, writing admirably detailed memoranda on such abstruse matters as the annual budget.[10] The ebullient Spring Rice took a lively if jaundiced interest in the political machinations of the Court.[11] His successor, Hugh O'Beirne, was a quiet but immensely talented official who played a critical role at the Embassy over many years. When Sir George Buchanan arrived at the Embassy, in 1910, the new Ambassador relied heavily on his deputy to advise him about the complexities of diplomatic and political life in the Russian capital. O'Beirne's departure from the Embassy in 1915 removed one of the most effective experts on Russia at a critical time in the country's evolution. His replacement, Francis Lindley, also quickly established himself as the Embassy's chief analyst of Russia's internal affairs, despite his lack of knowledge of the Russian language. His fortnightly summaries of political developments showed a remarkable grasp of the nuances and complexities of tsarist politics during the critical years of 1916 and 1917.

The backgrounds of the thirty six men who served as attachés and secretaries at the St Petersburg Embassy were also representative of the Diplomatic Service as a whole. A majority came from well-to-do professional families while some, such as Viscount Cranley, were scions of leading aristocratic families. Officials who entered the Diplomatic Service from the end of the nineteenth century onwards had almost invariably been educated at a major public school, while most had in addition attended Oxford or Cambridge. The same was true of many of those who joined the Diplomatic Service during an earlier period, although a number of them had been educated at home by private tutor rather than in formal educational establishments. The average length of posting to the Russian capital was around 30 months, while only a handful of diplomats served at the St Petersburg Embassy for more than four years. Around half the secretaries and attachés acquired a good enough knowledge of the local language to pass an exam entitling them to a special £100 allowance, although many of them did not in practice obtain the requisite level of proficiency until the final months of their posting. Few diplomats spent enough time in the city to develop an expert knowledge of Russia, while the small size of the Embassy staff meant that a new arrival was usually submerged in his daily duties from the very beginning. The debate about the wisdom of 'rotating' diplomats through posts is of course an old one. Those who favour the practice have traditionally argued that it allows officials to gain a wide range of experience and reduces the danger of parochialism. While there may be some justice in such an argument, there is also a danger that the peripatetic tradition makes it difficult for an individual to obtain a good knowledge of the country to which they are posted. British diplomats who served at the St Petersburg Embassy had to interpret developments in a country that was profoundly alien to them, despite lacking the time and resources that would have made their task much easier.

THE EMBASSY IN ACTION: IDENTIFYING THE KEY POLITICAL PLAYERS

British diplomats in St Petersburg faced many of the same pressures and dilemmas as their colleagues at other major diplomatic missions across Europe in the years before 1914. As representatives of the British government they were expected to defend and promote their country's interests *vis à vis* the tsarist government. As diplomats they were expected to conduct an on-going dialogue with their hosts designed to manage areas of tension and conflict. The Embassy's dealings with the tsarist government took place at many different levels and in many different forms, the texture of which was governed by a whole set of informal understandings as well as more formal conventions and agreements. The old diplomacy, as was suggested in Chapter 1, cannot be reduced to a set of principles or practices; it was instead a fusion of certain procedures and values.

There was a sharp distinction in the way in which British ambassadors to St Petersburg perceived their role. Hardinge and Nicolson were more interested than most of their predecessors and successors in influencing British policy towards Russia. When Frank Lascelles arrived at the Embassy in 1894 he hoped to reduce the tension between Britain and Russia, but his rapid disillusionment with the behaviour of his hosts soon made him sceptical about the possibility of strengthening the Anglo–Russian relationship.[12] Charles Scott was an instinctive russophile with many friends among the St Petersburg *beau monde*, but he had few ambitions to play a major role in influencing policy decisions back in London. Buchanan and O'Conor were both interested in questions of policy, routinely making proposals and suggestions in the dispatches and private letters they sent back to the Foreign Office in London, but neither man possessed such pronounced views as Hardinge or Nicolson. In practice, however, many of the problems faced by staff at the St Petersburg Embassy in carrying out their work continued regardless of who was in charge. The day-to-day operation of the Embassy was profoundly affected by the nature of the society in which it operated. A British diplomat in St Petersburg at the turn of the century had to go about his work in a very different way from his colleagues in Paris, given the contrasting social and political structures of liberal France and autocratic Russia. A posting to Russia created problems that could only be solved by summoning up considerable powers of endurance and ingenuity.

It was difficult for British diplomats posted to Russia to identify how domestic and foreign policy was made in St Petersburg, a vital task if they were to carry out their duties effectively. This was not simply because the culture of secrecy was so deeply embedded in tsarist political life. In the years between 1894 and 1914, policy making in the Tsarist Empire took place in an essentially *ad hoc* fashion, bringing together individuals and institutions in complex patterns of relationships that varied across time. In the years before 1905, Nicholas II depended on advice from a wide range of ministers, relatives and courtiers when making decisions about political matters. The new Fundamental Laws promulgated in 1906 ushered in an era of semi-constitutional politics that had considerable consequences for the way in which domestic and foreign policy was made. Both the Tsar and the Court continued to play a central role in domestic and foreign affairs throughout the period of the Constitutional Experiment, but the establishment of a new Duma and a reformed Council of Ministers led to a bewildering struggle for power and authority. British diplomats in St Petersburg therefore had to make sense of a series of a complex series of political changes that still remain confusing to historians almost 100 years after they took place.

The Court was always largely closed to the British Embassy, although a few members of the Russian royal family did establish social relations with members of the foreign diplomatic corps. While every ambassador had regular audiences with Nicholas II, these were usually formal occasions at which the sentiments of goodwill expressed by both sides were little more than diplomatic ritual. Charles Hardinge and George Buchanan probably came closest to developing a personal rapport with the Emperor, but neither man was under any illusions that they were on close terms with him. Nicholas's remoteness became even more pronounced following the outbreak of the Russo–Japanese War in 1904, which signalled the end of the elaborate Court receptions which had once formed an important part of the St Petersburg social calendar.[13] In the decade before the start of the First World War, ambassadorial audiences normally involved a trip to the palace of Tsarskoe Selo, some 15 miles from the capital. When Charles Hardinge went for his first audience after returning to St Petersburg as Ambassador, in the spring of 1904, he found himself caught up in an unfamiliar world of ritual, arriving at the palace in 'a gold coach with six white horses' that made him feel 'horribly shy'.[14] The retreat of Nicholas to a private world of family and friends was a matter of great concern to British officials, since they knew that many of the Tsar's advisers at Court were instinctive conservatives who favoured close relations with Germany rather than with the liberal powers like Britain and France. A number of the grand dukes were believed to act as a bulwark against any moves to build closer relations between London and St Petersburg. British diplomats were also concerned that senior members of the tsarist officer corps were particularly effective at winning the Tsar's ear, fearing that the generals were one of the major supporters of a 'forward' policy in Persia and the lands north of India.

The Embassy naturally had extensive dealings with the Foreign Ministry during the 20 years before 1914, but British diplomats always found it hard to gauge the influence of successive foreign ministers on tsarist foreign policy. Before the start of the Constitutional Experiment in 1906, it was generally assumed that the influence of the Foreign Ministry was small and that the 'The Court and the Military Party...are said to be anti-English'.[15] Six men served as foreign minister during Nicholas's reign. Some, like N.K. Giers, who left office in 1895, were well-regarded at the Embassy.[16] Others, like M.N. Murav'ev, were viewed with greater suspicion since they were believed (with some reason) to be instinctive anglophobes.[17] The three men who served as foreign minister between the start of the century and the outbreak of war in 1914, V.N. Lamsdorff (1900–6), A.P. Izvol'skii (1906–10) and S.D. Sazonov (1910–16) all managed to win a degree of respect at the British Embassy, although Lamsdorff was always seen as rather ineffectual and Izvol'skii as insufferably vain. However, while formal and informal contacts took place regularly between the Embassy and the Foreign Ministry throughout the years between 1894 and 1914, it was not until the negotiations for the Anglo-Russian convention got underway in 1906 that British diplomats and Foreign Ministry officials started to talk with any real frankness and warmth. Lamsdorff was anxious to maintain good ties with the British Embassy during his time as Foreign Minister, but his chronic shyness and fear of making any commitments on the basis of his own authority set limits to the closeness of the relationship. Izvol'skii, by contrast, came to office at a time when the Russian political system was in turmoil, and quickly revealed his determination to establish his influence on foreign policy; he was also more willing than his predecessors to speak openly to British officials about the problems he faced in carrying out his duties. The change in the tone of the relationship between the Embassy and the Foreign Ministry after 1906 was in large part a consequence of the improving relationship between Britain and Russia, but the process also had the effect of cementing the change. The development of a more open dialogue inculcated a degree of trust between British and Russian diplomatic representatives that had been largely absent in previous years.

The Embassy staff also developed links with other senior officials in the Russian Foreign Ministry. British diplomats usually classified Foreign Ministry officials along two dimensions: whether they were competent or incompetent, and whether they were instinctive anglophiles or anglophobes. Some officials such as N.G. Hartwig, who worked in St Petersburg before being appointed Russian Minister in Tehran in 1906, were respected for their ability but distrusted on account of their views about international relations. Other officials were seen as reasonably well-intentioned towards Britain but lacking in great ability or influence.[18] In the years before the Anglo–Russian convention, the officials most distrusted at the British Embassy were those believed to be sympathetic to the cause of a Russian forward policy in central Asia. In the years after 1907, attention focused instead on whether a particular official was committed to the Anglo–Russian *entente* or instead favoured the establishment of a closer relationship between St Petersburg and Berlin. During the last few years before the outbreak of war in 1914, there was widespread belief at the British Embassy that anglophile sentiments predominated among senior Foreign Ministry officials in

St Petersburg, but that many Russian diplomats in post abroad were considerably less friendly in their views.

While relations between the Embassy and the Foreign Ministry became increasingly warm as time went by, the significance of such a development was limited so long as a wide range of individuals and organisations were able to have an impact on Russian foreign policy. British diplomats in St Petersburg therefore had to attempt to establish a dialogue with all those who might be able to influence the policy making process. It has already been seen that the milieu of family and friends surrounding Nicholas at Court was often *terra incognita* for the Embassy staff during the years before 1914. They also found it difficult to establish good relations with most ministers who held office during the period. Individual ministers could be very influential even before the constitutional changes that took place in 1906. The intelligent and energetic Minister of Finance from 1894 to 1903, Sergei Witte – who exercised a great deal of influence on Russian foreign policy – frequently spoke 'off the record' to the British Embassy. He was, however, treated with a certain suspicion by British diplomats, who believed that Witte was instinctively pro-German.[19] The establishment of a reformed Council of Ministers in the spring of 1906 changed the structure of decision-making in St Petersburg, with the result that Embassy officials started to pay rather greater attention than before to establishing links with ministers believed to be well-placed to exercise an influence on policy making. Peter Stolypin, who served as Chairman of the Council of Ministers from 1906 to 1911, was particularly respected at the Embassy, in large part because staff there admired his efforts to combine domestic reform with the maintenance of public order.[20] During the five years he was in office, British diplomats probably had better access to information about politics in St Petersburg than at any other time before 1914. The assassination of Stolypin in 1911 undoubtedly made it much harder for the Embassy to keep track of developments in the Council of Ministers, which in turn meant that it was difficult for diplomats there to follow developments in Russian domestic and foreign policy.

British diplomats posted to Russia in the 20 years before 1914 were realistic enough to recognise that even the frankest interlocutor would be guarded in conversation with the representatives of a foreign power, with the result that they made great efforts to establish ways of obtaining information other than through direct interrogation of leading figures in the government. Embassy staff played an active role in the social life of the city, attending dinner parties, playing polo, and joining some of the city's more exclusive clubs. Supporters of the old diplomacy habitually justified these kinds of activities by arguing that the social round could provide an insight into the public mood, which could in turn facilitate a better understanding of the wider social and political situation. This argument was hard to sustain in late nineteenth- and early twentieth-century Russia. The world of the St Petersburg *beau monde* was radically divorced from the wider society. A casual conversation at a party or reception might well reveal something about the narrow metropolitan world to which the speaker belonged, but it was unlikely to provide any reliable insight into the attitudes of a wider public. Nor was a denizen of the St Petersburg *beau monde* likely to have any reliable information about developments taking place in the provinces. It was not even possible to argue that immersion in the social round was able to provide diplomats with good knowledge about the attitudes prevailing among the governing classes of the Tsarist Empire. The virtual retreat of the Court from St Petersburg after 1904 meant that there was a sharp divorce between high society and the milieu surrounding Nicholas at Tsarskoe Selo. Nor did senior government officials usually frequent the more fashionable salons and parties of St Petersburg. As a result, a British official could never be sure that the political opinions he heard expressed at the dinner table were in any sense shared by those responsible for making decisions. The value of the social round as a source of political information was certainly very considerable in a society like Edwardian Britain, where social, political and economic elites were fused together into a single 'Establishment'; it was of less obvious value in early twentieth-century Russia, where the boundaries between the rich, the powerful and the fashionable were less permeable.

Embassy staff also made use of the network of foreign representatives in St Petersburg, although relations with officials from other missions in the city were inevitably bound up with the wider pattern of international alliances and tensions. Members of the various foreign missions tended to go to the same round of dinner-parties and *soirées*; many of them also hunted or played polo together during their leisure hours. These social contacts could provide an important opportunity for the exchange of information and views, but since the pattern of such informal relationships was profoundly affected both by the personalities involved, along with the nature of the prevailing political relationship between the relevant governments, the configuration of the diplomatic network naturally changed over time. During the years between 1894 and 1904, the British Embassy maintained perfectly friendly relations with other missions, particularly when the ebullient Sir Charles Scott was in charge. Nevertheless, despite Scott's natural bonhomie, the ethos of 'splendid isolation' continued to exert its influence. Successive British ambassadors took some care to maintain a certain distance when dealing with other foreign representatives in the Russian capital. This pattern began to change somewhat following the establishment of the *entente cordiale* between Britain and France in 1904, which fostered an increasingly close relationship between the two countries' embassies in the Russian capital.

The French Ambassador in St Petersburg from 1903 to 1908, Maurice Bompard, was a staunch proponent of the Anglo–French *entente*, which he hoped to see complemented by the establishment of an Anglo–Russian convention. His successors, Georges Louis, Théophile Delcassé and Maurice Paléologue, were also committed to maintaining the London–Paris–Petersburg 'triangle', which was to become so pivotal in the summer of 1914. Bompard greatly respected both Hardinge and Nicolson, in large part because the two men shared his instinctive suspicion of Germany. When Hardinge served as Ambassador between 1904 and 1906, the French and British embassies kept each other closely informed about their dealings with the Russian government. The two ambassadors regularly briefed each other following meetings with Lamsdorff or the Tsar, as well as exchanging political gossip and news about the disorders sweeping across the country.[21] The relationship between the two embassies was even closer during the Anglo–Russian talks of 1906–7. Bompard provided Nicolson with detailed advice about how to prepare for the negotiations with Izvol'skii; Nicolson was in turn very frank with Bompard about the views of the Cabinet in London on Anglo–Russian relations, and kept his French colleague abreast of the progress of the talks.[22] Bompard's departure from Russia, which was in large part due to his hosts' suspicion that he was building too many links with members of the liberal opposition, did not fundamentally alter the relationships between French and British representatives in the Russian capital. By the time the First World War broke out in 1914, the British and French embassies in the Russian capital were already used to working closely with one another, which helped to foster cooperation between them during the era of alliance politics.

The attitude of the British Embassy towards its German and Austrian counterparts was also affected by the vagaries of international politics. The German Ambassador von Schoen, who arrived in St Petersburg a few months before the start of the formal negotiations between Nicolson and Izvol'skii, wrote many years later in his memoirs that 'I cannot recall without the deepest regret the fact that I was not destined to be more than an observant witness of the gradual rapprochement between Russia and England'.[23] In reality, von Schoen received repeated assurances from Izvol'skii that the negotiations with Britain were not directed against Germany, but the Ambassador always suspected that an agreement between London and St Petersburg on Asian questions would 'spill over' into the European arena. The formal relationship between von Schoen and Nicolson was perfectly good during the time when both men served in the Russian capital, but while Nicolson spoke well of the character of his 'gentle' German colleague,[24] there was none of the frankness which characterised his dealings with Bompard. The British Ambassador attended numerous receptions and parties at the German Embassy, but these were seldom the setting for any substantial exchange of views on questions of international politics. The relationship between the British and Austrian embassies during the establishment of the Anglo–Russian Convention followed the same pattern. Nicolson considered Count d'Aehrenthal to be 'amiable...but not brilliant', while he regarded Aehrenthal's successor, Count Berchtold, with still less favour. In return, neither man vouchsafed Nicolson with any great confidences, making few sustained attempts to transcend the formalities of diplomatic life when dealing with the Ambassador and his staff. The kind of informal exchanges and discussions that could breathe life into a diplomatic relationship, by helping to provide additional mechanisms and channels for resolving conflicts and securing agreement, never really evolved between British representatives in Russia and their colleagues from Berlin and Vienna. A rapport between two ambassadors could certainly help to foster greater understanding during times of tension, but personal chemistry alone could not smooth away the challenges posed by fundamental international differences. For much of the period before the outbreak of war in 1914, the relationship between the 'big four' ambassadors in St Petersburg was structured by the emerging fault-lines of international politics, a pattern that was heightened rather than ameliorated by the character of the personalities involved.

The British Embassy's attitude towards other foreign missions in the Russian capital predictably stood between these two extremes. The activities of senior representatives of other great powers such as Italy were monitored with some care, while exchanges of information between British and Italian diplomats took place on matters of mutual interest such as the disorders that spread across Russia in 1905. Informal conversations with foreign representatives could also serve as a useful source of information about more wide-ranging questions of international politics – information which was duly sent back to London by the Embassy for consideration by the Foreign Secretary and his officials there. The American Ambassador during the middle of the first decade of the twentieth century, George Meyer, a businessman who was not at all well-versed in the ways of professional diplomacy, occupied a rather singular position during his time in St Petersburg since his country stood aloof from many of the intricacies of European politics that so preoccupied his peers.[25] While Meyer played an important role in setting up the talks between Russia and Japan which led to the Portsmouth Treaty of 1905, he did not consult the British Embassy in any great detail about the subject, even though the existence of the Anglo–Japanese Treaty meant that Britain had a particular interest in the outcome of the war. The American Ambassador dined regularly with Charles Hardinge, and the two men did exchange political gossip and information, but the relationship never approached the closeness of the one between Hardinge and Bompard. The 'special relationship' before the First World War was very much one between the British and the French rather than the British and the Americans.

A number of British officials in Russia other than regular diplomats were also well-placed to help the Embassy carry out its work effectively. British consuls, whose role is discussed in detail in Chapter 4, reported extensively on developments in the provinces, while the military and naval attachés at the Embassy devoted considerable energy to cultivating contacts with Russian army officers in an effort to gain information about the secretive world of the tsarist officer corps. The position of the service attachés could be a difficult one, since their role was by its very nature ambiguous. As representatives of the War Office, who were temporarily under the authority of the ambassador, they could easily experience divided loyalties. The ambassador expected them to adhere strictly to the codes of behaviour expected from a diplomat, while the War Office demanded information that could not easily be obtained except through subterfuge and deception. Colonel de la Poer Beresford, who served as military attaché in St Petersburg at the start of the century, firmly declared that an attaché should never put himself in a position where he could be suspected of spying.[26] This could, however, be more difficult than it sounded. One naval attaché, Captain Aubrey Smith, was implicated in 1911 at the trial of a Russian Admiralty employee accused of purloining secret documents, although the Embassy indignantly denied that he had been involved in any kind of wrongdoing.[27] While the rights and wrongs of the Smith case are difficult to unravel, there is no doubt that the Embassy had been involved some years earlier in an attempt to bribe Russian officials to supply secret information and documents. Nor was this behaviour considered in any way unusual by Embassy staff, who recognised that such activities were part of the diplomatic game. Before the 1907 Anglo–Russian convention was signed, the British Embassy in St Petersburg was itself the repeated target of infiltration attempts by the tsarist secret police, whose operatives stole documents and bribed servants in an effort to obtain information.[28] The problems largely faded away with the signing of the convention, but the Embassy's mail continued to be opened right down to the start of the First World War.

Diplomats posted to the St Petersburg Embassy before 1914 usually tried to avoid having too many dealings with correspondents from foreign newspapers working in the city, since some journalists had contacts with individuals and groups that were anathema to the Russian government. The relationship between the *The Times* and the Russian government was particularly tense during the first few years of the century, following the expulsion of one of its correspondents for writing about 'the horror of the pogroms' and 'revolutionary tendencies'.[29] Senior Embassy staff were inclined to blame the inexperienced correspondent for the problems he encountered, resenting the tensions caused by an individual over whom they had no control. E.J. Dillon of the *Daily Telegraph*, who was on close terms with Sergei Witte, was a mine of useful information, although he too was not altogether trusted by the Embassy. Nevertheless, Dillon did provide British officials with many useful reports, particularly during the critical months following the promulgation of the October Manifesto in the autumn of 1905. The Embassy always faced something of a quandary when deciding how to deal with individuals and organisations that were viewed with distaste by the tsarist government. The problem was particularly acute after the launch of the Constitutional Experiment in 1906, given the potential influence of the Duma on Russian foreign policy. While British diplomats regularly attended sessions of the Duma, both Nicolson and Buchanan were reluctant to allow their staff to become too friendly with deputies who were critical of the government, fearing that it might damage the Embassy's relationship with ministers. It was largely for this reason that the Embassy made extensive use of two 'unofficial diplomatists' during the critical months and years following the 1905 Revolution, in an effort to gather political intelligence in a way that would not offend the susceptibilities of their hosts.

Donald Mackenzie Wallace and Bernard Pares both spent a good deal of time at the British Embassy in the period after the 1905 Revolution, at the invitation of senior officials there, allowing regular diplomats to draw on their undoubted expertise and knowledge. Wallace was an expert of many years standing on Russian affairs, an erstwhile foreign editor of *The Times* who was also able to boast a formidable array of political contacts back in Britain. Bernard Pares was an academic from Liverpool University, who had been familiar with Russia from his student days many years before. Since the two men were not professional diplomats, they could have dealings with a much wider range of people than most Embassy staff, ranging from liberal members of the Duma through to individuals suspected of involvement in the revolutionary movement. Wallace produced numerous reports for the Foreign Office about the organisation and operation of the Duma.[30] He also acquired a good knowledge of the activities of such revolutionary groups as the Social Democrats and the Socialist Revolutionaries, making use of pamphlets seized by the Russian secret police and handed to him by Stolypin. Pares similarly spent a good deal of time watching the progress of the Constitutional Experiment. The use of the two 'unofficial diplomatists' represented an ingenious attempt to overcome some of the constraints routinely encountered by diplomats at the St Petersburg Embassy as they attempted to go about their business.

THE EMBASSY IN ACTION

Conducting the Diplomatic Dialogue

It is hard to define something so nebulous and multi-faceted as the role of an Embassy, particularly since the boundaries between the various diplomatic functions are inherently permeable and shifting. The next two sections of this chapter focus on the negotiating and reporting role of the British Embassy in St Petersburg during the years before 1914. The notion of diplomatic negotiation is of course a complex one, since it is a process that can assume many different forms and take place in many different settings. Negotiations may take place at a highly organised summit meeting or in the more relaxed forum of a dinner party. They may revolve around specific proposals or take the form of a more casual exchange of views. The notion that a diplomat can never be 'off duty' is rooted in the very nature of the diplomatic career, since every conversation or meeting can represent an opportunity to exert influence or gather information. It is for this reason that the term 'diplomatic dialogue' is used so extensively in the following paragraphs: it reflects the fact that communications between an Embassy and the principal political actors in the country where it is located may occur in a wide range of patterns and places.

At one end of the diplomatic dialogue conducted by the British Embassy in St Petersburg were formal bilateral negotiations of the kind that took place between Nicolson and Izvol'skii in 1906–7, which were designed to secure a specific outcome: an agreement between the two countries about their role in central Asia. These set-piece negotiations were in fact the exception rather than the rule. When Sir Nicolas O'Conor was in charge of the Embassy, tentative *pour-parlers* took place about securing some kind of understanding between Britain and Russia in the Far East, but the talks never really progressed to formal negotiations.[31] The discussions that took place in London in 1903 between the Foreign Office and Benckendorff over a possible agreement on central Asia are similarly best-understood as an attempt to establish whether there was sufficient common ground between the two countries to make the start of formal negotiations worthwhile. The boundary between such *pour-parlers* and negotiations proper can never be a precise one, given that any preliminary talks will inevitably shape the subsequent proceedings. It is clear, however, that the dialogue between diplomats at the British Embassy and senior members of the tsarist government was 'continuous and confidential' – one of the features which Harold Nicolson believed defined the character of the old diplomacy.[32] The negotiations that took place in 1906–7 to secure the Anglo–Russian rapprochement are best understood as a kind of peak in an on-going diplomatic dialogue, distinguished primarily by their formal structure and orientation towards a specific goal rather than by the mere fact of their existence.

The structure of the 1906–7 negotiations between Nicolson and Izvol'skii, reviewed at some length in the previous chapter, illustrates some of the typical features of the old diplomacy. The detailed talks were for the most part conducted by the Ambassador and Foreign Minister in person (although Poklevskii-Kozell also played a significant role, discussing developments with Nicolson and keeping the Ambassador informed about Izvol'skii's dealings with other senior ministers and officials in St Petersburg). While the two men were able to call on their staff for information about a particular topic, they relied to a great extent on their own knowledge and judgement. The battery of experts that attend so many modern negotiations were conspicuous by their absence. At the same time, while enjoying a good deal of latitude in the conduct of the negotiations, Nicolson and Izvol'skii both faced significant political and administrative constraints on their freedom of manoeuvre. Nicolson was of course bound by the instructions given to him by the Foreign Office, although as one of the principal proponents of the Anglo–Russian agreement within the British diplomatic establishment his views were listened to carefully by Grey and Hardinge in London. Izvol'skii, as will be seen in Chapter 5, had to engage in a tortuous process of coalition-building in St Petersburg to win domestic consent for an agreement with the British government. The constraints faced by the two men had the paradoxical effect of strengthening their relationship, since they understood that they were engaged in a common effort to broker an agreement that would be acceptable to both their governments. Their dialogue encompassed many different levels of communication, ranging from formal exchanges of opening proposals through to 'off-the-record' discussions about possible areas of agreement. These informal discussions had the advantage of allowing each man to gauge the other's attitude without formally binding their governments to a particular position. The secrecy with which the detailed discussions were conducted helped to facilitate a fluidity and frankness that would have been much harder if the talks had been subject to greater scrutiny. In short, the 1906–7 talks illustrated many of the defining features of the old diplomacy – features which were seen by its proponents as strengths and its enemies as weaknesses. Critics of the old diplomacy considered that the culture of secrecy and diplomatic solidarity reduced public scrutiny of foreign policy and increased international uncertainty and tension; supporters believed that these were the very features which made it easier to secure agreements and promote peace.

If structured negotiations to achieve a formal agreement represented one end of the diplomatic dialogue, at the opposite extreme were talks designed to manage and defuse the various crises which erupted periodically in Anglo–Russian relations. Such talks were essentially reactive in character, driven by the need to respond promptly to the course of events rather than by a desire to secure well-defined objectives. The definition of an international crisis is itself somewhat problematic. It could, for example, be argued that Anglo–Russian relations were in a state of almost permanent crisis in the years before 1907, given the degree of tension engendered by conflicts in central Asia and the Far East. If a more restricted definition is used, however, then the most serious and celebrated crisis in Anglo–Russian relations during the 20 years before the summer of 1914 was probably the Dogger Bank incident of autumn 1904. When a number of British trawlers fishing in the North Sea were shelled by Russian warships, the incident immediately threatened to lead to a full-scale armed conflict, particularly since the outbreak of the Russo–Japanese War earlier in the year had already made relations between Britain and Russia very tense. The incident had all the ingredients of confusion and mendacity that are the hallmark of the typical war scare. A brief study of the way in which the two countries avoided war illustrates the way in which professional diplomats in general, and the British Ambassador in St Petersburg in particular, managed to sustain the diplomatic dialogue at a time when it threatened to be swamped on both sides by the rhetoric of war.

The British Ambassador in St Petersburg in the autumn 1904 was of course Charles Hardinge, while the Russian Foreign Ministry was headed by Count Lamsdorff, both of whom were fervently committed to preventing the outbreak of war between Britain and Russia. Hardinge had arrived in St Petersburg in the spring of 1904 determined to promote a closer relationship between the two countries,[33] while Lamsdorff was fearful that war might place unbearable strains on a Russian military establishment which had already been found wanting in the face of Japanese attacks in the Far East. Both men soon became acutely aware, however, that the Dogger Bank incident was likely to create patterns of political pressures that would make war more likely. A few days after the most acute phase of the crisis had passed, Hardinge wrote to Lord Knollys complaining that the British government's failure to impose an 'effectual restraint on public opinion' had made the crisis harder to resolve, since the aggressive tone of many newspapers in London undermined the prospects for compromise.[34] Lamsdorff in St Petersburg strongly suspected that important elements in the Russian military, along with a section of the political elite, were willing to countenance a war with Britain. Resolving the crisis peacefully therefore required senior members of both diplomatic establishments to maintain an effective dialogue aimed at finding a solution that would not be rejected out of hand by the more bellicose voices in their respective countries.

Senior members of the Russian and British diplomatic establishments at first seemed quite slow to recognise that the Dogger Bank incident could lead to war. As soon as the news arrived in London, Lansdowne told Hardinge to inform Lamsdorff about the scale of the 'indignation which has been provoked' by the shelling of the trawlers;[35] two days later, however, following a series of meetings with Benckendorff and his deputy, the British Foreign Secretary was in part mollified by the fact that the two men were clearly 'much distressed' by the news, even though they were at first reluctant to make any 'damaging admissions' in the absence of further details.[36] Meanwhile, Hardinge reported from St Petersburg that Lamsdorff was 'filled...with horror' and ready to hold an investigation into what seemed to be a tragic mistake.[37] King Edward in London wrote angrily about 'a most dastardly outrage', while newspapers in the British capital carried indignant accounts of how the Russian warships had failed to pick up survivors from the two trawlers that were destroyed, but the prevailing opinion at the two foreign ministries was that the incident lacked any wider political significance. While Lansdowne and Hardinge were both scathing about the failure of the Russian authorities to establish effective procedures for keeping in contact with their ships, which meant that ministers in St Petersburg could not provide a proper explanation for the incident from the admiral in charge of the Baltic Fleet, they were confident that the government in St Petersburg would soon be able to identify and punish the relevant officers.

The meetings which took place during this period between Hardinge and Lamsdorff in St Petersburg, as well as Lansdowne and Benckendorff in London, were inevitably tense, but the participants were united by a belief that war should and would be avoided. The crisis only entered its most dangerous phase some days after the incident in the North Sea actually took place, when the Russian admiral in charge of the Baltic Fleet finally sent his report of the incident to St Petersburg, claiming that the British trawlers had in fact been providing cover for two Japanese torpedo boats.[38] The admiral's account quickly received wide currency in St Petersburg, where resentment against Britain had for some months been fuelled by a widespread belief that Britain was offering tacit military help to its Far Eastern ally. It was, however, indignantly received in Britain, where Lansdowne quickly informed Benckendorff that it 'would not carry the slightest conviction...in this country',[39] while the Cabinet instructed the Admiralty to mobilise its ships 'to stop the Baltic Fleet, by persuasion if possible, but by force if necessary'.[40] As long as it had seemed that the action of the Russian warships was due to a tragic error for which the government in St Petersburg would eventually take responsibility, the prospects for a peaceful outcome seemed good. When the arrival of Rozhdestvenskii's report made it appear that the Russian government was likely to defend the action of its sailors, the whole complexion of the incident was changed immediately. The political pressures on both sides threatened to swamp the dialogue between members of the two diplomatic establishments and make it harder for them to avert the threat of war.

The arrival of Admiral Rozhdestvenskii's report in St Petersburg also transformed the political atmosphere in the Russian capital, where it was seized upon as evidence that Russian warships had behaved quite properly. The tone of embarrassed caution that Lamsdorff had adopted during the previous few days was quickly abandoned, as the Foreign Minister came under enormous pressure to take a much harder line with the British Ambassador. When Hardinge visited the Foreign Ministry on 27 October, he found that the 'air was charged with electricity.... The Russian government on finding themselves no longer in the role of the accused quite lost their heads and the general tone was decidedly bellicose'. Even the timid and polite Lamsdorff was 'so excited that he was very nearly rude'.[41] The British Ambassador was convinced that the hardliners were 'in a most dangerous frame of mind. They fully realised that if they went to war with us they would lose their Baltic Fleet, but they had got their backs against the wall and they were ready to risk anything in a general cataclysm'.[42] It was at this stage that Hardinge's behaviour probably played an important role in avoiding war, although the self-justificatory tone of his memoirs, letters and diary makes it difficult to gauge the exact situation. The Ambassador had no doubt that it was important to avoid putting the Russians in a situation where they could only salvage their pride and *amour propre* by going to war. He was privately opposed to the British Cabinet's decision to order the Royal Navy to shadow the Baltic Fleet, fearing that it would seem 'provocative' to the Russians in their 'present frame of mind'.[43] From the moment the crisis started, Hardinge had attempted to approach Lamsdorff 'as a friend' rather than as an Ambassador, in the hope that this more personal approach would make it easier to achieve their joint goal of 'maintaining friendly relations between the two countries'.[44] Following his difficult interview with the Foreign Minister on 27 October, Hardinge decided to return to the Embassy 'for I realized that he was not himself and that he was in an abnormal state...I said nothing beyond that I would see him the following day'.[45] In the hours following the meeting, the Ambassador apparently made a deliberate decision to avoid reporting back to London in detail about Lamsdorff's behaviour and words, instead simply telegraphing home that Lamsdorff and other senior members of the Russian government were 'excessively sensitive' to the complaints of the British.[46] The following day, Lamsdorff himself acknowledged that Hardinge's restraint during these critical hours had played a crucial role in preventing war, noting that he had been given instructions by the Council of Ministers that should the British Foreign Secretary or his representative 'utter one word of menace' he was to say that 'Well, you want war, and now you shall have it'. Hardinge's decision to respond calmly to Lamsdorff's outburst, and to report back selectively to London about his interview, helped to ease the tensions between Britain and Russia at a time when they threatened to explode.

The Dogger Bank crisis continued to rumble on during the rest of 1904. A proposal by Lord Lansdowne to establish an international tribunal to review the tragedy was taken up by Lamsdorff, who passed off the idea to the Tsar as his own. After the panic of 27 October, the Russian Foreign Minister himself quickly reverted to a far more cooperative approach, meeting with Hardinge on numerous occasions to discuss the tail-end of the crisis. He continued to face great pressure from the Russian Admiralty to take a harder line with the British, but once the immediate crisis surrounding the receipt of Rozhdestvenskii's report had been averted, Lamsdorff became more willing to defend the cause of moderation (although he was still on occasion forced to retract on certain agreements he had made as a result of pressure from hardliners both in the Foreign Ministry and beyond).[47] The political pressure began to drop in Britain as well, where the Prime Minister took advantage of a speech made at the end of October to express confidence that the Russian government was determined to make amends for the incident.[48] Lansdowne wrote to Hardinge on the evening of 29 October that during the previous two days 'the betting was about even as between peace and war',[49] but despite being worried that the Russian hardliners might once again get Russia into a 'scrape', he was confident that the immediate crisis had passed. A few weeks later, Hardinge sent a letter to Knollys which showed clearly that he had seen his role at the height of the crisis as that of a mediator between the two governments, rather than as a simple mouthpiece for the British government. He told the King's Private Secretary that he had throughout the crisis been 'firmly resolved to do everything I could to prevent war', and went on to criticise the more bellicose members of the British government, noting caustically that any military conflict would have 'involved [us] in a long and costly war in Central Asia, for which neither our military forces nor our finance appear to be in a fitting state of preparation'.[50] The Dogger Bank incident illustrated both the constraints and freedoms faced by a British ambassador, along with other members of the British and Russian diplomatic establishments, in dealing with an an acute international crisis that threatened to spiral out of control. Hardinge was for the most part successful in maintaining a cordial relationship with Lamsdorff and his colleagues, with the exception of the difficult meeting on 27 October. Benckendorff in London also managed to preserve a good relationship with the Foreign Office, while at the same time struggling to avoid offering an apology that might have exceeded his formal instructions. The most important actors in the dialogue between the British and Russian governments during the critical phase of the North Sea incident were professional diplomats and foreign ministry officials; relations between London and St Petersburg were handled almost entirely within the apparatus of formal diplomacy. Hardinge and his staff did not have many direct dealings with Russian officials from outside the Foreign Ministry during the final week of October (although the Ambassador did have an audience with the Nicholas II on 29 October at which the Tsar noted his great regret at the loss of life); Benckendorff similarly had few meetings except with Lansdowne at the Foreign Office during the most acute stage of the crisis. There was a consensus between senior members of the two diplomatic establishments on the need to avoid war, even though public and political discussion about the Dogger Bank affair was conducted in both countries in an atmosphere of indignation and self-righteousness which threatened to create tensions that could not be resolved within the framework of diplomacy. Professional diplomats in London and St Petersburg were not solely responsible for preventing the tragedy from escalating into war, but their ability to maintain a dialogue among themselves certainly helped to provide avenues for managing the immediate crisis and planning moves to lead to its resolution.

Formal negotiation and crisis-management were, as already noted, only two aspects of the diplomatic dialogue conducted by the British Embassy in St Petersburg in the years before the First World War. For most of the time, discussions between British diplomats and senior Russian officials were far more piecemeal in character, designed to provide the two governments with an insight into the other's position on a whole range of matters. Issues of specific bilateral concern, such as the future of Afghanistan, naturally figured prominently in this dialogue. The texture of global politics during this period meant, however, that many international questions were of concern to *all* the major powers. The combination of European rivalry and imperial ambition meant that the ability of one of the powers to defend and promote its interests across the world was a matter of vital consideration to all the others. The paradoxical nature of great power politics before 1914, characterised by a curious mixture of competition and cooperation, created a situation in which any minor conflict could quickly become a matter of general import. The dialogue between the British Embassy in St Petersburg and the Russian government was therefore not only about bilateral issues; it also provided an opportunity for discussion about other matters of major international concern. One of the principal tasks of the British ambassador in the Russian capital was to report to London about the St Petersburg government's attitude on all the major international questions of the day. The position of the tsarist government on matters ranging from disarmament through to the issues under discussion at the Algeciras Conference was routinely discussed in dispatches. Such matters were also discussed with the representatives of the other major powers posted to the Russian capital, who provided another valuable source of information. In an age when international questions were of concern to all the major powers, the various national capitals each provided a setting for important discussions and exchanges of views that helped to determine the dynamic of international politics. It was for this reason that the Foreign Office in London was careful to keep ambassadors in post abroad abreast of major developments across the spectrum of international relations, rather than treating them as 'specialists' dealing with a single bilateral relationship. The multilateral nature of great power politics meant that an embassy located in one of the major capitals formed part of a complex bureaucratic machine designed to gather information and assert British influence around the world.

The British Embassy in St Petersburg was, then, engaged in a multi-dimensional dialogue with a range of diplomatic and political actors, the purpose of which varied according to the prevailing circumstances. The dialogue could be designed to manage a crisis, to promote a formal agreement, or simply to exchange routine information about a range of international issues. The boundary between the classic diplomatic functions of reporting, representing and negotiating was highly permeable. A single conversation between a senior British diplomat and a member of the tsarist Foreign Ministry would often encompass a wide range of bilateral and multilateral issues. An important part of the diplomatic art consisted of assembling fragments of information and casual statements to allow a coherent analysis of the position of a foreign government on a particular issue. The reports sent back to London could then be combined with other information arriving at the Foreign Office to help the foreign secretary and his senior officials to grasp changes in the pattern of international politics.

Political Reporting

Political reporting was in some ways the most important task carried out by the British Embassy in St Petersburg.[51] The successful conduct of the diplomatic dialogue, in all its manifestations, depended on the acquisition of reliable information about the context in which Russian foreign policy was made. This was true whether Russia was viewed as a potential enemy or as a possible ally. The process of political reporting was continuous. Individual members of the Embassy staff sometimes compiled lengthy reports on such specific topics as the growth of student unrest and the state of provincial public opinion, which were then duly forwarded to London under the author's name. On other occasions, they drafted shorter memoranda for the ambassador, who decided whether to include the material in one of his dispatches to the Foreign Office. While political reporting took place at different levels and in different forms, the focus was usually on two specific areas. The first was the political process in St Petersburg, making sense of which required a careful analysis of the role of the Tsar, the Court, the ministries and, from 1906, the Duma. The second was the wider social and political scene, ranging from the activities of the various revolutionary parties through to the mentality of the peasantry in the Russian countryside. Reporting on each of these areas presented its own particular challenges and difficulties.

It was seen earlier that the Embassy found it difficult to cultivate good relations with many of the individuals who had the most immediate impact on the political development of the Tsarist Empire. The Tsar himself always remained something of an enigma to British diplomats. When Sir Frank Lascelles arrived as Ambassador in 1894, a few months before Nicholas II became Emperor, he was inclined to believe that the young Tsarevich was 'honest and well-intentioned'.[52] A few weeks later, following the death of Alexander III, the Ambassador wrote to Valentine Chirol that 'no one seems to know anything' about Nicholas and noted that 'there are the most contradictory reports as to what he is likely to do or not do'.[53] Lascelles was at first inclined to share the general view that the new Tsar would be more liberal than his father, but this impression soon faded as Nicholas took a 'very autocratic line', condemning those who called for the establishment of any form of representative assembly.[54] Lascelles in fact fell into the trap which snared many of those who tried to understand Nicholas's character. The Tsar's manifest decency and kindness were often taken as evidence that he was likely to reject the harsher elements of his autocratic inheritance in favour of a more liberal style of government. In reality, Nicholas was as firmly committed as his predecessor to the autocratic principle, which he defended with a stubborness that in the end had a devastating effect on his country's fortunes.

By the time the 1905 Revolution swept across Russia, ten years after Lascelles left the country to take up a new post in Berlin, the Embassy's collective view of Nicholas had acquired a familiar form. The Tsar was widely believed by British diplomats to lack the political skills needed to carry out his role effectively. Some diplomats were privately very harsh in their judgements. One of them believed that the Tsar had 'the brains of a sheep', while another official condemned Nicholas for deserting St Petersburg for Tsarskoe Selo where he played with his young son and tried to ignore the problems threatening to sweep away his dynasty.[55] Successive ambassadors tended to be more sympathetic in their judgements, perhaps because their personal dealings with the Tsar gave them an insight into his instinctive benevolence. Charles Scott was the kindest in his comments, doubtless because he was less interested in political questions than any other British ambassador who served in St Petersburg in the years before 1914. When Hardinge was appointed Ambassador, he already had a good knowledge of Nicholas's character, acquired during the years he served as Secretary of the Embassy. While not as harsh in his judgement of the Tsar as his deputy, Cecil Spring Rice, Hardinge had few doubts that Nicholas lacked the character and intelligence to deal with the burgeoning crisis facing Russia. He was also perturbed by the Emperor's instinctive conservatism and reluctance to contemplate the kind of reforms that might help to win the support of the population.[56] Arthur Nicolson echoed these views during his time in Russia, noting sadly that Nicholas did 'not always act with the required firmness and decision', while at the same time stubbornly refusing to listen to the counsel of his most able and intelligent ministers.[57] George Buchanan, who had his most extensive dealings with the Tsar during the critical years following the outbreak of war in 1914, was concerned above all by Nicholas's penchant for taking advice from his wife and such charlatans as Rasputin, which he feared alienated public opinion and drove policy in an increasingly conservative direction.

The Embassy faced even greater problems when reporting on developments beyond the official world of St Petersburg. In the city itself, revolutionary groups like the Socialist Revolutionaries and the Social Democrats were becoming more and more active during the early years of the twentieth century. The assassination of important ministers, such as the murder in 1904 of the Minister of Interior V.K. Plehve, provided graphic evidence of the revolutionaries' ability to cause chaos, although British diplomats found it difficult to provide London with accurate material about the revolutionary organisations. In the years leading up to the 1905 Revolution, the Embassy provided the Foreign Office with occasional reports about student unrest in the universities,[58] along with details of assassinations and bombings. Scott was on the whole inclined to believe that the challenge posed by radicals to the stability of the regime was overstated,[59] but by the middle of 1904 the Embassy took the prospect of revolution far more seriously. When Hardinge returned to St Petersburg in May, he was already concerned that popular discontent over Russian defeats in the Russo–Japanese War could serve as a catalyst for widespread disorder.[60] Spring Rice even believed that the Dogger Bank incident of October 1904 might be a deliberate attempt by hardliners in the Russian capital to provoke a war with Britain which would encourage a wave of nationalist euphoria calculated to increase the popularity of the government.[61]

The Embassy faced great difficulties in following the revolutionary upheavals of 1905–6, since the worst of the disorders took place thousands of miles from St Petersburg. While British diplomats were able to report at first-hand on such tragedies as 'Bloody Sunday', when troops opened fire killing hundreds of protesters marching on the Winter Palace, they found it was much more difficult to keep abreast of events in the provinces. The reports filed by British consuls, reviewed in Chapter 4, provided an important source of information, but many of the incidents of peasant insurrection and army mutiny still went unobserved. Since the causes of popular discontent were so wide-ranging, Embassy staff found it difficult to understand the scale of the crisis. In the first few months of 1905, Hardinge and his staff were confident that the disorders were largely spontaneous outbursts fuelled by local resentments, but by the late spring the dispatches and telegrams sent to London placed more emphasis on the role of the revolutionaries in fomenting discontent. The Ambassador himself did little to hide his frustration with the Russian government for failing to make the kind of reforms needed to ease tension. In February he wrote to Thomas Sanderson at the Foreign Office that Nicholas was living 'in a world apart' and was 'absolutely impervious to the danger'.[62] A few days later, he told Lord Knollys that catastrophe would follow if greater efforts were not made to respond to public dissatisfaction.[63] There was in fact some dispute between the Ambassador and his deputy, Spring Rice, about the nature of the upheavals – one of the few occasions in the years before the First World War when there was disagreement among Embassy staff about the significance of the changes taking place in Russia. Hardinge was inclined to see the upheavals as a natural expression of popular frustration with an autocratic and incompetent government, believing that political reforms and better administration could help to resolve the situation.[64] Spring Rice's characteristically bleak view of the Russian character led him to believe that events were being driven by an inexorable logic that would lead in time to an unknown and almost certainly unpleasant future.[65] Hardinge's optimism about the potential efficacy of political reform in Russia was for the most part more representative of senior British diplomats who worked in the country in the years before 1914.

Reporting the 1905 Revolution was one of the most challenging tasks faced by the Embassy in the decades leading up to the First World War. Critics of the old diplomacy in Britain habitually argued that it was precisely this kind of popular upheaval that professional diplomats found difficult to interpret, since they had little understanding of the public passions which increasingly determined the pattern of political development around the globe.[66] In reality, the major constraints faced by the St Petersburg Embassy when carrying out its reporting role during the years before 1914 were overwhelmingly *structural* in character. The small number of diplomats posted to the Russian capital simply did not have the time to travel round such a vast country, forcing them to rely instead on a combination of rumours, censored press articles, conversations with officials, and accounts from hard-pressed consular staff. Despite all these problems, however, the reports sent to London during 1905–6 were on the whole more striking for their comprehensiveness and accuracy rather than for their failings.

A clear theme ran through most of the political reports compiled by the St Petersburg Embassy during the opening years of the twentieth century, reflecting a delicate pattern of half-articulated assumptions and values that were common to most of the diplomats who worked there. While it is always difficult to speculate about the existence of something so nebulous as a collective institutional mind, most members of the British Diplomatic Service who served in Russia before the First World War shared Charles Hardinge's assumption that substantial political reform was required to restore stability to the Tsarist Empire. Indeed, George Buchanan made precisely this argument in his last-ever interview with Nicholas II, just a few weeks before the Romanov dynasty was overthrown in the spring of 1917.[67] While the Embassy staff were appalled by the violence that broke out in 1905–6, which threatened to sweep away the existing system of government, they had little sympathy with Nicholas's determined attempts to maintain the pattern of autocratic rule intact. Many of the reports sent to London in the years before 1914 were informed by a conviction that Russia should follow a 'whig' pattern of political development, in which the crown would slowly relinquish its prerogative powers to the more established and prosperous classes. The 1905 Revolution, and for that matter the March 1917 Revolution as well, were interpreted by the Embassy as a political explosion created by a conflict between unreasoning tradition and unthinking radicalism. A strategy of political gradualism was seen as the only form of political development that could extricate tsarist Russia from its crisis.

The whig instinct characteristic of Embassy staff helps to explain their reaction to the Constitutional Experiment set in motion via the election of the first Duma in 1906. The first two dumas were elected on a popular francise,[68] which resulted in the return of a large core of liberal Cadets and a smaller number of revolutionary deputies, who together gave the demands put forward by the new assembly a distinctively radical tinge. Officials at the Embassy were at first hopeful that the new Duma could provide an appropriate forum for integrating a wider proportion of the population into the political process, helping to foster a more peaceful pattern of political development, but the radicalism of the deputies and the instinctive conservatism of most ministers created a deadlock that fuelled a growth in bad-tempered rhetoric. Arthur Nicolson and his staff were initially inclined to blame both sides equally for the problems, but by the time the Tsar dissolved the second Duma, in 1907, the Ambassador placed most of the blame on the deputies. Both he and Mackenzie Wallace condemned the unwillingness of Duma members to engage in a constructive dialogue with the government.[69] It was for this reason that the Embassy broadly welcomed Stolypin's constitutional coup of July 1907, in which the Chairman of the Council of Ministers introduced a new electoral law providing that deputies to the third Duma would be chosen on the basis of a much more restricted franchise. The inevitable consequence of this was the return of a large number of deputies holding more conservative views, who were consequently less inclined than their predecessors to engage in the politics of obstruction. Nicolson also praised Stolypin for his willingness, at least during his early years as Prime Minister, to deal openly with the Duma, in marked contrast to his immediate predecessor, I.L. Goremykin, who had failed to make any serious efforts to cooperate with deputies. The support of the Ambassador and his deputy, Hugh O'Beirne, for the constitutional arrangements set in place following Stolypin's 'conservative revolution' – which was strengthened by their admiration for the agricultural reforms he introduced around the same time – informed the tone of the Embassy's political reporting right down to 1914. While Stolypin's readiness to use savage measures of repression to crush the periodic outbursts of rebellion was condemned by Nicolson, he was inclined to overlook such abuses as a regrettable necessity. Although George Buchanan treated Stolypin with somewhat greater caution when he became Ambassador, he quickly came to endorse his predecessor's view, describing the Prime Minister's assassination in 1911 as a tragedy that would have serious consequences for Russia's political development.[70] Like Nicolson and Hardinge before him, Buchanan was vigorously critical of both revolutionaries and conservatives, believing that Russia's future could only be assured by inculcating the values of political moderation and agreement. The problem was, of course, that the divisions in Russian society were far too deep to be managed within the kind of institutional and political framework that existed in the country on the eve of 1914.

Critics of the old diplomacy believed that members of the British Diplomatic Service were ill-prepared to meet the challenges which faced them during the turbulent years before 1914. The history of the St Petersburg Embassy suggests that the real situation was less clear-cut. The men who worked at the Embassy between 1894 and 1914 were certainly typical representatives of the British Diplomatic Service, that is members of well-established professional or landed families who had received the kind of education normal for young men of their class. They were committed to a professional ethic that emphasised the value of secrecy in the day-to-day conduct of diplomatic relations, along with the importance of building a dialogue with their counterparts in other diplomatic establishments that was based on a high degree of trust and integrity. While the six men who served as ambassador in St Petersburg between 1894 and 1917 differed in the way they viewed their ambassadorial role, each of them to a greater or lesser degree believed that they had both the right and the duty to advise the British government on matters of policy. Their outlook in most matters was essentially conservative. In the international arena, they considered that the role of the diplomat was to manage the tensions and conflicts that continually developed between states. They accepted uncritically the existing structure of the international order, dominated by a handful of great powers, and believed that the maintenance of peace depended on securing a balance between their competing interests. In the domestic arena, British ambassadors and other senior officials posted to St Petersburg were instinctively committed to the view that the most efficacious pattern of social and political development in all countries was one which combined moderate change with the preservation of public order and established patterns of class privilege. In this sense, then, the men who worked at the St Petersburg Embassy before the First World War were undoubtedly 'guilty' of many of the charges levelled against them by their critics: they were representatives of a socially privileged milieu, committed to the notion that diplomacy was most effectively conducted far from the public gaze. At the same time, however, British diplomats serving in the Russian capital before 1914 were not, as many of their critics believed, untrained dilettantes lacking the skill and judgement to thrive in the contemporary international environment.

Most diplomats posted to the St Petersburg Embassy were dedicated to their work, toiling for long hours at tasks that were far more boring and routine than their critics ever realised. This was particularly true in the decade before 1914, when important changes in both the international environment and the Russian domestic political system created a great deal of extra work for the Embassy. While British diplomats moved easily in the *beau monde* of the Russian capital, the social round only commanded a small proportion of their time and energy. Most of the day was instead spent writing reports, wading through newspapers, or meeting with senior tsarist officials and diplomatic representatives from other countries. A handful of diplomats were expected to produce, with very little assistance, detailed reports on subjects ranging from the structure of the Russian government through to the state of the budget and the economic development of the Tsarist Empire. Nor did staff based at St Petersburg only concentrate on 'high politics' at the cost of more prosaic economic and commercial subjects – one of the favourite charges of the critics of old diplomacy. The Embassy files show that they actually spent a good deal of time reporting back to London on subjects ranging from the construction of railways through to the expansion of the Moscow tram system. The sheer scale of the Embassy's activities in the years before 1914 therefore destroys any notion that a diplomatic career was suitable for a dilettante; a diplomatic career instead demanded a high level of flexibility and intelligence, as well as a readiness to undertake a good deal of tedious work that could easily have been carried out by a clerk or secretary. While the men who worked at the St Petersburg Embassy were committed to the values and procedures that characterised European diplomacy before 1914, they were not the ineffectual amateurs written about with such contempt by many critics of the old diplomacy.

NOTES

1. For a brief review of the attitudes of British officials posted to Russia before 1900, see Michael Hughes, *Inside the Enigma*, pp. 1–12.
2. *Diaries and Correspondence of James Harris, First Earl of Malmesbury*, Vol. 1, 173.
3. The plans of the building, along with other relevant material, are located in Public Record Office, WORK 10/25–1.
4. FO 65/1678, Scott to Lansdowne, 7 January 1904.
5. FO 800/17, Lascelles to Kimberley, 15 August 1894.
6. Hughes, *Inside the Enigma*, p. 23.
7. Among the numerous memoirs and accounts concerning preparation for the exams, see Maurice Baring, *The Puppet Show of Memory*, pp. 154–5; Nevile Henderson, *Water Under the Bridges*, p. 18.
8. The biographical information presented in the following paragraphs is compiled from the relevant editions of the *Foreign Office List*, *The Dictionary of National Biography* and *Who's Who?*.
9. For comparative data about the composition of the British elite, see W.L. Guttsman, *The British Political Elite*, pp. 75–108.
10. FO 65/1640, Memorandum by Hardinge on 1902 budget, encl. with Scott to Lansdowne, 6 March 1902.
11. A large number of Spring Rice's letters, containing pithy comments on various aspects of social and political life in the Russian capital, can be found in Stephen Gwynn (ed.), *The Letters and Friendships of Sir Cecil Spring Rice* (2 vols).
12. Lascelles's growing unease about the Russian government was in part a response to the appointment in 1895 of Lobanov-Rostovskii as the new Foreign Minister in place of Giers; see FO 800/17, Lascelles to Kimberley, 19 June 1895.
13. Sir George Buchanan, *My Mission to Russia and Other Diplomatic Memoirs*, Vol. 1, p. 173.
14. Hardinge Papers, 6, Hardinge to Lady Salisbury, 26 May 1904.
15. Hardinge Papers, 6, Hardinge to Lansdowne, 25 May 1904.
16. FO 800/17, Lascelles to Kimberley, 1 August 1894.
17. Sir Frank Lascelles was at first quite complimentary about Lobanov-Rostovksii, though his doubts began to grow after the prince had been in office for a few months. See, for example, FO 800/17, Lascelles to Woodhouse, 23 February 1895; Lascelles to Kimberley, 19 June 1895.
18. FO 800/17, Lascelles to Kimberley, 15 August 1894.
19. See, for example, FO 800/72, Spring Rice to Grey, 1 March 1906.
20. See, for example, the comments of Arthur Nicolson, in Harold Nicolson, *Lord Carnock*, p. 225; and of Charles Hardinge in Royal Archives (RA) X22/44, Memorandum by Hardinge on the Visit by Edward VII to Russia in 1908.
21. See, for example, *BD*, Vol. 4, Hardinge to Lansdowne, 4 October 1905 (doc. 195); Hardinge to Lansdowne, 14 October 1905 (doc. 198).
22. Maurice Bompard, *Mon Ambassade en Russie*, p. 255; *BD*, Vol. 4, Nicolson to Grey, 13 January 1907 (doc. 245).
23. Wilhelm Edward von Schoen, *The Memoirs of an Ambassador*, p. 37.

24. Nicolson, *Carnock*, p. 211.
25. A great deal of useful information about Meyer, including original letters and diary entries, can be found in M.A. de Wolfe Howe, *George von Lengerke Meyer: His Life and Public Services*. For a useful brief account, see David Mayers, *The Ambassadors and America's Soviet Policy*, pp. 60–3.
26. Colonel C.E. de la Poer Beresford, 'Kundschaftsdientse', *National Review*, Vol. 56, pp. 954–64.
27. The papers on the Smith affair are located in FO 371/1215 (various documents).
28. Henderson, *Water Under the Bridges*, pp. 30–2; Hardinge, *Old Diplomacy*, pp. 107–8. More detailed information about attempts by the British Embassy to counter attempts by the Russian authorities to obtain information illicitly can be found in Public Record Office, HD 3/128; HD 3/132; HD 3/133.
29. *The History of the Times*, Vol. 3, p. 382.
30. Wallace Papers, 15 (various papers).
31. The relevant documents are reprinted in *BD*, Vol. 4 (docs 181–2).
32. Harold Nicolson, *The Evolution of Diplomatic Method*, p. 75.
33. See, for example, Hardinge's words to Lamsdorff during their first meeting, in Hardinge Papers, 5, diary entry for 17 May 1904.
34. Hardinge Papers, 6, Hardinge to Knollys, 24 November 1904.
35. *BD*, Vol. 4, Lansdowne to Hardinge, 24 October 1904 (doc.6).
36. *BD* Vol. 4, Lansdowne to Hardinge, 24 October 1904 (doc. 8); Lansdowne to Hardinge, 25 October 1904 (doc. 12); Lansdowne to Hardinge, 26 October 1904 (doc. 13).
37. *BD*, Vol. 4, Hardinge to Lansdowne, 24 October 1904 (doc. 7).
38. The text of the admiral's report is contained in *BD*, Vol. 4, Lansdowne to Hardinge, 27 October 1904 (doc. 16). For Hardinge's view of the 'twist' in the crisis, see FO 65/1729, Hardinge to Lansdowne, 27 October 1904, in which the Ambassador argued that 'The matter now enters on a new phase'.
39. *BD*, Vol. 4, Lansdowne to Hardinge, 27 October 1904 (doc. 16).
40. *BD*, Vol. 4, Admiralty to Vice-Admiral Channel Fleet (Gibralta), 27 October 1904 (doc. 19).
41. Hardinge Papers, 5, diary entry for 12 November 1904.
42. FO 800/141, Hardinge to Lansdowne, 5 November 1904.
43. Busch, *Hardinge of Penshurst*, p. 82.
44. FO 65/1729, Hardinge to Lansdowne, 26 October 1904.
45. The following paragraph is in part drawn from the material and argument in Briton Cooper Busch, *Hardinge of Penshurst*, pp. 80–1.
46. *BD*, Vol. 4, Hardinge to Lansdowne, 27 October 1904 (doc. 15).
47. Hardinge Papers, 5, diary entry for 24 November 1904.
48. Benckendorff still found some of Balfour's words offensive in his speech at Southampton; see *BD*, Vol. 4, Lansdowne to Hardinge, 29 October 1904 (doc. 23).
49. FO 800/141, Lansdowne to Hardinge, 29 October 1904.
50. Hardinge Papers, 6, Hardinge to Knollys, 24 November 1904.
51. For a more detailed discussion of the reports compiled by British officials in Russia during these years, see Hughes, *Inside the Enigma*, pp. 35–52.

52. FO 800/17, Lascelles to Kimberley, 10 October 1894.
53. FO 800/17, Lascelles to Chirol, 8 November 1894.
54. FO 800/17, Lascelles to Kimberley, 31 January 1895.
55. Hughes, *Inside the Enigma*, p. 26.
56. Hardinge Papers, 6, Hardinge to Sanderson, 15 February 1905; Gwynn, *Cecil Spring Rice*, Vol. 1, p. 458.
57. *British Documents on Foreign Affairs (henceforth BDFA)*, 1A, Vol. 4, Annual Report for 1906.
58. See, for example, FO 65/1620, Memorandum by Graham dated 20 March 1901.
59. FO 65/1620, Scott to Lansdowne, 21 March 1901.
60. Hughes, *Inside the Enigma*, p. 37.
61. BM, Add. Mss 49747, Spring Rice to Louis, 5 November 1904.
62. Hardinge Papers, 6, Hardinge to Sanderson, 15 February 1905.
63. RA W45/120, Hardinge to Knollys, 1 March 1905.
64. *BDFA* 1A, Vol. 3, Hardinge to Lansdowne, 4 July 1905.
65. RA W46/3, Spring Rice to Knollys, 2 May 1905.
66. *BPP 1914–16*, 11 (cd 7749), Appendices to the Fifth Report (of the MacDonnell Commission): Minutes of Evidence, Qus 38,062, 38,108.
67. George Buchanan, *Mission to Russia*, Vol. 2, p. 49.
68. For a valuable survey of the political reforms following the 1905 Revolution, see Geoffrey Hosking, *The Russian Constitutional Experiment*.
69. RA W51/55, Wallace to Knollys, 28 March 1907.
70. *BDFA*, 1A, Vol. 6, Buchanan to Grey, 20 September 1911.

4 British Consuls in Russia

THE CRITICS OF THE CONSULAR SERVICE

The British consular services became the target for a good deal of public criticism during the late nineteenth and early twentieth centuries.[1] This was particularly true in the case of the 'wretched and despised' General Service, whose members staffed consular posts throughout Europe and America. When the Board of Trade set up a committee in 1898 to examine the 'Dissemination of Commercial Information', a number of the witnesses who submitted evidence were extremely harsh about the poor calibre of consular officials. One witness from the Sheffield Chamber of Commerce spoke for many of his colleagues when he observed that 'it wants to be drilled in the Consuls that they must become trained experts and cover their ground'. Members of the Wakefield Chamber of Commerce were adamant that 'Consuls should in all cases be commercial and practical businessmen, and well up in commercial education and knowledge', while their counterparts in Birmingham agreed that 'All Consuls should have some commercial experience'.[2] The prevailing view was that no amount of tinkering with regulations could improve the quality of commercial information unless there was a radical shake-up in the personnel who manned consular posts abroad.

The scale of the criticism prompted Lord Lansdowne to establish in 1902 a new committee to recommend reforms of the consular services, which was chaired by Sir William Walrond.[3] The Walrond Committee was generally sympathetic to the complaints made by British businesses over the previous few years. Its final report proposed that the consular services should be reorganised along more professional lines, adopting new recruitment and promotion procedures designed to attract 'capable young men' with a business background. These recommendations rapidly assumed the status of conventional wisdom, and were echoed by later inquiries including the 1914 MacDonnell Commission on the Reform of the Civil Service. In reality, however, the problems confronting Britain's consuls in the early years of the twentieth century were a good deal more complex than many of their critics realised. They were *not* simply a consequence of poor organisation and a lack of qualified personnel. Many British businesses had quite unrealistic expectations about the level of help that could be provided by consular officials. A number of witnesses to the 1898 Board of Trade inquiry wanted consuls to pursue bad debts run up by overseas buyers; others wanted consulates to become 'centres of commercial information' for use by British traders and firms. Some members of the various committees set up to examine the consular services did acknowledge the need to reduce business expectations to more reasonable levels, but few of them really understood the scale of the problems facing consuls in post abroad. Even the most energetic official was not always able to meet the demands that were placed upon his time.

British consuls were expected to carry out a wide range of tasks in the years before the First World War.[4] As well as reporting on commercial and economic affairs, they were expected to perform numerous routine administrative tasks such as issuing passports and dealing with tourists who had lost their money or fallen foul of the local police. Consuls were also required to provide the Foreign Office with a regular flow of political and military reports about the region in which they were based, while those serving in major seaports were expected to report regularly on the movement of naval vessels. Despite the scale of these demands, however, the resources allocated to most consular posts were extremely meagre. Even a consul-general – the most senior consular rank – often had just one or two clerks to help him carry out his work. Any verdict about the effectiveness of British consuls at the beginning of the twentieth century must therefore recognise the difficulties under which they laboured.

THE ORGANISATION OF THE BRITISH CONSULAR SERVICE IN RUSSIA

While the role of British consuls was extremely wide-ranging, there was universal agreement that the promotion of British trade represented one of their most important tasks. Although most consuls lacked the resources to provide the level of service sought by British firms, the General Instructions issued to officials early in the century emphasised the importance of keeping abreast of such things as 'the laws and usages of commerce and shipping' and 'questions of labour, wages, workpeople, cooperation, strikes, conciliation boards'. The reports sent back to London were expected to provide the sort of information about local economic and commercial conditions which could provide British businesses with the information needed to help them identify commercial opportunities and challenges.

Table 4.1 Value of the Total Exports of the Produce and Manufactures of the United Kingdom 1895–9 (£ million)[5]

Country	1895	1900	1905	1910	1914
Russia	7.01	11.00	8.17	12.52	14.44
Germany (*)	20.5	28.00	29.70	37.02	23.08
France (*)	13.87	19.97	16.05	22.46	25.78
Total Exports (**)	226.31	291.19	329.81	430.38	430.04
British exports to Russia as a % of all exports	3.1	3.78	2.48	2.91	3.36

*Excludes exports to French and German overseas territories,
**British exports to foreign countries and dependencies.

During the late nineteenth and early twentieth centuries, Russia was a significant market for British goods of various kinds, although it still lagged behind a number of other countries in importance. British exports to Russia in 1905 were lower than exports to France, Germany, the United States, the Netherlands, Belgium, Italy, Argentina and India. Although the expansion of Russian industry from the early 1890s led to an increase in British exports to Russia, the rise was not much greater than the average rise in total exports to all other countries. However, British sales were concentrated in a small number of sectors, which helped to increase the importance of the Russian market for British companies. The export of agricultural machinery and new plant for the country's burgeoning factories featured prominently among the goods shipped to Russia from Britain. A considerable number of small firms, manufacturing consumer products ranging from bicycles to umbrellas, also hoped that the Russian market would grow in importance as industrialisation fostered the emergence of a more prosperous middle class. There was also a good deal of British investment in the country, particularly in the textile mills around Moscow and the oil business in the southern provinces. In any case, growing international competition in the years before 1914 made the whole question of trade very sensitive for both business leaders and politicians in Britain. Every opportunity for promoting British interests was seen as important in a world where American and German competition was becoming more intense with every passing year.

During the two decades leading up to the Great War, there were on average some 12 or 14 *paid* British consular officials based in the Russian Empire.[6] There were also 20 or so unpaid vice-consuls and consular

Table 4.2 Cost of Maintaining British Consular Establishment in Various Countries (1910)[7]

Country	Exports of UK Produce (£ million)	Cost of Consular Establishment (£)	Total Cost of Consular Establishment per million pounds of trade (£)
Russia	12.405	12 998	1 048
Germany	36.922	9 969	270
France	22.500	12 489	555
USA	32.801	35 706	1 088

agents, who spent most of their time dealing with their own business affairs, setting aside a few hours each week to attend to consular business. The British consular presence was minute in comparison with its German counterpart; the German Consulate in St Petersburg, for example, had a budget five times greater than its British equivalent. At the same time, however, the cost of maintaining the British consular presence in Russia was considerably greater than the cost of maintaining a British consular presence in other European countries – something which of course in large part reflected the sheer size of the country.

British consular offices were dotted around the Tsarist Empire, although a majority were concentrated in areas of economic importance including the major sea-ports. There was a marked concentration of officials in south Russia and the Ukraine. By contrast, the only consulates in Siberia were located in Vladivostok and Omsk, despite the growing commercial and strategic importance of the whole region following the construction of the Trans-Siberian Railway. Robert Hodgson, who served in Vladivostok for many years during the early twentieth century, repeatedly tried to persuade the Foreign Office of the need to expand British representation in the area, but his efforts met with little success. The distribution of British consular offices in Russia in 1914 was very similar to the pattern that existed 20 years earlier, despite the major economic and military changes that had taken place during the period.

Most consular officials in Russia received some form of office allowance, ranging from £100 to £450 in 1905 and £100 to £600 in 1910. However, consular officials of all ranks, from unpaid vice-consuls through to consul-generals, complained that it was far too low to allow them to run their offices effectively. A few officials like Charles Bayley, the Consul-General in Warsaw and Moscow from 1908 to 1913, possessed sufficient private means to supplement their expenses out of their own pocket, but such men were the exception rather than the rule among paid members of the consular services. When Robert Bruce Lockhart first arrived as a young vice-consul in Moscow in 1912, he was shocked to find that the Consulate there 'was housed in surroundings of which a Malayan Sanitary Board inspector would have been ashamed'.[8] Lockhart's new boss, Montgomery Grove, was perenially short of money and in no position to pay for improvents to his shabby office. Some officials lobbied hard to receive extra expenses. When Robert Erskine took over as Consul in Helsingfors (Helsinki) at the beginning of 1911, he found to his dismay that it was 'quite impossible to keep the office expenses within the limit of the grant, without seriously affecting the efficiency of the consulate'. His request for a rise of 150 per cent was predictably refused, but he did succeed in obtaining an increase in the office allowance to £200. The extra money allowed Erskine to hire a new clerk for a few hours a week to deal with routine correspondence and filing.[9] However, like his colleagues, Erskine was never able to afford enough clerical assistance to liberate him from the more mundane aspects of his job. Most paid British consular officials based in the Russian Empire found it extremely difficult to carry out the diverse work required of a member of the consular services, and were continually frustrated by the need to seek approval for the expenditure of even the most trivial sums of money.[10] So much of their time was spent dealing with minor clerical tasks that they had to struggle to find the time to fulfil the various duties set down in the General Instructions.

Despite these problems, a career as a paid consul was still popular during the years before 1914. The promotion prospects were poor, since the number of senior positions was limited, but a man who succeeded in becoming a consul-general could expect to receive a salary that was roughly on a par with a senior official at an Embassy. In 1904, Alexander Murray, the Consul-General in Warsaw, was paid £800 *per annum*, just £100 less than Cecil Spring Rice received for his services as Secretary at the St Petersburg Embassy. However, it was not only financial incentives that attracted prospective applicants, which helps to explain why so many men were willing to work as unpaid officials. When an unpaid consul at Kiev died in 1911, the Foreign Office was lobbied by a number of men hoping to take his place, since they believed that a good deal of prestige could be derived from holding such a position.[11] This, in turn, could help to advance their business affairs by providing them with a higher profile in the local community. As the Foreign Office took considerable trouble to ensure that appointees for unpaid posts commanded respect and a reputation for probity among the local British community, appointment as a consul offered a valuable *imprimatur* of respectability.

Membership of the General Consular Service never commanded the same degree of social prestige enjoyed by members of the more illustrious Diplomatic Service. Nevertheless, by the end of the first decade of the twentieth century, during which time a serious attempt was made to improve the calibre of consular recruits, most applicants for a paid position were drawn from the ranks of the professional classes. The majority had attended a public school, while many had been to one of the ancient universities.[12] However, whereas most new diplomats had attended Eton or Harrow, consular recruits were drawn from a wider range of public schools; most of them were educated at one of the newer nineteenth-century institutions such as Ardingly or Marlborough. A career in the consular services offered these young men the prospect of adequate pay and interesting work overseas; it also offered them a career that commanded a reasonable measure of social respect in the closeted world of Edwardian Britain. Bruce Lockhart was not the only young man whose entry into the General Consular Service was brought about by parents anxious to see their offspring settled in a secure job capable of providing a steady income.[13] Most newly-appointed paid vice-consuls sent to Russia during the decade before 1914 were, like Lockhart, young men in their early 20s who expected to spend a lifetime in their chosen career. By contrast, paid consular officials already serving in Russia at the beginning of the century had normally started their consular career at a later stage in life. While a number of these older men had worked in some form of business or trade, many came from a non-commercial background. A considerable number had served in the army. Both Alexander Murray in Warsaw and Charles Smith in Odessa had military backgrounds; so too did Montgomery Grove in Moscow, who had first learnt Russian during his time in the Indian Army.

Critics of the consular services seldom considered at length whether the qualities required by a consul might vary according to the country in which he was posted. This was perhaps surprising, since there already existed separate Far Eastern and Levant services whose members were recruited to work in these areas precisely because the work was deemed

Table 4.3 Russian Experience of Consular Officials in Post on 1 July 1913

City	Rank	Name	Time Served in City During Current Posting (yrs)	Total Time Served in Russia (yrs)
Moscow	Consul-General	Bayley	0	5
Petersburg	Consul	Woodhouse	6	22
Warsaw	Consul	Grove	0	14
Riga	Consul	Bosanquet	2	16
Batum	Consul	Stevens	22	31 (*)
Odessa	Consul-General	Smith	14	14
Average			7.3	17

*Includes time served as consular clerk.

to demand special linguistic and cultural knowledge.[14] Consular posts in the Russian Empire were by the beginning of the twentieth century staffed by members of the General Service. There was periodic talk of setting up a dedicated 'Russian' Consular Service, but nothing came of these discussions during the period. In practice, however, consuls posted to Russia early in their career usually spent most of their working life in the country, something which was in sharp contrast to the peripatetic career structure characteristic of the professional Diplomatic Service. This pattern can be seen by an examination of the consulates and consulates-general in Moscow, St Petersburg, Warsaw, Odessa, Batum and Riga.[15]

The average figure for 'time served in current post' was sharply reduced by the exchange of posts between Grove and Bayley that took place in July 1913; even so, the normal tenure in post was still twice as high as for diplomats at the Embassy. The final column of Table 4.3 indicates that consular officials were frequently transferred between posts *inside* the Russian Empire, with the result that they often spent many decades in the country. There was even a tendency to limit transfers to particular regions of the country, most notably in south Russia, where moves between the various consulates dotted along the shores of the Black Sea were commonplace. The significance of this *de facto* emergence of a set of consular officials with particular experience of Russia was considerable. A knowledge of the local language and culture could not make up for ignorance of economic and commercial matters, but it did help consuls in Russia to become very familiar with their district. When

Charles Smith gave evidence to the Royal Commission on the Civil Service in 1914, he rightly noted that an understanding of the local language was vital if a consul were to carry out his duties effectively.[16] And, as the final part of this chapter will suggest, long experience of Russia was instrumental in allowing British consuls to report on the political upheavals which swept through the Tsarist Empire during the years before the First World War.

THE PASTORAL ROLE OF BRITISH CONSULS IN RUSSIA

The full-time consular officials who served in Russia before 1914 carried out the same multifarious set of tasks performed by their colleagues working in the countries of Western Europe or North America. A significant proportion of their time was spent dealing with British travellers or residents who had somehow managed to get themselves into financial or legal difficulty. Although a section of the British community in Russia was extremely wealthy and well-established, there were also many impoverished governesses and domestic servants of British nationality living in the country. If they fell ill, or their employment unexpectedly came to an end, these people often found themselves destitute and lacking the financial means to buy a ticket back to Britain. Consular officials like Grove in Moscow and Murray in Warsaw were on occasion forced to give money to such people from their own pockets, something which neither man could really afford. While the Foreign Office did usually reimburse them for such expenditure, any delay in payment could make their own parlous financial position even more critical. Alexander Murray, in particular, was perennially short of funds, and was forced on more than one occasion to plead for extra money from the Foreign Office so that he could avoid the indignity of having to borrow from the Jewish money lenders who were his only local source of credit.[17] Consular officials based at the various ports faced the additional problem of dealing with the problems posed by the crews of visiting British ships. Since the local authorities, particularly in the south of the country, were concerned that revolutionary agitators might attempt to come and go from Russia by sea, they often proved unhelpful when dealing with foreign vessels whose crew were deemed to lack suitable identity papers. This in turn enraged British masters and shipowners, who automatically appealed to the nearest consul for support and assistance in their battles with recalcitrant bureaucrats.[18] The riotous behaviour of British seamen could also create difficulties for consular officials in port cities like Odessa. Many sailors were arrested after getting into fights while on shore-leave, forcing the local consul to intervene with the police in an effort to expedite their release before their ship left Russian waters. Since tsarist police officials were not noticeably effective at carrying out their work in a speedy fashion, dealing with these cases was often a bureaucratic nightmare for the luckless official summoned to deal with the self-imposed plight of his unruly compatriots.

The political turbulence of tsarist Russia in the years before 1914 created particular problems for British consular officials that were not faced by their counterparts in other countries. Some British nationals established contacts of various kinds with underground organisations, which brought them into conflict with the tsarist authorities. Since many of these people were from *emigré* families of one kind or another, a good deal of time often had to be spent establishing whether they were in fact entitled to help from the British Embassy and consulates. Such cases could easily become politically explosive, since the cause of the detained person was often taken up by their friends and relatives back in Britain, while Russian officials were reluctant to show any lenience to individuals whom they believed were guilty of revolutionary activities. When a certain Kate Malecka was arrested in Warsaw in 1911, on suspicion of conspiring to overthrow the Russian government, the Consul-General Charles Bayley found himself squeezed between the authorities, who refused to give him permission to visit Malecka, and the vigorous representations made to him on her behalf by vocal relatives and radical groups back in Britain.[19] It was a dilemma that became familiar to several of his colleagues in other Russian cities.

The political unrest that was endemic in the Tsarist Empire during the years before 1914 had further consequences for the work of British consular officials, besides forcing them to deal with their fellow-nationals suspected of involvement in revolutionary activities. During the upheavals of 1905, they had to spend a good deal of time and energy defending the interests and safety of British citizens unfortunate enough to be caught up in the disturbances. The violence created widespread panic among British residents and travellers in Russia, along with their relatives at home, with the result that diplomats and consuls alike were bombarded with requests for help and information. The hapless Montgomery Grove, who had to deal with the large number of British nationals in Moscow, was particularly hard hit by the pressure of this additional work, given the size of the British community in the

Russian capital. When the British press published dramatic accounts of the violence that broke out in the city during the last months of 1905, he received dozens of letters asking for information about friends and relatives in the Moscow area.[20] He also received requests for money from British citizens anxious to leave the country. Since consular officials like Grove were unable to deal properly with the financial and administrative burden of such demands, the Embassy became increasingly involved in the repatriation of British citizens, using money from the secret service vote in an effort to keep the preparations secret from the Russian authorities.[21] Nevertheless, Embassy diplomats were loathe to accept sole responsibility for the plight of British subjects caught up in the turmoil of 1905, with the inevitable result that consular officials across the country continued to receive many time-consuming requests for help and information.

THE COMMERCIAL ROLE OF BRITISH CONSULS IN RUSSIA

British consular officials in the Tsarist Empire, like their counterparts elsewhere, were expected to provide reports about local economic conditions along with details of possible commercial opportunities available to British companies in their region. Many of the reports were in practice sent to London long after they were due. The Foreign Office regularly complained about the practice, but its protests had little impact since many consuls maintained that they simply lacked the time to complete them on schedule. Routine inspections of consular posts were designed to ensure that individual officials were running their offices properly, but since these were usually carried out by the supervising consul-general they were seldom particularly effective. Charles Smith in Odessa regularly toured the consular posts in south Russia, but his inspections were primarily 'audits' concerned with mundane administrative and accounting issues rather than more substantial considerations of the effectiveness of a particular consul or vice-consul. Since Smith himself found it difficult to carry out on schedule many of the tasks expected of him, he doubtless judged the performance of junior officials more sympathetically than an independent inspector less familiar with the problems.

Some British consuls in Russia did make a determined effort to report on commercial opportunities of interest to British firms. The *Board of Trade Journal*, which was circulated to large businesses and chambers of commerce, routinely carried such entries as:

The British Vice-Consul at Batum reports that air compressors are proving an economical and efficient means of raising oil under certain conditions. Those so far in use are all of American manufacture, and the Vice-Consul laments that all the orders for this class of machinery, for which there is a growing demand, should go to the United States.[22]

Another entry in the same journal noted a recommendation by the Consul-General in Warsaw that 'British firms, and more especially makers of agricultural machinery and implements, should very seriously consider opening up business connections' with the many new agricultural improvement societies that were being established in Poland.[23] The Consul in St Petersburg reported in the same year on a whole array of export opportunities for British firms in areas ranging from cutlery and china to timber and typewriters. Despite the criticism advanced by British traders against members of the Consular Service, it seems that officials working in Russia made a real effort to identify and report on commercial opportunities that could be exploited by British firms.

The demands placed by British businesses on consular officials can be seen by means of a brief review of the files of the Moscow Consulate of Montgomery Grove. Until 1912, when Bruce Lockhart first arrived in Moscow, Grove was the only paid member of the Consular Service resident in the city.[24] He had little clerical assistance and was personally responsible for gathering most of the commercial and economic information included in his reports to London. During the turbulent 12 months between July 1905 and June 1906, when the lurid reports appearing in the papers in London about events in Russia might have been expected to discourage any business interest in the country, Grove continued to receive a huge volume of letters from British firms asking for help and advice. The most common request was for information about local market conditions. During the first few months of 1906, for example, Grove was asked to provide details about the demand for products including electrical machinery, linoleum, dried fish and bicycles. Other requests were made for information about the local production of turpentine, leather goods and furniture. He also received a constant stream of letters asking him to chase companies who had delayed payment during the political turmoil of 1905. The Moscow files for 1904 reveal a similar pattern.[25] One business producing cold storage facilities wanted Grove to supply them with the names of all the local suppliers of kippers, eggs, butter, bacon and game. Another company wanted to know what method was used in the Moscow region for harvesting hay.

Moscow was the most important commercial centre in the Tsarist Empire, and the workload of the Consulate there was certainly higher than at British consulates located in other cities in Russia.[26] Nevertheless, the competing pressures faced by Grove were also experienced by many of his full-time colleagues, albeit in a less extreme form. Critics of the consular services in London failed to understand the time-consuming nature of many activities carried out by consuls. At least some officials were so weighed down with the press of daily business that they found it impossible to respond to all the demands that were placed upon them.

CONSULS AS POLITICAL REPORTERS

While routine business occupied most of the working day for consular officials across the globe, a number of them also carried out other work of a very different kind. British consuls were expected to submit regular reports to the Foreign Office containing information about social and political affairs in their area. Most of them, however, did not see the compilation of such reports as one of their principal responsibilities, only commenting on social and political questions in response to a direct request for information from London or the Embassy in the country to which they were posted. Before the early years of the twentieth century, British consular officials in Russia followed this general pattern. Although they would submit accounts of strikes or labour unrest in their area, their reports usually focused on the commercial significance of the disturbances. This situation changed rapidly when Charles Hardinge became Ambassador in 1904. In June of that year, Hardinge wrote to the consuls in Riga (Arthur Woodhouse), Moscow (Montgomery Grove) and Warsaw (Alexander Murray), noting that:

> From an examination of the correspondence received from your Consulate during the past few years it appears that little, if any, information of a general or political nature relating to events in your Consular District has been furnished to this Embassy.
>
> There may have been special reasons in the past for the absence of any reports of this kind, but it is evident that much information of an interesting nature could be supplied to H.M. Rep[resentati]ve by H.M. Consuls without in any way departing from their proper attitude of intelligent observation and without exceeding their legitimate function as consular officers.[27]

Hardinge's note, which was sent in a rather different form to other consular officials, was written just a few months before the Bloody Sunday incident that signalled the beginning of the 1905 Revolution. The Ambassador's comments were prompted by a recognition that his own staff lacked the time and opportunity to track events in the provinces, where repeated bouts of unrest were already serving as harbingers of impending disorder. He was shrewd enough to realise that the consular network could provide his staff with valuable information about the looming social and political crisis.

British consuls were not of course trained in the art of political reporting – though nor for that matter were professional diplomats. However, since the compilation of political reports was acknowledged as one of the most important skills performed by a diplomatic mission, most new entrants to the British Diplomatic Service went through a kind of unofficial apprenticeship during their early postings, gathering information and preparing drafts under the supervision of more experienced staff. Despite their lack of experience, a large number of consular officials in Russia responded enthusiastically to Hardinge's request for reports including 'information of a general or political nature'. In the following years, consuls in the Russian Empire submitted hundreds of reports describing in vivid detail the breakdown of authority in the provinces. Among the most enthusiastic 'reporters' were Murray, Grove and Woodhouse, the recipients of Hardinge's original note chiding them for failing to address social and political questions in their reports. During the period 1905–6, British consular officials in the Tsarist Empire proved themselves to be shrewd political observers, as capable as many diplomats at interpreting the crisis that threatened to rip apart the country in which they lived.

British consuls in Russia had been aware of the anarchy latent in the countryside since the middle of the nineteenth century, although their reports only dwelt on the subject at times of peasant upheaval and rebellion. Consular officials based in the major towns had also recognised for many years the depth of the tensions created by industrialisation and the growth in urban population. However, like the staff at the Embassy in St Petersburg, most of them were taken aback by the events of 1905. Montgomery Grove in Moscow played a particularly important role during this period, keeping the Embassy and the Foreign Office in London informed about the challenge facing the government in Russia's ancient capital. Since the city's many factories were a focus for economic and political unrest, he compiled numerous reports detailing the growth of the strike movement among the workers. Grove was at first convinced that the disorders were economic in origin, fuelled by popular resentment about poor wages and working conditions, but he quickly changed his mind once activists from the various revolutionary organisations attempted to take advantage of the strike movement to extend their influence over the urban working class. Unlike some of his fellow consuls in Russia, however, Grove consistently questioned the strength and appeal of the revolutionaries. Even at the height of the Moscow uprising, in December 1905, he argued in a report to Hardinge that there was an unbridgeable gap between the workers and the agitators who were attempting to mobilise them against the regime.[28] In the event, Grove was proved right. The lurid accounts of the violence which appeared in the Russian press underestimated the Russian government's ability to respond to the challenge; by the beginning of 1906, the army had defeated the rebels and taken control of the city. Without Grove's reports, it would have been very difficult for diplomats and Foreign Office officials to follow events in Moscow, since the Russian press was severely censored while the British press was filled with alarmist and inaccurate reports. Although Spring Rice arrived in Moscow at the height of the unrest to see the situation there for himself, during his visit he relied on Grove to provide him with detailed briefings about the local political situation.

The reports sent by British consuls from the provinces during 1905 were in some ways even more important than those submitted by Grove in Moscow, since diplomatic staff at the Embassy found it impossible to obtain reliable information about such distant regions. This was particularly true in the south of the Empire, where many of the worst outbreaks of violence took place. Among the most assiduous writers of political reports was Patrick Stevens, who served as Consul at the port of Batum, on the eastern shore of the Black Sea. Stevens already had several years' experience obtaining secret intelligence for the British authorities when the disorders broke out in his region in 1905. Like Grove, he initially believed that the upheavals were a product of economic misery, created by the shortage of land available to the local peasantry and the low wages paid to workers in the towns. In the early part of 1905 he wrote to the British Embassy in St Petersburg, predicting that the collapse of trade in his area would create growing poverty and lead to violent 'excesses' among all social classes as they began to feel the 'pinch of absolute want'. By the end of June, he was convinced that 'further developments of a grave character are in store', particularly as tension mounted between the Christian and Muslim populations. Throughout the remaining months of 1905, Stevens's dispatches chronicled in detail the breakdown of order in his district and described the failure of the local authorities to re-establish control over the situation.[29] His pessimism was shared by Charles Smith in Odessa. Smith received information from the network of British consuls and vice-consuls serving throughout the Ukraine and southern Russia, and was well-placed to report on the peasant uprisings which spread across the Tsarist Empire's richest agricultural region. In a series of detailed dispatches, he described the collapse of tsarist authority in the Russian countryside and the turmoil in the towns.[30] Many similar reports were sent to St Petersburg and London by consular officials in the Finnish and Polish provinces of the Empire, where social and economic tensions were heightened by nationalist resentment against Russian imperial power. On some occasions, British consulates themselves became targets for attack. Extra guards had to be posted in cities such as Odessa and Warsaw, while two officials requested extra money from the Foreign Office in order to buy weapons to protect themselves against possible violence.[31] Nor were these fears imaginary. One unpaid vice-consul was shot in the arm during the disturbances which took place in Baku on the Caspian Sea, although since the bullet only grazed his arm he was lucky enough to avoid serious injury.

The upheavals of 1905–6 were exceptionally turbulent even by the standards of pre-revolutionary Russia. During the following years, the tsarist government was able to restore a measure of order throughout the provinces. As peace returned, most British consular officials scaled back their political reporting and once again devoted their energies to more routine duties. The most important exception was Montgomery Grove in Moscow. During the years following the 1905 Revolution, Moscow became an important centre for the liberal opposition parties founded after Nicholas II issued the October Manifesto promising to establish the new Duma. Grove was well-placed to report on the changing tempo of political life in Russia's ancient capital.[32] Although he did not have many personal contacts with those involved in the new parties, he monitored their publications and sent regular summaries of the local press to the Embassy in St Petersburg. He reported at length on the disturbances which continued to break out on the streets of the city from time to time, describing in one report how the local police were forced to turn it into a 'military camp' in an effort to maintain order. Charles Smith in Odessa also continued to write a large number of political reports, many of which contained information about the violent activities of the various revolutionary groups in the southern provinces of the Empire.[33]

The scale of consular reporting on social and political affairs began to increase sharply once again in the critical period leading up to the outbreak of war in 1914. The reports sent to Sir George Buchanan in St Petersburg contained important information about the increasingly radical mood of workers in cities like Riga.[34] However, while Charles Hardinge had been instrumental in encouraging consular officials to provide the Embassy with this sort of information when he was in charge of the Embassy during 1904–6, his successors were less interested in reading reports provided by men whom they did not believe were well-versed in the art of political reporting. Bruce Lockhart recalled in his memoirs that the Embassy paid little attention to the dispatches which the Moscow Consulate forwarded in the critical years leading up to the First World War.[35] Lockhart may in fact have exaggerated the lack of interest in consular dispatches, since the Foreign Office archives contain many letters from successive ambassadors to Russia praising the quality of the reports they received from consular officials. Nevertheless, at least some British diplomats in Russia, along with many of their colleagues posted to other countries, treated members of the Consular Service with considerable social and professional disdain. In doing so, they marginalised an important source of information which could have provided them with a better insight into the social and political tensions which ripped apart pre-revolutionary Russia.

BRITISH CONSULS AND THE COLLECTION OF SECRET INTELLIGENCE

Foreign Office staff in London usually placed a greater value on the political reports submitted by British consuls in Russia than their diplomatic counterparts in St Petersburg;[36] the information contained in them was read by senior officials and regularly published in the confidential print. The Foreign Office also sometimes used consular staff to perform functions far removed from the ones set down in their formal instructions, namely, the collection of secret intelligence about the activities of the Russian military. This was particularly true during the years before the establishment of the Anglo–Russian Convention marked an effective end to the era of the Great Game. During the years before 1907, each government devoted considerable time and energy to collecting information about the other. It was seen in Chapter 3 that the Embassy in St Petersburg was a target for the tsarist secret police, while British diplomats themselves occasionally engaged in activities that were at odds with their diplomatic status. However, since the British government was always keen to emphasise that its diplomats did not engage in clandestine activities – a sentiment that was strongly echoed by most members of the Diplomatic Service themselves – there were very real limits on the extent to which the Embassy staff could involve themselves in the collection of secret intelligence. The same considerations ought to have applied in the case of consuls who, as representatives of a foreign government, should not have been engaged in any form of activity that smacked of espionage. It is clear, however, that these scruples were on occasion put aside both in London and on the ground in Russia.

At the beginning of the twentieth century, Britain's intelligence-gathering capacity across the globe was still quite rudimentary.[37] The number of staff employed in military and naval intelligence was very small, while the secret service vote did not amount to more than £50 000. Nevertheless, a considerable slice of these resources was devoted to obtaining secret information about Russia's military and naval forces. Given the tsarist secret police's formidable counter-intelligence capacity, this task was by no means straightforward. The Foreign Office and War Office both recognised that commercial activities could be a useful front for the acquisition of secret intelligence, with the result that during the years before the First World War the British government on occasion allocated money to business ventures across Europe which provided a suitable cover for the collection of intelligence.[38] In Russia, the legendary spy Sidney Reilly used expenses from the Special Intelligence Service to set himself up as a commercial representative for a munitions manufacturer, employing his position to obtain vital information about Russian and German military equipment.[39] As British consuls across Europe frequently had a large number of commercial contacts in the countries where they were based, they too could be well-placed to gather intelligence. The author of a secret 1903 War Office memorandum noted that British consuls were in a good position to provide London with vital information, and observed that because Britain had a much smaller 'army of spies' than its neighbours it had to rely far more than most continental countries on the reports of 'a few intelligent observers at the Capitals and chief seaport towns'.[40] The Foreign Office and War Office were not slow to exploit this potential.

Some consular officials in Russia were ready to gather clandestine information without any prompting from the Foreign Office. At the beginning of 1904, Charles Cooke, the British Consul at Helsingfors, decided on his own initiative to carry out a private surveillance operation of the Russian fortress at Svaeborg, rumoured to be the setting for some important naval and military manoeuvres. He made his way through the snow to the fortress, where he noted down the layout of the buildings and recorded details of preparations being made to launch the torpedo boats based there. Cooke then returned to town, taking care to avoid the numerous guards posted in the area, and wrote an account of his observations for the Embassy in St Petersburg. However, his activities met with a rather chilly response from Sir Charles Scott, who was nervous at the thought of any British representative doing something which could be deemed incompatible with his official position. In a covering note sent to London with Cooke's report, the Ambassador noted that he could not vouch for its accuracy. He also expressed concern that Cooke might find it difficult to conduct his normal consular duties if he exposed himself 'to the suspicion of the military authorities by undertaking secret observations of fortresses'. While Scott praised the Consul's 'zeal and diligence', he did not believe that information gathered under such circumstances could justify the harmful consequences that would result if the Russian authorities were to catch redhanded an official British representative engaged in such activities.[41]

The Foreign Office did not authorise the activities of Charles Cooke in Finland, but the situation was very different in the south of the country, where at least two British consular officials received special payments in order to finance the acquisition of secret intelligence. Since most of this information was reported directly back to London, Embassy officials in St Petersburg were probably unaware of the whole business. Russian military manoeuvres in the area around the Black Sea and Caspian Sea were of enormous interest to the authorities in London, since any mobilisation there could threaten British interests in Persia or India. At the end of the nineteenth century, however, British military intelligence still only had a limited capacity for obtaining information in the region, with the result that consular reports about the movements of Russian naval vessels and troops were of great importance. The Foreign Office and War Office were both keen to support any moves which might improve the quality of the dispatches sent by British consuls based in the southern provinces of Russia. Even so, a majority of initiatives designed to promote this goal did not originate in London but were instead prompted by consular officials themselves. The most important of these was Patrick Stevens, the Consul at Batum, whose reaction to the disorders of 1905 was examined earlier. In March 1898, when he had already been in post for a number of years, Stevens wrote to the Foreign Office in London urging the need to improve Britain's capacity for collecting information about naval and military affairs in south Russia. He went on to note that he knew of 'a man' at Baku, on the Caspian Sea, who would be willing to make regular reports on this subject in return for a payment of six or seven pounds a month.[42] The letter was forwarded to the War Office, who agreed that it would be valuable to receive reports from Baku since they had no agents in any of the Caspian ports. A senior official added that they would welcome reports from other towns situated in militarily sensitive regions. Stevens was therefore given permission to recruit his prospective informant at Baku, whom he described as 'an Englishman who has been residing there for many years past and... [is] therefore all the better able to keep a strict watch on things without attracting attention, or arousing suspicion'.[43] A few weeks later he went on to obtain the services of a second agent in the town of Petrovsk, further to the east, apparently on the same terms. The British Consul also paid small sums, initially out of his own pocket, to a Russian dock worker who was able to 'knock about the quays' and provide useful information.[44] By the end of 1898, Stevens had already established a small network of agents and informants capable of providing London with details about the military potential of Britain's principal rival for power and influence in Asia.

During the next few years, Stevens became a pivotal figure in Britain's intelligence-gathering operations in southern Russia. By 1900, the Batum Consul employed at least one agent who 'travels between Petrovsk and Baku... and reports... by word of mouth';[45] it is not certain, though, whether this individual was one of the two men first employed by Stevens in 1898, or represented instead an additional appointment. There was certainly considerable turnover in the informants used by the British in southern Russia during these years, in part because many of them were businessmen whose affairs took them away from the region for long periods of time. Stevens therefore continued to recruit people who could provide him with information about the Russian military. In March 1904, at a time when Anglo–Russian tension was on the increase due to events in the Far East, he wrote to the Foreign Office asking whether 'it would be prudent to increase our vigilance on the other side of the Caspian', since 'the man employed by us can only be in one place at one time'.[46] This proposal, like most of those put forward by Stevens during these years, was sanctioned by London, where arrangements were made to double the 'special funds' available to him. A few months later, in October, Stevens put forward an even more ambitious scheme. He told Sir Thomas Sanderson at the Foreign Office that his 'special agent' might be able to obtain a contract to build an electricity-generating plant at Tashkent in central Asia, designed to power a military printing press there. As a result, the agent would 'have constant access to the printing office...which circumstance will place him in a particularly advantageous position for obtaining prompt and accurate information on all subjects of military interest to us'.[47] However, the whole plan was conditional on the British government advancing the money required to purchase the generating equipment for the new plant. Senior Foreign Office officials were concerned about the proposal, partly because of the costs involved and partly because discovery of the plan would encourage the tsarist authorities to take even more determined measures to stamp out espionage by foreign governments. Nevertheless, the scheme was eventually sanctioned after Stevens's agent had agreed to sign a mortgage bond as 'a security for the accurate and diligent performance of the services required'. Over the next year, he developed good contacts with the Russian military in Tashkent, even requesting extra money in order to entertain senior officers. By the beginning of 1906, though, the agent had for some reason begun to attract the attention of the military authorities and was forced to flee Russia.[48] The impact of this discovery on the flow of intelligence from the region is not clear. At least one other agent in central Asia reported to Stevens, but his reports were deemed to be 'very poor' by officials in London. It therefore seems certain that the information obtained by Stevens from central Asia was of a lower quality at the end of 1906 than a year earlier, although he still had a number of active informants in the Transcaucasus. Since Anglo–Russian relations were rapidly improving at this time, the loss of intelligence reports was less significant than it would have been a few years earlier. In any case, the British had another set of agents in central Asia who were apparently 'working well', presumably a reference to activities organised by the Meshed consulate in Persia. By the summer of 1906, the cost-conscious authorities in London had already decided to reduce their expenditure in the region so that they could use the money to employ an additional agent in South Africa.

The records do not provide much evidence about the quality of the intelligence obtained through Stevens; nor do they say a great deal about the ways in which his agents passed on their information. Some reported direct to the British Consul in person, travelling to Batum for the purpose, while others passed on messages via British travellers in the region. Stevens does not seem to have forwarded any written documents from them to London, choosing instead to incorporate the information in his own reports. Even so, despite these precautions, he did on occasion attract the attention of the tsarist authorities, who were well-versed in the techniques of *contre-espionage* and kept a close watch on all the representatives of foreign powers; even the entirely innocent Montgomery Grove reported on one occasion during the Russo–Japanese War that 'I am looked on as a spy'.[49] In March 1904, Stevens was sent an anonymous letter offering to sell him a complete set of maps of the Batum region, showing the location of all the forts and artillery batteries in the area. He did not follow up the offer, writing to London that he believed it was 'a trap set by the authorities with a view to getting in hand proof of my attempts to obtain secret papers'.[50] His caution was approved at the Foreign Office in London, where officials knew that 'it was a constant practice...to make such offers as a trap'. Stevens's discretion therefore prevented the authorities from gaining firm evidence of his activities – evidence which could have made his own position extremely difficult, while at the same time creating a diplomatic incident between London and St Petersburg.

Although Stevens was a pivotal figure in the Britain's intelligence effort in south Russia, he was not the only consular official in the region who received money from London to pay for confidential information. In 1906 Charles Smith in Odessa told the Foreign Office that he was 'not satisfied with the reports which I have been able to make lately', and went on to ask Sanderson if it was worth 'opening relations with a man who seems able to hear something of what is happening'. He reassured the Permanent Secretary that there was not the 'slightest risk' in his proposal, and noted that the cost was unlikely to exceed £20 *per annum*.[51] Since the sum of money was so small, the plan was approved. The British representative in Odessa had a reputation in London for being 'very cautious', and officials at the Foreign Office did not believe that he would propose any initiative that could create problems with the Russian authorities. Smith had in any case previously received payments from London designed to cover the expenses of consular officials who had been instructed to obtain particular 'information' of various kinds.[52] Although the records are incomplete, it seems that in at least some cases these costs were incurred by staff travelling to meet informants who were paid by the British government for their services. While Smith was far less involved than Stevens in organising the collection of secret intelligence, he too recognised that the defence of British interests in south Russia and central Asia required the acquisition of material which the tsarist government would have preferred to keep to itself.

The collection of clandestine information by Stevens and Smith only formed a small part of their workload. The information obtained by the two men related almost exclusively to the deployment of Russian military and naval forces, and seldom shed much light on the tensions that convulsed south Russia during the first decade of the twentieth century. The dispatches they sent to St Petersburg and London on social and political questions were instead largely based on material that they had obtained legitimately or through their own observation. They were not able to rely on close contacts with the local authorities as a means of acquiring information, and were forced to rely a good deal on a study of the press and casual conversations with Russian friends and acquaintances. Nevertheless, their determination and commitment helped them to produce political reports of a quality that would have done credit to a young professional diplomat blessed with far more time and opportunity to monitor developments in the country to which he was posted.

A SPECIALISED CONSULAR SERVICE FOR RUSSIA?

The distinctive problems faced by consular officials posted to the Tsarist Empire were on occasion recognised back in London. The members of the Levant Consular Service, who staffed posts in south-eastern Europe and the Near East, had by the end of the nineteenth century already established themselves as something of an elite among British consuls, on account of their superior training and specialised knowledge of the regions in which they worked. Following the outbreak of the First World War, Russian consular posts were for a time brought under the umbrella of the Levant Service, since the linguistic and cultural demands of service in the Tsarist Empire were deemed to require the same kind of specialisation as posts in countries like Bulgaria or Turkey.[53] A number of proposals were also made before 1914 for changing the organisation of consular representation in Russia. The most important of these was put forward by Bernard Pares in 1911.[54] Pares was convinced of the need to establish a dedicated Slavic Consular Service, arguing in a lengthy memorandum that men who possessed a good knowledge of the Slavic world would be far more effective at fulfilling their duties than men who arrived in post without any prior training. He proposed that a special scheme be established to provide recruits with the necessary language skills, suggesting that his own university in Liverpool was best-suited to provide the training – a point that was not lost on those critical of his proposals. The professor showed little interest in preparing men for carrying out consular functions *per se*; he believed instead that a period of academic training was necessary to familiarise future consuls in the Slavic lands with the local culture and language. The academic ethos of the programme suggested by Pares was in reality out of touch with the prevailing ideas about reform to the various consular services, which were usually far more utilitarian and prosaic in tone.

Pares's proposals met with a range of responses. Most senior officials at the Foreign Office were sceptical about the idea, suggesting that the much-vaunted success of German businesses in Russia was due to their employees' energy and initative rather than the efforts of their consular representatives. Since 'Neither commercial attachés nor consuls *create* trade', they did not believe that spending money on training a new cohort of officials would produce very good results. Officials in London instead believed that it would be more sensible to enhance the quality of consular officials in Russia by a process of incremental change, 'improving the present system, widening it rather than narrowing it, increasing the attractions of Russia as regards pay and staff'. Officials at the Board of Trade agreed with their colleagues at the Foreign Office that a programme of piecemeal reform was more sensible than the introduction of a new specialist service that would cost a good deal of money and which might not yield the expected benefits.

Some other responses to Pares's proposals were more positive. George Buchanan in St Petersburg believed that they merited 'very serious consideration', since men with good language skills were likely to be more effective at promoting the interests of British commerce. The Ambassador made no secret of his belief that 'our Consular Service is at present very inadequately equipped for the duties which it is called on to perform'. Senior members of the Consular Service serving in Russia also agreed that reform was overdue, but they understandably tended to focus on questions of resources rather than the quality of personnel. Montgomery Grove urged that more consular posts should be established, particularly in areas where the Russian economy had expanded rapidly during the course of the previous decade. He also suggested that special commercial, financial and agricultural *attachés* should be appointed, each with an assistant; the task of these new appointees would be to provide reports about key sectors of the economy. Arthur Woodhouse also responded favourably to Pares's proposals, particularly the introduction of more training for consular staff prior to appointment, and suggested that the principle could be extended to those destined to serve in other countries beside Russia. Like Grove, he argued that more resources should be provided to allow the recruitment of extra clerical staff at the major consulates, in order to allow career consuls to spend less time on mundane administrative work.

The Pares proposals were in one sense a logical solution to the whole problem of preparing consular officials for service in countries where the language and culture were very different from anything to which they were accustomed. However, while the professor's scheme was lucidly presented, it contained a number of important flaws. Pares was primarily concerned with questions of *training* rather than resources, even though shortage of clerical staff was the principal problem identified by consular officials with direct personal experience of service in Russia. In any case, while the professor was obviously right to argue that a thorough knowledge of language and culture could help a consul to perform his duties more effectively, he was too inclined to gloss over the whole question of how young men could best be prepared for carrying out their actual consular duties. Nor did Pares make a serious effort to define the role of the new breed of consular officials who would be posted to Russia and the other Slavic countries, a major weakness given that public criticism of the Consular Service was in large part rooted in the excessive expectations of those businesses who considered that consuls should be required to serve as a kind of unpaid functionary for companies seeking to promote their exports. The greatest weakness with Pares's scheme was, however, that it failed to recognise that a *de facto* Russian Consular Service had already developed over the previous few decades. It was seen earlier that the average tenure of a paid consular official in Russia was far longer than that of a professional diplomat, while some men like Woodhouse and Stevens spent virtually all their career in the Tsarist Empire. Most consular officials who were resident for more than a short period of time developed a working knowledge of Russian, as well as a good understanding of the texture of daily life in the Russian provinces. A number of them were married to Russian women, which helped to integrate them still further into the society in which they lived. It is true that some young consular officials only served in Russia for a short period of time, but these men were the exception rather than the rule; in general, the considerable experience of members of the General Consular Service in the Tsarist Empire helped them to carry out their work with a good degree of efficiency.

It was suggested in Chapter 1 that critics of the old diplomacy in Britain fell into two distinct camps. Some radically-minded politicians and writers were primarily concerned about the promotion of democratic control and the adoption of more egalitarian recruitment practices, while other more moderate figures were most interested in promoting greater efficiency. Consular officials were largely spared the diatribes of the radical critics of old diplomacy, since the various consular services were universally seen as less powerful and prestigious than the Diplomatic Service and Foreign Office. They were, however, subject to attack from many other sources. Business people spoke scathingly about the service they received from consuls. Members of the Foreign Office and Diplomatic Service looked down on men who performed the least glamorous of all the tasks carried out by Britain's overseas representatives. Politicians were only too willing to seek a convenient scapegoat in an age when concern about Britain's economic decline *vis à vis* its major international competitors was growing rapidly. In the early years of the twentieth century, the British consular services had few friends and many powerful detractors.

It is hard to generalise about such a diverse body of individuals as the men who made up the General Consular Service before the First World War. Some of them were paid, others were unpaid; some were able and energetic officials, others were incompetent and lazy; some of them had a good understanding of commercial affairs, while others knew almost nothing about the subject. The previous pages have suggested, however, that some of the charges made against the General Consular Service may have been too simplistic, at least if the men who served in the Tsarist Empire were in any sense representative of their colleagues. Paid British consuls in Russia seldom had a strong background in commerce, but most of them were in post long enough to develop a thorough knowledge of the region to which they were posted. They provided London with reports about local economic conditions and struggled dutifully to respond to requests for more specific information from individuals and companies. They carried out numerous minor administrative duties and gave help and assistance to British nationals who called for it. When called upon to produce political reports of the sort normally compiled at the Embassy, they showed themselves able and willing to fulfil a quasi-diplomatic role even though there were many other demands on their time. Despite their lack of resources and status, they struggled hard to perform their duties as effectively as possible.

NOTES

1. See, for example, J.H. Longford, 'The Consular Services and its Wrongs', *Quarterly Review*, April 1903. The best general history of the consular services can be found in D.C.M. Platt, *The Cinderella Service: British Consuls since 1825*.
2. *BPP, 1898*, 33 (cd 8962), 'Report of the Departmental Committee Appointed by the Board of Trade to Inquire into and Report Upon the Dissemination of Commercial Information'.
3. *BPP, 1903*, 55 (cd 1634), 'Report of the Committee appointed to Inquire into the Constitution of the Consular Service'.
4. For a list of duties performed by consuls, see the *General Instructions for His Majesty's Consular Officers* (1907).
5. Figures compiled from the various 'Annual Statements of the Trade of the United Kingdom with Foreign Countries and British Possessions', in *BPP, 1900*, 86 (cd 187); *BPP, 1905*, 80 (cd 2626); *BPP, 1910*, 88 (cd 5298); *BPP, 1914–1916*, 65, (cd 8069).
6. Information derived from the relevant editions of the *Foreign Office List*.
7. Figures compiled from FO 371/1214/34234, Stanley (Board of Trade) to Foreign Office 1911. The figures provided by Stanley on the level of British exports diverge very slightly from those given earlier in this chapter.
8. R.H. Bruce Lockhart, *Memoirs of a British Agent*, p. 64.
9. FO 369/404/14935, Erskine to Grey, 3 February 1911.
10. See, for example, FO 369/406/17957, Smith to Grey, 8 May 1911, seeking approval for the expenditure of thirty shillings to bind five volumes of the consular archives in Sevastopol.
11. The relevant documents are located in FO 369/404.
12. The following data is compiled from various sources, including the *Foreign Office List*, *The Dictionary of National Biography* and *Who's Who?*, as well as data compiled by the Walrond Committee and the MacDonnell Commission.
13. Lockhart, *Memoirs of a British Agent*, p. 35.
14. On the history of the Far Eastern and Levant Services, see Platt, *Cinderella Service*, pp. 125–230.
15. Details derived from the relevant editions of the *Foreign Office List*.
16. *BPP, 1914–16*, 11 (cd 7749), qu. 40,115.
17. Hughes, *Inside the Enigma*, p. 33.
18. FO 181/818, Storm to Bosanquet (Odessa), 19 July 1904.
19. For details of the Malecka affair, see the relevant documents in FO 371/1215.
20. Grove was so overloaded by the requests that Alexander Murray in Warsaw wrote to London offering to go to Moscow to assist his colleague. FO 369/36, Murray to Grey, 3 January 1906.
21. Public Record Office, HD 3/133 (various letters from Spring Rice to Grey).
22. *Board of Trade Journal*, 37 (April–June 1902), p. 339.
23. *Board of Trade Journal*, 37 (April–June 1902), pp. 530–1.

24. Henry Cooke, the British Commercial Agent in Russia, did spend a good deal of time in Moscow, but does not seem to have dealt with any of the more prosaic duties carried out by Grove.
25. The examples of requests to the Moscow Embassy for 1906 are taken from FO 447/29–32; those for 1904 are taken from FO 447/26–27.
26. Valuable comparative figures about the workload of the Helsingfors Consulate for 1908 can be found in FO 369/36/25669, Cooke to Grey, 1 July 1909.
27. FO 181/825-2, Hardinge to Consular Officers at Riga, Moscow and Warsaw, 29 June 1904.
28. FO 181/844, Grove to Hardinge, 27 January 1905; Grove to Hardinge, 6 March 1905; Grove to Hardinge, 25 December 1905.
29. FO 181/832, Stevens to Spring Rice, 22 May 1905; Stevens to Hardinge, 20 June 1905.
30. See, for example, *BDFA*, 1A, Vol. 3, Smith to Lansdowne, 30 September 1905 (including encls).
31. FO 369/36, Smith to Grey, 6 January 1906; Stevens to Grey, 8 February 1906.
32. See, for example, FO 800/340, Grove to Nicolson, 13 November 1907; 28 November 1907.
33. FO 181/920, Smith to Grey, 15 January 1907.
34. FO 371/2090/4265, Woodhouse to Grey, 27 January 1914.
35. Lockhart, *Memoirs*, p. 78.
36. For a different view, see Platt, *Cinderella Service*, pp. 54–5.
37. See Christopher Andrew, *Secret Service: The Making of the British Intelligence Community*, Chapters 1–2.
38. See, for example, the proposal to establish various coal agencies abroad, contained in documents found in HD 3/118.
39. Robin Bruce Lockhart, *Reilly: Ace of Spies*, pp. 59–70.
40. HD 3/124, Memorandum on 'The Secret Service in the Event of a European War'.
41. FO 65/1679, Scott to Lansdowne, 3 January 1904 (including Cooke's report).
42. HD 3/109, Stevens to Salisbury, 16 March 1898.
43. HD 3/109, Stevens to Sanderson, 10 August 1898.
44. HD 3/109, Stevens to Sanderson, 24 December 1898.
45. HD 3/117, letter dated 11 July 1900.
46. HD 3/125 Part 1, Stevens to Sanderson, 3 March 1904.
47. HD 3/125 Part 2, Stevens to Sanderson, 20 October 1904.
48. HD 3/133, Stevens to Sanderson, 1 February 1906.
49. FO 181/818, Grove to Hardinge, 31 August 1904.
50. HD 3/125 Part 1, Stevens to Sanderson, 3 March 1904.
51. HD 3/132, Smith to Sanderson, 9 January 1906.
52. HD 3/131, Smith to Lansdowne, 19 June 1905; HD 3/133, Smith to Hardinge, 22 February 1906.
53. Platt, *Cinderella Service*, p. 169.
54. The documents relating to Pares's proposals, along with the various responses they elicited, can be found in FO 371/1214.

5 The Russian Ministry of Foreign Affairs 1894–1914

THE POLITICAL AND ADMINISTRATIVE CULTURE OF TSARIST RUSSIA BEFORE 1914

The previous chapters have shown that the organisation and operation of the British diplomatic establishment before 1914 were profoundly influenced by changes in the wider administrative and political environment. While the liberal political structures and values inherent in the British constitution placed constraints on the ability of Foreign Office officials and diplomats to set the course of the country's foreign policy, their impact on the policy making process at any particular time was governed by a complex matrix of domestic and international circumstances. A focus on institutional structures and constitutional norms cannot therefore alone reveal the true character of the British diplomatic establishment. The Russian diplomatic establishment can be analysed through a similar intellectual prism. By examining the formal organisational structure of the tsarist Ministry of Foreign Affairs (*Ministerstvo inostrannykh del* or *MID*), as well as its changing role in the formulation of Russian foreign policy in the years before 1914, it is possible to see how the operation and influence of the country's diplomatic establishment were affected by a wide array of factors.

The political culture and constitutional order of tsarist Russia changed considerably in the 20 years before 1914, complicating any analysis of the role and organisation of the country's diplomatic establishment. The autocratic system of government, which had existed for centuries, faced a severe challenge by the beginning of the twentieth century. Both Alexander III and his son Nicholas II, who was Emperor from 1894 until the collapse of the tsarist regime in 1917, were deeply wedded to a traditionalist interpretation of their role, resisting any proposals that might impinge on their authority. The instincts of both men were forged by the ideology of 'Official Nationality', a semi-articulated set of ideas that emphasised the centrality of orthodoxy (*pravoslavie*), national identity (*narodnost'*) and autocracy (*samoderzhavie*) to all aspects of Russian social and political life.[1] These values also commanded a good deal of currency among many ministers and members of the Court, although there were naturally important differences between individuals. While it is problematic to apply such inherently simplistic terms as 'conservative' and 'liberal' to members of the political elite of late Imperial Russia, a marked distinction always existed between those who were reluctant to recognise the need for constitutional reform and those who believed that the pace of economic and social development demanded changes in the institutional structure of the tsarist state.

The ideology of Russian autocracy was predicated on the assumption that the Tsar's powers were given to him by God, with the result that his decisions could not be legitimately challenged by any individual or institution. The real position was, however, more complex, even before the launch of the Constitutional Experiment in 1906 led to the establishment of new political institutions whose members claimed a right to be involved in decisions about public policy.[2] Not only were the Tsar's powers circumscribed by law and custom; they were also constrained by the practical problems involved in governing a vast empire. The famously chaotic state of Russian government in the nineteenth and twentieth centuries was in part rooted in a conflict between constitutional theory and political practice. Since no individual – certainly not one as instinctively timid and vacillating as Nicholas II – could manage in detail all the affairs of state, a degree of delegation to ministers and officials was inevitable. At the same time, the formal commitment to autocracy hindered the emergence of institutions and processes capable of facilitating an orderly process of delegation. The policy making process therefore tended to be *ad hoc* in character. Individual ministers and other senior officials could sometimes enjoy a considerable degree of autonomy, particularly when dealing with issues that were of no great interest to Nicholas. On other occasions, by contrast, the Tsar could by-pass the responsible ministry altogether, relying instead on members of the Court or other private individuals to give him advice. In such a system, the role of the ministries, and the men who worked in them, was extremely poorly defined.

The institutional structure of the tsarist state was sharply altered by the launch of the Constitutional Experiment. The establishment of a new Parliament (Duma) in 1906, albeit with rather narrowly-defined powers, expressed in institutional form the principle that some degree of public control should be exercised over the government. At the same time, the attempt to establish a more unified form of administration, via the establishment of a revamped Council of Ministers, was designed to promote greater coordination between ministries and allow a whole range of public policy to come under collective scrutiny. Ministers and other senior officials had to operate in a new political environment in which the old 'rules of the game' no longer applied. In reality, however, the Constitutional Experiment did not mark such a radical change with the past as at first appeared. The Tsar continued to have considerable – if ambiguous – powers, particularly in the areas of foreign policy and defence. The role of the Duma was marginalised by the use of 'emergency powers' and by tinkering with the franchise in order to ensure the election of deputies who were sympathetic to the government. As was the case before 1906, the policy making process remained extremely fluid, with the result that an analysis of formal structures alone cannot provide a complete understanding of its character.

The role and organisation of the tsarist Foreign Ministry between 1894 and 1914 can only be understood against the backdrop of this wider political and administrative setting. Before 1906, the implicit constitutional role of Russian foreign ministers was to advise the monarch and implement his decisions on matters of foreign policy. In reality, though, since matters of foreign policy touched on the interests of several ministries and numerous individuals, successive foreign ministers found themselves caught up in a complex network of personal and political relationships. In the years after 1906, the constitutional status of the foreign minister was altered by the nominal establishment of 'unified government', but his role and influence was still governed by a complex network of formal and informal relationships with other important political actors.[3] Any study that attempts to understand the role and organisation of the MID before 1914 therefore has to focus both on the Ministry's internal structure and its operation within the wider Russian state apparatus.

THE CRITIQUE OF OLD DIPLOMACY IN RUSSIA

The constitutional and political changes ushered in by the 1905 Revolution provided a new forum for attacks on Russian diplomats and international diplomacy of a kind that were becoming increasingly audible in Britain and France during the same period. The relaxation of censorship provided journalists and deputies with new opportunities for criticising Russian foreign policy and the men responsible for implementing it. Employees of the tsarist Foreign Ministry, whether working in St Petersburg or at a mission abroad, had generally occupied an ambiguous place in the public mind during the years before 1905. A successful career at the MID was for the most part only open to young men who enjoyed the kind of connections and contacts necessary to compete for the more desirable posts. At the same time, however, a diplomatic career in late imperial Russia never commanded quite so much prestige as in some other European countries. Members of the Russian diplomatic establishment were often viewed with a certain suspicion by large sections of the public. One aspiring young diplomat recalled that when he returned to his home town of Kharkov shortly after winning entry to the Foreign Ministry, in 1894, he was looked at with 'ill-disguised coolness' by many of his erstwhile friends for whom 'a diplomat was the symbol of pretense, vanity, and sheer stupidity'.[4] In Court circles, a career in one of the better-known guards regiments was usually regarded as more prestigious than a post in the MID. The political changes that took place after 1906 provided fresh opportunities for these somewhat inchoate suspicions of the Russian diplomatic establishment to be articulated. At a time when every institution of the tsarist state was coming under growing scrutiny and pressure, the employees of the MID could not avoid falling victim to the burgeoning critique of established institutions.

Attacks on the tsarist diplomatic establishment *per se* were often associated with a battle to control the course of Russian foreign policy.[5] The establishment of the Anglo–Russian *entente* in the late summer of 1907, for example, directed considerable attention towards the MID. Since the agreement with Russia's traditional imperial rival was controversial in some quarters, having been the subject of bitter dispute among senior officials in St Petersburg throughout the previous year, it served as a catalyst for more general reflections in the press about the course of Russian foreign policy and the quality of the country's diplomatic establishment. Although a number of articles had appeared on this subject during the previous few months, the agreement with London helped to trigger a far more intense debate about the organisation of Russian diplomacy that continued for several years. The Anglo–Russian *entente* itself was generally welcomed by the leading Russian periodicals, even though some of the more conservative publications had previously run articles criticising the idea of an agreement with London. An editorial in the most influential of these newspapers, the daily *Novoe Vremia*, acknowledged that an understanding with London could reduce international tension and secure Russian interests in Asia, but the author also took the opportunity to launch a stinging attack on the country's diplomatic establishment. He noted in his article that 'Life is changing. The factors of international politics are changing [along with] the very essence of the diplomatic profession and the demands which are placed upon it'. He then went on to suggest that diplomacy was no longer a profession suitable only for the scions of well-established families versed in the arts of intrigue. The kind of men capable of dealing with the demands of the modern world had to be 'broadly educated' and possess an 'understanding of national interests'. The author of the *Novoe Vremia* editorial then suggested that a new generation of diplomats ought to be recruited for their broad experience and outlook. While he acknowledged that the diplomatic establishments of all the major European powers required reform, he argued that rapid change was of particular importance in Russia since the Foreign Ministry was in a state of complete chaos.[6]

The *Novoe Vremia* editorial attacking the Foreign Ministry was part of a journalistic assault that took place in both the liberal and conservative press in the years after the beginning of the Constitutional Experiment. The liberal newspaper *Rech'*, which usually echoed the sentiments of the more moderate Cadet deputies in the Duma, had already carried an article similar in tone to the one that subsequently appeared in *Novoe Vremia*, suggesting that the Foreign Ministry needed to be reformed to meet the demands of a new and complex international environment. The author of the *Rech'* article was, in true liberal spirit, insistent that a full public debate should take place about the organisation of the Ministry, a sentiment that was probably inspired by a knowledge that senior officials in the MID were considering a reform plan of their own. He was particularly concerned about the inefficiency and duplication of work in the central Ministry in St Petersburg. The *Rech'* editorial also attacked the irrational distribution of Russian missions overseas, acidly pointing out that Russia still maintained missions at the various German courts, even though the country had been unified since 1870, while a solitary diplomatic mission was maintained in the whole of South America. Its author was even more critical about the absence of Russian diplomatic missions in the Far East, where economic and political developments were of vital importance for the prosperity and security of the Tsarist Empire.[7]

Over the next few years, both *Rech'* and *Novoe Vremia* returned to the attack time and again, a pattern that was also evident in other newspapers such as *Golos Moskvy*. The authors of these articles were particularly critical of the gulf that existed between the central Ministry and the various diplomatic missions abroad, which meant that officials working in St Petersburg often had little understanding of foreign countries, while diplomats 'in the field' were too detached from the views and sentiments of their fellow-countrymen.[8] Numerous attacks were also made on the supposed 'snobbism' and laziness of many MID employees.[9] Writers in *Novoe Vremia*, in particular, believed that organisational reform could not produce benefits without a determined effort to get rid of many of the men already in post. The paper also expressed concern about the low status of Russian consuls abroad, who were often forced to work in such dilapidated surroundings that they attracted derision from the local population, making it harder for them to carry out their core functions of protecting Russian nationals and promoting Russian trade.[10] By 1908 or 1909, it had become an article of faith among many Russian journalists and members of the Duma that their country's diplomatic establishment was failing to carry out its duties effectively.

THE MINISTRY OF FOREIGN AFFAIRS, 1894–1914: ORGANISATIONAL STRUCTURE AND STAFFING

When A.P. Izvol'skii was appointed Foreign Minister in the spring of 1906, taking over from the shy and reclusive Count V.N. Lamsdorff, he was already convinced that the Foreign Ministry in St Petersburg was hopelessly inefficient and riven by internecine bureaucratic conflict. He also recognised that the major changes taking place at the time in the political and administrative structures of tsarist Russia were likely to increase the opportunity to promote reforms within the MID. Like five of the six men who served as foreign minister in the twenty years before 1914, Izvol'skii had made his career almost exclusively at overseas diplomatic missions, and was instinctively suspicious of the parochial mentality which he believed characterised many of the Ministry *chinovniki* (officials) in St Petersburg.[11] He had for some time been inclined to believe the stories which circulated in the Russian capital about the nepotism and corruption prevailing at the MID. It was largely for this reason that he quickly appointed a special Commission, headed by K.A. Gubastov, the assistant Foreign Minister, to recommend possible reforms to the organisation of the central Ministry. Izvol'skii also moved quickly to put in place a number of other reforms designed to promote the effectiveness of the organisation, including the establishment of a new Press Bureau to deal with the public relations aspect of the Ministry's work.[12] The Gubastov Commission and its successors took far longer than expected to complete their work, with the result that the final proposals were not forwarded to the Duma for legislative approval until the end of 1910.[13] The proposed reforms were designed to promote greater efficiency by achieving a more orderly distribution of business within the MID, so that the function of each department and section was clearly-defined. Other proposals related to pay and staffing levels. In this sense, then, the changes proposed by Gubastov and other reform-minded officials in the MID were very much in the spirit of the 'rationalising' reforms associated with Hardinge and Crowe at the Foreign Office in London and Berthelot at the *Quai d'Orsay* in Paris. Administrative reform was designed to promote the orderly conduct of business at a time when the demands placed on the Foreign Ministry were rising rapidly. Even though the proposals seemed to be a sensible response to many of the criticisms made in the Duma over the previous few years, deputies there were in fact very dilatory in considering them, with the result that the changes had still not been properly implemented when war broke out in the summer of 1914. The operation of the central Ministry in St Petersburg remained chaotic right down until the collapse of the tsarist regime in the spring of 1917.

A tradition of piecemeal change had characterised the MID ever since it was established in 1802, the year when Russia's central administration was first organised on ministerial lines.[14] The culture of bureaucratic traditionalism that was a hallmark of tsarist Russia right down to the 1917 Revolution helped to forestall major administrative changes throughout the period. Nevertheless, when trying to understand the role and influence of the MID in the 20 years before 1914, it is not sufficient to focus on formal institutional structures alone. In a political system where the authority and stability of the principal institutions were always in question, it is also important to focus on other factors such as the role of individual personalities and the existence of competing perceptions about where foreign policy decisions should be made. There was in tsarist Russia no such formal distinction between a 'Foreign Office' and a 'Diplomatic Service' as the one which existed in Britain before their merger in 1919. An official could in theory be posted from St Petersburg to a mission abroad once he had passed the requisite diplomatic examinations (although such transfers were in practice quite rare). While most young men were attracted to the MID by the glamour of a career abroad, a lack of posts meant that many who passed the diplomatic examinations were in practice doomed to spend their entire working lives in the Russian capital. Obtaining a position at a foreign mission, or indeed securing rapid promotion within the central Ministry in St Petersburg itself, usually depended as much on contacts and networking skills as on the diligent performance of duties. It could also depend on luck. One young official who managed to obtain a post at the London Embassy believed that his success was due to the impression made on his superiors by his fabulous borzoi dog which accompanied its master to work every day![15]

The lack of regular transfers between the central Ministry and missions abroad was a frequent target for critics, who argued that it fostered a narrow perspective that impeded a good understanding of international affairs among officials based in St Petersburg. Ironically, some commentators even compared the situation unfavourably with the one that existed in Britain, apparently ignorant of the fact that transfers between the Foreign Office and Diplomatic Service were also comparatively unusual.[16] Nor were contributors to newspapers like *Novoe Vremia* entirely correct when criticising the low status of Russian consular officials *vis à vis* diplomats. There was actually greater movement between consular and diplomatic posts in the Russian diplomatic establishment than in its British counterpart. When the future Minister to Tokyo, Baron Rosen, opted to become Consul-General in New York during the reign of Alexander III, he was ready to take a post 'much below the preferment that I had a right to expect in the diplomatic line' since it was located in a city of enormous interest to him.[17] A British diplomat would seldom have been willing or able to make such a choice. Nor was Rosen an isolated case. A.D. Kalmykov moved from the Consulate in Tabriz to the Legation in Teheran, while Konstantin Nabokov served as Consul-General in India from 1912 to 1915 before being appointed Counsellor at the London Embassy. It appears that scholars who have suggested that there were particularly rigid boundaries between the various branches of the MID in the years before 1914 may have paid too much attention to critical articles appearing in the contemporary Russian press.

The statute that established the MID on a new legislative footing in 1906 largely preserved its formal structure intact, despite the dramatic changes taking place in the wider political and administrative environment. The statute set down that the central Ministry should consist of the Minister, an assistant Minister, the Departmental Council, the Chancellery and three Departments dealing with Asiatic affairs, internal relations and staffing. In practice, however, the structure of the Ministry seldom corresponded with the actual distribution of responsibilities. The Asiatic Department – a name that was formally changed to the First Department in 1897 – had a much wider remit than its title suggested, dealing with most areas of the globe other than Western Europe (which came within the province of the Chancellery).[18] The division of responsibilities was in practice often confused; even the official literature produced by the Ministry struggled to define where particular tasks should be carried out.[19] There was often a considerable duplication of effort, with the result that it was by no means uncommon for individuals to make conflicting decisions about the same issue.[20] The formal hierarchical structure of the Ministry concealed considerable tensions between the various departments and sections. The Chancellery was usually staffed by socially well-connected individuals who looked askance at their peers in other departments, considering them to be 'from a social point of view, inferior'.[21] Officials working in the Asiatic Department were in turn inclined to resent this patronising attitude and responded by emphasising their own expertise and diligence. There was also frequently a high degree of fragmentation *within* departments.[22] The inevitable problems created by the poor integration between different parts of the Ministry were compounded by a culture of bureaucratic parochialism. While some senior officials worked valiantly to take advantage of such forums as afternoon tea to supplement or bypass the formal channels of communication, they were seldom able to overcome the forces making for administrative atrophy. Indeed, to make matters worse, such informal conversations often only served to fuel the atmosphere of intrigue and mistrust which itself damaged the cause of cooperation between officials.

The men who worked in the Foreign Ministry during the reign of Nicholas II varied sharply in their assessment of the organisation, but there was a common concern among the more thoughtful of them about the bureaucratic ethos that prevailed there. Complaints about red tape (*volokita*) were legion in the memoirs written by former members of the MID.[23] The concept of bureaucracy is of course a complex one, particularly since everyday usage of the term tends to contrast sharply with its use in scholarly discourse. The Ministry in St Petersburg was undoubtedly bureaucratic in the sense that officials working there generated a vast amount of paper and found themselves caught up in a system that appeared to lack well-defined objectives. It was certainly *not* bureaucratic in the more formal Weberian sense of the term: regulations were frequently ignored while the division of labour was not geared to promote the achievement of particular goals.[24] Although the MID was organised in a formal hierarchy, many senior *chinovniki* found it hard to establish authority over their subordinates. Personal rivalries and differences over policy led officials to vie with one another to promote their own interests. Many officials sought the support of important patrons, both inside and outside the MID, whom they hoped might be able to promote the development of their career or provide support for a favoured policy. Some ministers, most notably Lamsdorff, seemed to thrive in this atmosphere of intrigue (although Lamsdorff himself was ironically roused to fury at attempts by the Tsar and other members of the royal family to promote their favourite candidate for a particular post irrespective of the normal promotions procedures).[25] Other ministers, including Izvol'skii, found it much harder to operate in such an environment. Nevertheless, while Izvol'skii was bitterly critical about the state of the MID under his predecessor, the culture of intrigue and bureaucratic infighting was not simply the consequence of the personal style of a particular minister; nor was it even the inevitable consequence of an autocratic political system that emphasised the importance of individuals over institutions in the formulation of policy. It was instead uncertainty about the MID's proper role in the foreign policy making process, both before and after the changes wrought by the 1905 Revolution, which helped to create a climate in which individual officials believed that their influence and career prospects depended as much on their ability to win influential patrons and bureaucratic battles as on their ability to carry out their assigned duties.[26]

One of the most serious problems resulting from the organisational fragmentation of the central Ministry was the absence of effective procedures for allocating work between departments and individuals. The MID in St Petersburg was over-staffed by almost any criteria; it certainly employed more officials than its counterparts in the major capitals of western Europe. One official recalled in his memoirs that a diligent official was a 'rare breed' during the time he served in the capital early in the twentieth century, while Kalmykov spoke of the 'leisurely mode of life' which prevailed in the Asiatic Department when he worked there in the 1890s.[27] The actual situation was, however, rather more complicated. Some senior officials such as D.A. Kapnist, who headed the Asiatic Department during Kalmykov's time, were extremely lazy and only came to the office when it was absolutely unavoidable.[28] The same was true of Prince P.A. Golitsyn, who for many years headed the MID archives in Moscow. Some of their colleagues were, by contrast, extremely hard working. Count Lamsdorff himself went to the Ministry every day, including Saturdays and Sundays, even before he was appointed Foreign Minister, a routine which allowed him to develop a formidable knowledge of the bureaucratic minutiae which governed the life of his subordinates.[29] The position of junior officials was more complex. The dominant culture of the central Ministry emphasised the virtue of an 'attitude of assumed nonchalance' and disparaged displays of 'excessive zeal', even among those who were in reality extremely diligent, with the result that some of the more critical comments about the laziness of a typical MID official should probably be discounted.[30] Some young officials who were well-connected certainly arrived late in the morning and left half-way through the afternoon without greatly damaging their career prospects.[31] Others, by contrast, found themselves weighed down with a mountain of paperwork that could not be properly dealt with by a single individual. There was without doubt 'spare capacity' in the central Ministry right down to 1914, but since the work was all too often allocated in an illogical and haphazard way, it was quite common for one official to be forced to struggle under a huge burden while another had almost nothing to do.

Since the Foreign Ministry in St Petersburg employed several hundred officials in the years before the First World War, it is difficult to generalise about the background and character of the men who worked there. Ever since the days of Peter the Great, members of the tsarist bureaucracy had been organised into an elaborate series of ranks (*chiny*), a process which helped to inculcate and perpetuate the bureaucratic mentality which permeated Russian society right down to 1917. While social prestige in late Imperial Russia rested on a complex matrix of rank, birth and money, a senior post in one of the more desirable ministries certainly commanded considerable social *cachet*. Dmitri Abrikossov, the scion of a wealthy merchant family, wanted to pursue a diplomatic career at the beginning of the twentieth century, in large part because it offered the kind of social prestige that could not be achieved in commerce.[32] Other individuals such as Nicholas de Basily joined the MID because a career in diplomacy was part of a long family tradition; both his father and grandfather had occupied senior diplomatic posts abroad.[33] A handful of recruits, including Kalmykov, entered the MID because they hoped to have an opportunity to develop a knowledge of foreign countries which had first been stimulated by their university studies.[34] The diversity of motives for seeking to join the Foreign Ministry therefore makes it difficult to talk meaningfully of an MID 'type'.[35]

There were several changes in the regulations governing recruitment to the MID during the years before 1914, but they do not seem to have made much impact on the social composition of the Ministry. The regulations published in 1912 laid down that a candidate who wanted to pursue a diplomatic career abroad, or to carry out diplomatic work in St Petersburg, had to pass a preparatory test and obtain a recommendation from the head of the department he proposed to enter; he subsequently had to pass a more wide-ranging examination which required a knowledge of foreign languages, world history, international law, and the like.[36] The entrance examinations were in reality always much less formidable than they appeared. Few candidates felt the need to go through the kind of cramming process that was normal for young Britons hoping to enter the Foreign Office or Diplomatic Service in the early years of the twentieth century.[37] Most examinations were conducted on a face-to-face basis before a panel of senior officials, with the result that the selection process tended to reward candidates with the most appropriate social and personal skills. Abrikossov recalled that when he sat the examinations, the examiners were more concerned with 'evaluating general behaviour, appearance, and quick thinking' than a knowledge of the required subjects.[38] While it was possible to defend such an approach on the grounds that character and personality were of great importance for a career in diplomacy, these informal barriers discriminated against candidates who had not been schooled in the appropriate social *mores*. The Russian higher education system was comparatively egalitarian in ethos by the end of the nineteenth century, but graduates who applied to the MID seldom came from humble backgrounds. An element of self-selection among potential candidates, when combined with the discrimination inherent in the recruitment process, meant that the MID remained, for the most part, a preserve for individuals who came from the upper reaches of Russian society.

While the young men who succeeded in passing the diplomatic examination were usually drawn from moderately prosperous and well-connected families, the composition of the MID was by no means homogenous. Differences in social and educational background could have considerable implications for an individual's later career. A disproportionate number of the most coveted posts abroad, along with the more senior positions in the central Ministry in St Petersburg, were filled by men who had graduated from the prestigious Imperial Alexander *Lycée*. The *Lycée* did not provide its students, who normally graduated around the age of 20 or 21, with a particularly advanced level of education when compared with the universities; nor was the curriculum geared to the study of subjects likely to be of value for those considering a career in foreign affairs.[39] Access was, however, for the most part limited to boys from well-connected familes, whose members commanded a good deal of influence and prestige in Russian society. The *Lycée* was also effective at inculcating a certain *esprit de corps* among its graduates, as well as promoting certain core values centred around the importance of patriotism and the duty of serving one's country. Graduates of the *Lycée* who entered the Foreign Ministry therefore formed a distinct cohort, whose members used their extensive contacts both with each other and with other important patrons to secure the most desirable posts. Four of the six men who served as foreign minister between 1894 and 1914 were graduates of the Lycée (Giers, Lobanov-Rostovskii, Izvol'skii and Sazonov); the same was true of half the men who served as assistant minister during the same period. On the eve of the First World War, both the foreign minister and his deputy were graduates of the *Lycée*, along with the heads or acting heads of mission in Paris, Berlin, Athens, Bucharest, Peking and Tehran.

Graduates of institutions other than the *Lycée* certainly believed that they were at a disadvantage when seeking posts abroad or promotion at home. A young man arriving to work at the Foreign Ministry for the first time quickly became aware that his career was likely to suffer if he did not have the kind of contacts enjoyed by the typical *lycéen*. Abrikossov, who was himself a graduate of Moscow University, wrote rather acidly in his memoirs that *lycéens* dominated the Chancellery in St Petersburg where they 'stuck together tyrannically and did not admit any outsiders'. When he started work in the MID, Abrikossov was received with little warmth by officials who looked askance at this 'merchant from Moscow', whose family name was synonymous with jams and confectionary rather than an illustrious tradition of state-service.[40] P.S. Botkin, a graduate of St Petersburg University, also found the atmosphere cold and forbidding when he first arrived to work in the Ministry in the reign of Alexander III.[41] At the same time, however, while the possession of a well-known name and graduation from the *Lycée* could help to advance an individual's career, it was still possible to progress without such advantages. Botkin and Abrikossov both managed to carve out good careers for themselves, while an individual such as N.G. Hartwig, who enjoyed few social advantages at the time he first joined the MID, was able to become Director of the Asiatic Department and subsequently Minister in Tehran and Belgrade. Diligence and careful cultivation of contacts and patrons could allow an MID official to advance his career even when he lacked the advantages of the typical *lycéen*.

It was seen in previous chapters that while members of the British diplomatic establishment were usually drawn from the aristocracy or well-to-do professional familes in the years before 1914, they were also expected to establish their intellectual credentials via a recruitment process that became increasingly competitive in the years before the outbreak of the First World War. The situation in the Russian Foreign Ministry was more complex. The entrance examination was less demanding, while membership of a well-established noble family, along with the possession of good contacts among the official world of St Petersburg, were undoubtedly of great importance in allowing an individual to build a successful career. And, as has already been seen, the leisurely ethos that was on the wane in the British diplomatic establishment by the end of the nineteenth century still prevailed for at least some members of the MID. There seems to have been a greater degree of heterogeneity in the Russian diplomatic establishment when compared with its British counterpart. Experts and ignoramuses, specialists and dilettantes, could all be found working for the Russian Foreign Ministry in the years before 1914. Individuals who had won the gold medal for academic prowess during their time at the *Lycée* were certainly admired for their intellectual ability, but the MID also had room for officials who found it difficult to summon up the energy and willpower to draft a coherent memorandum. The recruitment and promotion procedures in place before the First World War did not provide candidates with any strong incentive to develop areas of knowledge likely to be of value in their work, since the various examinations they took did not in practice require great expertise to pass. A good knowledge of foreign languages was helpful, but given that French was in wide use in the *beau monde* of St Petersburg, and that many MID officials were from families of German origin, obtaining the requisite level was not normally a great problem for candidates. Candidates who had studied the more obscure languages could even sometimes feel that they were at a disadvantage in their career, since they were likely to be stuck carrying out routine work on the relevant desk in St Petersburg.[42]

It is of course possible to paint too bleak a picture of the men who worked for the tsarist Foreign Ministry before 1914, either in St Petersburg or at one of the missions abroad. During the twenty years before 1914, the Ministry always had a number of officials, such as Lamsdorff, who were well-versed in the complexities of internal procedures – a knowledge that was vital in allowing the MID to continue to function despite its organisational shortcomings and problems. These 'typical bureaucrats' were not, however, necessarily well-versed in foreign affairs, since they had usually spent their whole life working in St Petersburg.[43] The members of the MID who had the best knowledge about the complexities of international relations proper can be loosely divided into 'generalists' and 'experts'. The generalists, rather like their British counterparts, prized the possession of a particular diplomatic 'nous' rather than a specialised knowledge of a certain country or issue. Among the 'experts' were such men as P.M. Lessar, who served as political agent in Bokhara before subsequently serving as minister in Peking, during which time he acquired a reputation among his colleagues as a leading expert on Asian affairs. Another senior official, Pokotilov, proved to be such an expert on economic questions in the Far East that he was eventually poached by the Ministry of Finance to head the new Russo-Chinese Bank. One of their more cynical junior colleagues observed in his memoirs, however, that Lessar and Pokotilov 'were practically the only men...who knew and understood the East' – a statement which was not strictly true, although a majority of senior members of the MID certainly preferred to focus their energy on European affairs. Even D.A. Kapnist, who headed the Asiatic Department in the early 1890s, was 'unable to retain correctly in his memory a single Oriental name'.[44]

The Foreign Ministry also went to considerable trouble to obtain the services of leading specialists on questions of international law, since few MID officials or diplomats could hope to have a detailed knowledge of such an abstruse subject. F.F. Martens, Professor of International Law at St Petersburg University, and author of the influential *Contemporary International Law of the Civilised Peoples*, served for many years as legal adviser to the MID. His successor to the chair of International Law at St Petersburg University, Baron Taube, also advised the Ministry on matters of international law, before being asked by Lamsdorff to serve as deputy Director of the Second Department (in which capacity he played an important role in preparing the Gubastov reforms).[45] Nor was the practice of bringing outsiders into the Ministry particularly unusual. When Izvol'skii established a new Press Office in 1908, he selected as its chief the head of the St Petersburg Telegraph Agency, while Sazonov appointed Prince G.N. Trubetskoi to a senior position in 1912, even though he had spent the previous six years as a gentleman-journalist penning numerous articles on international affairs rather than as a serving member of the MID.

The officials who worked in the tsarist Foreign Ministry before 1914 were, then, a diverse set of men with a range of backgrounds and talents. The possession of a well-respected aristocratic name certainly helped an individual to rise to the top of the service, but it was by no means a prerequisite for professional success. A good deal has been written in the last 20 years or so about the emergence of a schism in late imperial Russia between the traditional landed elites and the state bureaucracy. Although the evidence remains inconclusive, it appears that most MID officials were not large landowners. For a majority of them, service in the Foreign Ministry provided a large part of their income as well as a psychological focus for their daily lives.[46] At the same time, however, while there was a certain degree of 'professionalisation' taking place at the MID during the late nineteenth and early twentieth centuries, in the crude sense that service there was increasingly important financially to its members, there was little professionalisation in the sense that a career in international relations was deemed to require particular patterns of knowledge or experience. The ethos of the dilettante was more pronounced in the Foreign Ministry in St Petersburg than at the Foreign Office in London during the years before 1914.

THE DIPLOMATIC MISSIONS AND THE LONDON EMBASSY

At the end of the first decade of the twentieth century, Russia had eight embassies abroad headed by a full ambassador (two more than in 1894), along with 30 or so other diplomatic missions.[47] Seven of the embassies were situated in Europe.[48] The diplomatic missions were staffed in the normal way by a complement of secretaries graded by seniority. While the central Ministry in St Petersburg was larger than the Foreign Office in London, the same was not true of Russian missions abroad. The Russian embassies in Paris, London and Berlin typically employed one first secretary and two or three other secretaries, in addition to the ambassador, the counsellor and the naval and military *attachés*. The number of clerical staff at Russian missions was usually very small, with the result that the more junior diplomatic secretaries had to spend a good deal of time on comparatively mundane administrative duties.

The various critical attacks made on the Russian diplomatic establishment after 1906 usually focused on the central Ministry in St Petersburg rather than on diplomatic missions abroad. Nevertheless, a good deal of criticism was directed against the distribution of Russian missions, which was condemned by newspapers such as *Rech'* for not reflecting the changing configuration of international power and wealth.[49] This charge was certainly in large part fair, given the paucity of representatives in areas such as South America, although the number of Russian missions and consulates had grown enormously in the course of the nineteenth century. When the MID was established in 1802, there were just 44 Russian embassies, missions and consular establishments under its authority; by 1902 there were 173.[50] Diplomats working abroad did not escape criticism altogether in the press; they were routinely condemned in newspaper articles for idleness and spending too much time at receptions and parties.[51] A post abroad was certainly prized by officials working for the Foreign Ministry; indeed, competition for the more coveted positions was an important element in fuelling the atmosphere of intrigue that was such a hallmark of the culture of the MID. Since the best-connected officials tended to be most successful in the battle to win an assignment to a diplomatic mission abroad, Russian diplomats *en poste* were typically more 'blue-blooded' than the average MID official. The embassies at London, Berlin, Paris and Vienna were normally viewed as the most attractive assignments. Copenhagen was also an attractive post, since members of the Russian royal family frequently visited the city, allowing diplomats posted there to develop good relations with Nicholas II and his entourage. The handful of men who were particularly interested in developments in central Asia and the Balkans, such as Hartwig, naturally welcomed an assignment to such missions as the ones at Belgrade or Tehran, but most members of the Foreign Ministry posted abroad preferred the ambience and amenities of European cities. Many tsarist diplomats even chose to retire abroad at the end of their career, since years of service outside Russia meant that they no longer felt any great affinity for their own country.

The London Embassy was a popular posting for Russian diplomats in the late nineteenth and early twentieth centuries, except for men who were irredeemably committed to the notion that Britain was their country's 'natural' enemy. Diplomats who wanted to feel involved with the complexities and challenges of international politics celebrated the fact that they were working at the heart of the British Empire, which was still the most formidable global economic and naval power; those who were more interested in the social round could enjoy living in 'the most gorgeous city in the world, with the riches and pride of the English aristocracy apotheosized'.[52] In the late nineteenth and early twentieth centuries, London society still commanded an unrivalled international reputation for style and wealth. The two men who served as ambassador in the 20 years between 1894 and 1914, Baron G.G. Staal and Count A.K. Benckendorff, were both confirmed anglophiles who mixed easily in the late Victorian and Edwardian *beau monde*. Staal first arrived in London as Ambassador in 1884, and remained there until 1902, although ill health and absence at the first Hague Conference on disarmament meant that he was rather detached from the day-to-day work of the Embassy towards the end of his time there. He was replaced by Benckendorff, who remained at the Embassy until his death a few weeks before the collapse of the tsarist *ancien regime* in the spring of 1917. The length of time spent by both men at the Embassy was exceptional, but Russian ambassadors posted abroad did normally stay *en poste* for a good deal longer than their British counterparts; Prince N.A. Orlov served at the Paris Embassy from 1871 until 1884, while his successor also served there for 13 years.[53] During the 33 years that Staal and Benckendorff served at the London Embassy, no less than eight men served as ambassador at the British Embassy in St Petersburg. More junior Russian officials also usually remained in a particular post for comparatively long periods of time, with the result that the turnover of secretaries at the Russian Embassy in London was rather lower than the turnover of their British counterparts in St Petersburg.

The *modus operandi* of the London Embassy under Staal and Benckendorff was in most respects typical of the era of old diplomacy. Benckendorff was considered by his subordinates to be 'the most elegant man in London society', while Staal was described by another senior Russian diplomat as a 'distinguished diplomat of the old school', instinctively attuned to the social rituals of his chosen profession.[54] Both men were adept at mixing in the best circles in British society, and they encouraged their staff to attend the most important social events of the day in the hope that it would allow them to collect valuable information. They also hosted numerous receptions and balls at the Embassy itself, which was situated in two large houses near Hyde Park. Since the boundary between the social and political elites of late Victorian and Edwardian Britain was extremely porous, occasions such as the Henley Regatta and Cowes week provided valuable opportunities for informal discussions between Embassy staff and leading British politicians and civil servants. It also allowed Embassy staff to assess the mood of the British Establishment on important domestic and international issues. Staal, in particular, spent a great deal of time studying the state of public and political opinion in Britain, using his wide range of contacts to obtain information and news. The dispatches and letters he sent back to Russia often contained detailed reports about divisions in the Cabinet or the mood of the House of Commons[55] – reports that were as often as not based on material gleaned at a dinner party or a conversation at Ascot. Benckendorff also established a formidably wide range of contacts in influential social and political circles, where he was generally viewed with a good deal of sympathy and respect. The Ambassador regularly visited Windsor Castle, speaking frequently with Edward VII about international affairs, as well as attending house-parties hosted by leading politicians from both major political parties. Although Benckendorff was less interested in the intricacies of British domestic politics than

Staal, he too made a concerted effort to keep St Petersburg informed about the state of public opinion and the views of the major political parties on important international questions.

While the ambassadorial status of Staal and Benckendorff provided them with access to leading social and political circles, the same was not automatically true of the diplomats who served under them. Even though diplomats representing the major foreign powers commanded a certain amount of prestige and status in London society, they could not rely on an automatic *entrée* to the most exclusive house-parties and dinners. Winning acceptance in the snobbish *beau monde* of late Victorian and Edwardian Britain required a good deal of effort and perseverance. Some diplomats at the Russian Embassy went to extraordinary lengths to achieve this goal. The wealthy S.A. Poklevskii-Kozell, who had for many years desperately wanted a posting to a major embassy, before finally being appointed as Counsellor at the London Embassy, was mortified to discover on arrival there that 'English society did not attach any importance to the mere fact that a person was a member of some Embassy'.[56] He therefore spent huge amounts of money renting a large house, where he gave numerous parties entertaining a wide variety of the social and political *cognoscenti* in an effort to gain acceptance in London society. He also managed to gain an entry into the exclusive circle surrounding Edward VII. The position of Benckendorff and Poklevskii undoubtedly helped to raise the profile of the Russian Embassy in London during the early years of the twentieth century, with the result that their more junior colleagues found themselves 'invited everywhere'. Nevertheless, while participation in the social world of the British capital helped to promote the status and influence of the Embassy, it could sometimes have painful consequences for the men who worked there. The expense of keeping up a position in London society was of no great concern to wealthy individuals like Poklevskii, but it could be ruinous for individuals with smaller fortunes. One unfortunate individual even had to be relieved temporarily of his duties so that he could have time to deal with the debts he had incurred during his time in London.

The day-to-day operation of the Embassy naturally varied according to the particular constellation of circumstances and personalities. While Staal and Benckendorff moved easily in the London *beau monde*, they both considered themselves to be working ambassadors charged with the effective conduct of a critical international relationship; neither man was content to confine himself to the ceremonial aspect of his duties. In the best traditions of the old diplomacy, they did not make any firm distinction between their public and private lives, recognising that an ambassador was effectively on duty even in the informal surroundings of a dinner or house-party. Benckendorff found some of the procedural minutiae associated with diplomatic life to be rather tedious and boring, and was even sometimes inclined to sign reports drafted by his subordinates without reading them properly. This may have been no bad thing, since the Ambassador's own dispatches were dreadfully verbose, doubtless in part a reflection of the fact that Russian was not his first language; like many of his colleagues at the London Embassy, he was born into a Baltic German family and spoke French and German – and perhaps English – better than he spoke Russian. Benckendorff often preferred to use private correspondence rather than formal dispatches to express his views about important international issues, particularly when Izvol'skii was Foreign Minister, a pattern that was of course characteristic of the era of old diplomacy in most countries. Staal was also inclined to rely on private correspondence, although it does appear that he drafted his own dispatches with great care, at least until his final years in London when overwork and ill-health meant that he had to rely more on the assistance of his staff.

The remaining diplomats posted to the London Embassy varied in the way they approached their work. The more senior diplomats such as Poklevskii and the future Foreign Minister, Sergei Sazonov, who both served as Counsellor at the Embassy in the first decade of the century, spent a good deal of time on their official duties. Not all their colleagues were so assiduous. Some treated their duties in a very relaxed fashion, preferring to pass their time at parties and receptions, although others spent long hours conscientiously compiling reports and filing correspondence. The level of administrative support available to diplomatic staff was very modest: in the early years of the twentieth century, there was just one ancient typewriter which had to be shared between officials. The Chancery itself was crammed into two small rooms, where the secretaries were expected to decipher telegrams and copy by hand the dispatches of the ambassador, tasks which could be agonisingly time-consuming at periods of tension and crisis. Benckendorff suspected that some of his staff were inclined to shirk their duties, a view that was shared by a number of the more diligent secretaries. When the self-righteous Dmitrii Abrikossov first arrived in London he was appalled by the deplorable state of the Embassy archives. He also noted disapprovingly that a number of his colleagues spent too much time on their 'social obligations' rather than in carrying out more mundane duties.[57] Despite these tensions, however, a strong *esprit de corps* seems to have developed among the Embassy staff, particularly when Benckendorff was in charge. The Ambassador encouraged his staff to dine with him as often as they wished, and made great efforts to ensure that they were given access to the more influential figures in London society.

Both Staal and Benckendorff were closely involved in debates about Russian foreign policy, a subject which is discussed in greater detail later in this chapter. The same was true, to a lesser extent, of the men who served as counsellor at the London Embassy in the years before 1914. The two ambassadors were confirmed anglophiles, committed to promoting the cause of Anglo–Russian friendship. Staal repeatedly urged the then Foreign Minister in St Petersburg, Count M.N. Murav'ev, to avoid taking advantage of Britain's diplomatic isolation over South Africa at the start of the twentieth century.[58] Benckendorff played a significant role in the various diplomatic manoeuvres which led to the 1907 Anglo–Russian rapprochement, promoting the cause of an agreement in Britain and returning to St Petersburg at a critical stage in the negotiations to help Izvol'skii in his battle to promote the policy at home. Neither Staal nor Benckendorff were, however, inclined to discuss foreign policy at great length with their more junior colleagues. For this reason, the duties of the secretaries were almost entirely routine in character. While they were encouraged to write reports about such questions as the state of opinion within the various political parties, they were not encouraged to write briefing papers on important matters of foreign policy. The counsellors alone were expected to involve themselves in such matters, and even they sometimes felt largely excluded from discussions about important international questions. Konstantin Nabokov, who served as Counsellor during the First World War, recalled that at that time Benckendorff 'very seldom imparted to me the tenor of his confidential talks with Sir Edward Grey',[59] although the Ambassador was more forthcoming ten years earlier with Poklevskii when the Anglo–Russian rapprochement was under negotiation. It was the ambassador as an individual, rather than the Embassy as an institution, which exercised a potential influence on policy deliberations back in St Petersburg.

The Russian Embassy in London was in most respects typical of other tsarist embassies. Receptions, musical evenings and dinner parties were as common in Washington or Berlin as they were in London. Most Russian diplomats, whether senior or junior, relished the social and ceremonial aspect of their job, and were well-suited to thrive in the cultural milieu characteristic of the old diplomacy. Nor were Staal and Benckendorff unusual in believing that they had both a right and a duty to make recommendations about matters of policy. Just as Benckendorff used his position to promote the cause of Anglo–Russian rapprochement in 1906–7, so his counterpart in Constantinople tried to encourage St Petersburg to take a more aggressive line in negotiations with the British in order to win concessions over the straits.[60] Far from being supine recipients of instructions issued by the Emperor or foreign minister in St Petersburg, most senior tsarist diplomats believed that they had the right and duty to influence the making of Russian foreign policy.

THE RUSSIAN CONSULS

Many journalists who wrote critical articles about the MID in the years after the 1905 Revolution were convinced that Russian consuls working abroad lacked the status and resources needed to carry out their work effectively.[61] The actual situation was, however, more complicated than many of them realised. The duties carried out by full-time Russian consular officials varied sharply from post to post. Officials posted to the countries of western Europe in which there existed full Russian diplomatic missions usually spent most of their time carrying out a narrow range of strictly consular functions. In countries where there was no diplomatic mission, by contrast, they performed numerous quasi-diplomatic duties.

Members of the Russian diplomatic establishment moved more frequently between diplomatic and consular posts than their British counterparts. The regulations published in 1912 set down that a young official seeking a post abroad would normally be assigned to consular or diplomatic duties according to his particular talents and aptitudes,[62] although in practice good connections both inside and beyond the MID were of greater importance in determining the allocation of particular posts. The regulations did, however, permit transfers to be made, particularly when an official was still at an early stage of his career. The duties of a consul laid down in the 1912 regulations were very wide-ranging. He was expected to answer questions from government officials and private firms about trading conditions in the country to which he was posted, as well as filing regular reports about local economic conditions. He was also required to assist any Russian nationals who asked him for assistance, in addition to performing a host of other routine duties. Consular officials received very little clerical and administrative support from the Russian government; nor were most of them willing or able to use their own money to relieve the situation. Many full-time Russian consuls therefore found it difficult to carry out their manifold duties properly – a situation that Chapter 4 showed was also true for British consuls as well.

A brief look at the role of Russian consular officials in Britain, India and Persia can put some flesh on these comments. There were in Britain at the end of 1894 one Russian consul-general and three consuls, at Hull, Newcastle and Liverpool; there were in addition some 35 vice-consuls and seven consular agents, most of whom were British nationals employed to carry out routine consular tasks on a part-time basis.[63] The Russian government maintained more vice-consuls in Britain than in the other major countries of western Europe, presumably because all Russian trade with Great Britain was carried by sea, which meant that every port of significance required a consular presence. The number and distribution of Russian consular officials in Britain did change somewhat over the following 20 years, but the basic pattern remained intact. Between 1894 and 1914 there were fewer Russian nationals employed full-time on consular duties in Britain than British nationals employed to carry out consular duties in Russia.

Even the career Russian consular officials based in Britain seem to have spent most of their time dealing with routine consular affairs, although they spent longer than the part-timers compiling lengthy reports on economic and trade issues. The edited collections of consular reports compiled annually by the MID provide a useful insight into the role of consular officials. The 1898 edition contained articles on a wide variety of topics, ranging from the amount of trade passing through the port of Hamburg to a description of recent archaeological excavations in Mesopotamia.[64] Articles submitted by consular officials in Britain included one by the Consul in Liverpool on the availability of agricultural credit in Ireland, and another by the Consul-General in London on the state of the gold-mining industry across the globe. The Consul in Newcastle, a certain Brunner, provided a more prosaic report on the local trade in large-horned cattle. A few of the published reports by Russian consuls in Britain did touch on broader economic and social themes. Brunner himself wrote a detailed report about a strike by British engineering workers who were demanding a reduction in the working week from 54 to 48 hours. The report on agricultural credit in Ireland mentioned earlier also contained a great deal of information about social problems in the country. A simliar pattern was visible in the consular reports published by the MID in 1899. Most reports were concerned with narrow economic issues, but a number, such as one written by Baron Ungern-Sternberg (the Consul-General in London) on the situation in Rhodesia, were concerned with more overtly political questions. In general, however, the importance of consular reports as sources of political information was limited. Since Britain was a comparatively small country, with excellent communications between the centre and the provinces, Russian diplomats at the Embassy in London found it much easier to keep abreast of developments across the whole country than did their British counterparts in St Petersburg.

While full-time Russian consular officials in Britain seem to have spent most of their time on core consular duties, the same was not always true of their colleagues posted elsewhere. In countries where there was no Russian diplomatic mission, consuls inevitably tended to have a broader range of duties than was the case in countries where there was an embassy or legation. When Konstantin Nabokov was appointed as Russian Consul-General in India, a few years before the outbreak of the First World War, his duties were in some respects not very different from those of a minister or ambassador. India was of course something of a special case. While the Viceroy did have a special committee advising him on questions of foreign affairs, formal diplomatic relations were conducted through London with the result that there were no direct contacts between St Petersburg and the Indian government. Nevertheless, India was of such enormous significance to Russia that its representatives there were expected to take on a quasi-political role. Nabokov himself observed in his memoirs that while the Consul-General in India was nominally a trade agent, 'in fact, of course, he had the opportunity of doing political work of the highest importance...keeping his Government informed on all questions of the middle East affecting the interests of Russia, in particular in Persia and Afghanistan'.[65]

Nabokov was himself very much schooled in diplomatic rather than consular work. He served in the Russian Embassy in Washington D.C. prior to his transfer to India, and was appointed Counsellor at the London Embassy following his departure at the end of 1915. During his years in India, Nabokov not only emphasised the importance of his quasi-diplomatic reporting role: a convinced anglophile, he also sought to strengthen Anglo–Russian relations, which at times remained less than cordial in southern Asia despite the *entente* between the two countries established in 1907. Suspicion of Russian intentions in the region ran very deep among British officials in India, many of whom remained immersed in the attitudes of the Great Game. Nabokov therefore worked hard to persuade his own government in St Petersburg that 'our interests are in every way identical with those of Great Britain' and that 'political questions affecting both countries can only be settled if they are approached in a spirit of sincere friendship and frank discussion'. He also sought to convince senior British officials that their 'forebodings' about Russian intentions in the region were groundless.[66] Nabokov's influence was in reality quite negligible, since the issues which had most direct impact on the Anglo–Russian relationship in the years immediately before 1914 were European rather than Asian in character. Nevertheless, his belief that the holder of a consular post could exercise quasi-diplomatic functions illustrates how the boundary between the roles of Russian diplomats and consuls could evaporate under certain circumstances.

Nabokov's anglophilism was not shared by all Russian consuls working in areas where Anglo–Russian rivalry had been endemic in the nineteenth century. Consular officials from both Britain and Russia were deeply involved in the struggle between their respective governments for power and prestige in Persia; indeed, the activities of 'Russian consuls' in the country were a major concern for many British officials during the early years of the twentieth century. Since the battle between Britain and Russia for influence in Persia often took a directly economic form, touching on issues ranging from the provision of loans through to the construction of railways, the boundary between economic and political issues was particularly confused. The British used their consulates in Meshed and Seistan as centres for the collection of secret intelligence, running agents throughout Persia and south Russia. A number of Russian consular officials responded in kind, employing native agents to gather information about British activities throughout the region.

Russian consuls in Persia were particularly assiduous in promoting the influence of their country in the years before the Anglo–Russian convention divided the country into well-defined British and Russian 'spheres of influence'. In 1898, the Russians appointed a consul to Seistan, an area in which there were few Russian nationals and little Russian trade, in a step that was 'clearly calculated to demonstrate to the British that they had no monopoly on south-eastern Persia'.[67] The British government countered by transferring Percy Sykes to Seistan, so that he could observe his Russian 'colleague'. The bad-tempered relations that developed between British and Russian officials could sometimes border on the farcical. In the town of Nosratābād, the British Consul held a weekly gymkhana in an apparent attempt to impress the local population, while his Russian opposite number responded by holding a counter-attraction 'in the shape of a native band with a performing monkey'.[68] The Russian official also showed little sensitivity to the refined sensibilities of his British colleague, turning up drunk at a reception designed to mark the King's birthday. Many Russian consuls in Persia made little secret of their anglophobia. I.F. Pokhitinov, the Russian Consul-General at Tabriz, was far from alone in having a reputation for 'detesting everything English'. Since Pokhitinov commanded good links with senior officials at the MID, as well as among the wider St Petersburg bureaucracy, he was able to exercise at least some influence on the development of Russian policy in the region. The formal conclusion of the Great Game in 1907 might have helped to relieve the tension between the British and Russian governments, but the struggle 'on the ground' continued with a considerable degree of vitriol and bad temper for some years afterwards.

By the time the First World War broke out in 1914, there was growing anxiety among senior Foreign Ministry officials in St Petersburg about the effectiveness of Russian consuls serving abroad. Concern was focused in particular on the competence of 'non-state' consuls, that is the hotch-potch of Russian and non-Russian nationals who filled consular posts on a part-time basis. A lengthy circular issued by the MID in February 1913 noted that greater attention should be given to the selection and supervision of such men, since there was evidence that too many of them had been carrying out their duties with little care. In future, the circular noted, all non-state consular officials would be expected either to be Russians or to have a good knowledge of the Russian language; they would also be expected to keep abreast of the various regulations and notes issued by the Ministry. It concluded by asking for any information about individuals who were particularly incompetent in carrying out their duties.[69] In the same year, the Ministry of Trade and Industry established a network of commercial agents abroad who were charged with carrying out a wide variety of tasks, although there was a good deal of confusion about how their role would relate to that of regular consular officials.[70] Once the war broke out, Russian consular officials abroad continued to report avidly on a range of economic and political issues. In 1915, for example, around 600 reports of this kind were sent to the Ministry of Trade by consular officials; a quarter were compiled by officials based in the British Isles.[71] Most of these dealt with such arid issues as the amount of land given over to wheat growing, but the Consulate-General in London also filed reports on such matters as the attempts by the British government to promote pro-Russian sentiment among the population. Consular officials throughout Europe filed numerous reports containing information they had received locally about economic developments in Germany. Russian consuls could, like their British counterparts, prove on occasion to be a valuable source of vital economic and political information for their government.

THE ROLE OF THE RUSSIAN FOREIGN MINISTRY IN FOREIGN POLICY MAKING

The debate about the tsarist diplomatic establishment which took place in Russia after 1906 was in one respect very different from the debate that occurred in Britain during the same period. The authors of articles in newspapers like *Novoe Vremia* and *Rech'* were concerned above all with questions of competence and efficiency. They were afraid that officials who worked for the MID did not possess the sort of talents and aptitudes that were needed to thrive in a changing international environment; they were seldom, if ever, concerned that the MID was becoming too powerful *qua* institution. The same was largely true of deputies in the Duma. Even those who attacked the foreign policy pursued by the government usually assumed that it was the Tsar or his ministers who were responsible for making decisions; the Foreign Ministry itself was never demonised in the way that the Foreign Office was demonised by many writers in Britain. The machiavellian image of 'the diplomat', so dominant in the writings of men like Brailsford or Morel, did not really have a counterpart in Russia.

The Russian Foreign Ministry did not have a strong corporate identity in the early twentieth century, since organisational fragmentation and personal rivalries prevented the emergence of a strong *esprit de corps* among its members. There were nevertheless certain well-defined patterns of tension *between* the major ministries in St Petersburg during the years before 1914. Kalmykov wrote in his memoirs that during the early years of the twentieth century, 'Good relations with the Ministry of Finance were one of the traditions of the Russian Foreign Office, just as distrust of the War Ministry was another'.[72] This analysis was too simplistic. Under the formidable Sergei Witte, the Finance Ministry developed during the 1890s into such a powerful ministry, with its own international interests and perspectives, that it served as an institutional rival to the MID. At the same time, officials at the Ministry of War did on occasion cooperate closely with staff at the Foreign Ministry. And, as will be seen later, the heads of all three ministries were quite capable of working with one another when they believed that their power and influence was being usurped by non-ministerial advisers who had succeeded in capturing the Tsar's attention. There was in reality a good deal of uncertainty in tsarist Russia *both* before and after 1906 about how and where foreign policy should be made.

The MID was not organised in a manner calculated to facilitate the formulation of coherent decisions on foreign policy. This was in part due to its chaotic internal structure, but it was also a consequence of a more general ambiguity about the correct constitutional role of the MID in the foreign policy making process. When its basic structure was established during the early nineteenth century, the Foreign Ministry was intended to serve primarily as an administrative and executive organ. At the same time, however, because foreign ministers were required to advise the Tsar on important matters of policy, consideration of possible courses of action necessarily formed an important part of the duties of senior officials. Only the most senior officials in the central Ministry in St Petersburg were normally involved in discussion of questions of policy. Junior officials working in the Asiatic Department and the Chancellery were almost entirely concerned with carrying out routine work such as filing documents and enciphering telegrams; they were not expected to make any comments on incoming dispatches or telegrams. A young official arriving to work at the Ministry in St Petersburg for the first time soon found that all his 'illusions about diplomatic life were quickly dispelled', since nobody 'took any notice' of him while discussion about all important questions of policy took place 'behind closed doors'.[73]

The influence of the officials who sat 'behind closed doors' varied a good deal according to the instincts and talents of a particular individual, something which was even true of the six men who served as head of the Foreign Ministry in the 20 years before 1914. The political and constitutional changes that took place following the 1905 Revolution undoubtedly gave ministers more opportunities than before to exercise influence on the policy making process, but the birth of the Constitutional Experiment also created new constraints on their power. In the years before 1905, the Tsar took a great deal of interest in foreign affairs, carefully reading a large amount of the correspondence arriving at the MID and annotating it with numerous comments and instructions.[74] When Izvol'skii arrived at the Foreign Ministry in the spring of 1906, the position of Nicholas was politically and constitutionally much weaker than in previous years, while the new Foreign Minister had a definite programme which he wished to pursue, predicated on the establishment of a rapprochement with Britain and a growing focus on European rather than Asian affairs.[75] His successor, Sergei Sazonov, similarly believed that whoever served as foreign minister should exercise a major influence on foreign policy; indeed, it was probably during his tenure that the Foreign Ministry acquired its greatest autonomy and influence. By contrast, Izvol'skii's predecessor, Count Lamsdorff, instinctively took a less assertive view of his role than his successor, frequently deferring on questions of foreign policy both to the Tsar and to the energetic Sergei Witte at the Finance Ministry (at least until the latter's dismissal in 1903). Lamsdorff had spent his entire career in the central Ministry in St Petersburg, and while his instinctive penchant for the world of bureaucratic minutiae helped him to establish considerable influence inside the MID, he lacked the presence and determination needed to defend his views against Nicholas or other ministers. One French ambassador who served in Petersburg described Lamsdorff as a '*Russian* Foreign Minister, which is to say that he did not have direction of foreign policy, but only of the diplomacy of Russia'.[76] Such a bald judgement inevitably fails to capture the full complexity of the Foreign Minister's position. Lamsdorff did have decided views on important questions of foreign policy, and was on occasion willing to assert himself against Nicholas, perhaps most notably in 1905 when he refused to accept the infamous treaty of Björko signed between the Tsar and the Kaiser without the prior knowledge of the MID. Nevertheless, as will be seen later, Lamsdorff never really succeeded in establishing himself as the principal channel for providing the Tsar with advice about foreign affairs. His predecessor as Foreign Minister, Murav'ev, even went so far as to make a virtue of passivity, boasting that his role consisted of nothing more than the implementation of the imperial will[77] (although Murav'ev showed himself in practice to be perfectly capable of defending and promoting the policies which he believed in). Not every foreign minister who served Nicholas II in the years before the 1905 Revolution was so supine. Prince Lobanov-Rostovskii, who had himself enjoyed a long diplomatic career abroad before returning to St Petersburg to head the Foreign Ministry in 1895, spent a good deal of time and energy trying to educate Nicholas in the subtleties of international affairs during his time in office, as well as offering forthright advice about the most important questions of the day.[78] His predecessor, N.K. Giers, lacked the cachet and influence which Lobanov-Rostovskii enjoyed by virtue of belonging to a distinguished aristocratic family, but he too worked hard to defend his views on important matters of policy. Foreign ministers with the necessary determination and talent could exercise considerable influence on their country's foreign policy even during the years when the autocratic structure of the tsarist state was still formally intact.

The influence of other senior officials in the central Ministry depended as much on their personal qualities and ambitions as on their formal position in the hierarchy. When D.A. Kapnist headed the Asiatic Department in the 1890s, he treated the post as a sinecure which did not require much time or attention;[79] he was therefore not in a position to exercise much influence over questions of policy, even on matters relating to the countries which came within the purview of his department. By contrast, when Hartwig headed the Department a few years later, his energy and initative allowed him to play a major role in internal debates about policy within the MID. The influence of the men who served as assistant minister during the decades before 1914 also varied sharply. N.P. Shishkin, who occupied the post in the 1890s, made a poor impression on his subordinates and colleagues and does not seem to have had very much influence on policy.[80] K.A. Gubastov, however, who served as deputy to Izvol'skii, played an important role in planning the organisational reform of the MID discussed earlier. Izvol'skii was also willing to allow Gubastov's successor, Sergei Sazonov, to have access to all important documents and meetings.[81] Discussion of policy questions inside the MID therefore took place on a rather *ad hoc* basis throughout the 20 years before the outbreak of war in 1914. While members of the Ministry's Council were charged with reviewing 'all business that the Minister believes should be submitted to it for deliberation',[82] such a formulation was in practice loose enough to allow the Minister considerable discretion. Most important discussions of policy took place outside the confines of the Council, in private meetings between senior officials, while even those debates that took place at formal Council meetings were dominated by individuals who had the ability and diligence to master the issues under review.

The influence of diplomats posted abroad on policy also varied a good deal. There was, not surprisingly, a marked tendency for them to lay stress on the importance of improving relations between St Petersburg and the government to which they were accredited. It has already been seen that Staal and Benckendorff made a considerable effort to promote better Anglo–Russian relations during their extended tenure in London. Other senior diplomats who worked at the London Embassy were also usually strong anglophiles. Poklevskii-Kozell and Sazonov, who both served there as Counsellor in the early years of the twentieth century, believed that the interests of the Tsarist Empire in

154   *Diplomacy Before the Russian Revolution*

Europe and beyond depended on establishing greater trust between London and St Petersburg. Russian diplomats in Paris also became strong advocates of the cause of a Triple Entente following the formation of an Anglo–French *entente* in 1904, which helps explain why the embassies in London and Paris cooperated closely with one another during the period of the Anglo–Russian negotiations in 1906–7.[83] Anglophile sentiment was not, however, characteristic of the whole Russian diplomatic establishment. Senior diplomats posted to Vienna and Berlin were almost invariably supporters of building closer relations with the central powers, a sentiment that commanded widespread support among many conservatives back in Russia, both inside and outside the MID.[84] The same pattern was evident beyond Europe, where diplomats at Russian missions similarly tended to look at international politics through a parochial prism. The Ambassador in Constantinople forcefully argued during the negotiations for an Anglo–Russian *entente* that Britain should be expected to make concessions over the navigation of the straits in return for an agreement over central Asia.[85] In Persia, Russian ministers such as A.N. Speyer often had a reputation for being strong anglophobes.[86] Nor did the Anglo–Russian agreement of 1907 itself immediately reduce the tension that had traditionally prevailed between the British and Russian missions in Tehran. When Hartwig served as Minister in Tehran in the years after the signing of the Anglo–Russian convention, he intervened frequently in local politics in an attempt to establish his influence over the Persian government. The tension was heightened by the fact that the instinctively russophobic Cecil Spring Rice was the British Minister in Persia during these years. Relations between the two missions became so bad that the problem was only eventually resolved when both men were withdrawn from the country. While the British and Russian governments might have been able to agree to cooperate over Persia, their representatives on the spot found it much harder to overcome the legacy of the Great Game, a telling example of how sentiments in both diplomatic establishments were not neatly amenable to orders from above.

The final section of this chapter briefly examines a number of case-studies designed to illuminate the shifting role of the MID in the foreign policy making process during the first decade of the twentieth century. The first of these explores the development of Russian foreign policy in the period leading up to the outbreak of the Russo–Japanese War in

The Russian Ministry of Foreign Affairs 155

January 1904, when the MID under Lamsdorff – along with other ministers who normally exercised an influence over foreign policy – proved unable to persuade the Tsar of the dangers inherent in an expansionist policy in the Far East. The second case-study looks at the way in which Izvol'skii succeeded in defending the cause of the Anglo-Russian rapprochement against its opponents during 1906–7, taking advantage of the malleability of the new political and administrative system to marginalise his critics. The third case-study focuses on the role of the Foreign Ministry in the years immediately following Izvol'skii's departure. None of these brief case-studies can of course capture the full complexity of the foreign policy making process in the years before 1914, but they can cast light on the way in which the influence of the MID shifted according to the configuration of personalities and circumstances involved.

THE MINISTRY OF FOREIGN AFFAIRS, THE FOREIGN MINISTER AND POLICY MAKING

Case-Study 1   Lamsdorff and Russia's Far Eastern Policy, 1903

In January 1904 Japanese warships launched an unexpected attack on Port Arthur, after a long and fruitless series of negotiations failed to resolve the differences between the governments in St Petersburg and Tokyo over their differences in the Far East.[87] In the following months, Russian forces suffered a series of catastrophic defeats that played an important role in undermining public confidence in the tsarist government and fomenting the social and political tensions that exploded in the 1905 Revolution. Lamsdorff subsequently faced a good deal of criticism for not pursuing policies that might have prevented the outbreak of the Russo–Japanese War, and for failing to persuade the Emperor to ignore the counsels of those who urged the pursuit of an expansionist policy in the Far East. Such a charge was in large part unfair. The Russian foreign policy making process in general – and the making of policy towards the Far East in particular – was influenced by a wide array of powerful individuals and bureaucratic departments in the years before the 1905 Revolution. This in turn made it difficult for the Foreign Minister to assert the role of his Ministry as the primary location for determining policy or, perhaps more realistically in an autocratic system of government, for serving as the main source of authoritative information and advice for the Tsar. Even Baron Rosen, a bitter critic of Lamsdorff, who served as Minister in Tokyo during this period, acknowledged in his memoirs that:

> We must never lose sight of the fact that the Government of Russia, although nominally an 'autocracy' or rather an autocratic bureaucracy, was far from being invested with the omnipotence which one associates with the idea of 'autocracy' or 'Tsarism'. [It was instead] in the words of one of our wittiest statesmen, 'a powerless federation of independent departments whose relations to each other were not always friendly, or even neutral, and sometimes partaking of the character of almost open hostility'.[88]

Charles Hardinge, one of the most perceptive of foreign observers, agreed, writing at the end of 1904 that in Russia each minister ran

> ... his own Department on his own lines, regardless of his colleagues, his sole object being to obtain the Emperor's favour.... The present ministers are the most worthy and well-disposed lot and individually one can have a certain amount of confidence in them, but there is no cohesion amongst them at all, and consequently they have no real power.[89]

The Far East was widely seen in Russian society as a natural arena for imperial expansion and influence, a sentiment created by a mixture of racial arrogance and shrewd *realpolitik*. Since any expansion in the region would have a vital economic and military dimension, senior officials at the Ministries of War and Finance considered that they had a right to be involved in the making of Russian policy in the region. The Ministry of Finance was headed, at least for the first eight months of 1903, by the bombastically brilliant Sergei Witte, whose enormous energy and ability gave him great influence in St Petersburg. During his ten years at the Ministry of Finance, Witte had turned the institution into a massive and elaborate structure, with representatives posted in many countries where they worked for such pseudo-independent organisations as the Russo-Chinese Bank and the Far Eastern railway.[90] As a result, he often received reports from abroad – and particularly from the Far East and Persia – that were as detailed and reliable as any received by Lamsdorff at the Foreign Ministry. The same was true of General Aleksei Kuropatkin at the Ministry of War, who was sent reports by the commanders of troops deployed along the borders of the Tsarist Empire and, in some cases, actually on foreign soil. In the 'age of imperialism', Russian economic and military penetration of supposedly sovereign countries like Korea and China took place in a way that minimised the influence of the MID on the process, a phenomenon that was compounded by the fact that most senior members of the Foreign Ministry, including Lamsdorff, did not have much real knowledge about Far Eastern affairs. The pattern of bureaucratic politics and information flows made it impossible for the MID to act as a 'gatekeeper' capable of establishing itself as the principal institution determining policy towards the Pacific region.

While the interest of ministries other than the MID in foreign affairs always threatened to create tensions between different parts of the formal ministerial bureaucracy, there was by the beginning of 1903 considerable agreement between Lamsdorff, Witte and Kuropatkin over policy in the Far East (something which had certainly not been true in earlier years). The Foreign Minister's instinctive fear of pursuing policies that might lead to tension with foreign powers was endorsed by the Minister of Finance, who was anxious about the cost of any military conflict which he believed would outweigh the benefits of further expansion in the region. Kuropatkin was also reluctant to support any 'forward' policy that might create a huge strain on Russian forces, with the result that he was willing to countenance a limited withdrawal of troops from Manchuria, something that was fervently desired by most of the other powers who were intensely suspicious of Russian ambitions in the Far East. Nevertheless, while there was a considerable degree of agreement between the triumvirate in the early months of 1903, they were still not able to determine the course of Russian policy in the Far East, a stark illustration of the extent to which foreign policy making could on occasion take place outside the formal ministerial structure.

The most effective way of influencing policy in an autocratic system was to capture the attention of the Tsar and persuade him to adopt a particular course of action. Ministers and other senior officials had to reckon with a whole host of other potential imperial 'advisers', ranging from relatives of the Tsar through to individuals who for some reason or other had ideas or opinions that attracted Nicholas's interest. From the end of the nineteenth century onwards, Nicholas had shown himself to be consistently sympathetic to demands for the adoption of a forward policy in Korea and Manchuria, designed to take advantage of the various economic concessions which had been obtained by Russian merchants and companies there during the previous few years. In the years after the Russo–Japanese War, many of those involved in the débâcle claimed that the conflict was almost entirely brought about by the activities of a handful of 'adventurers', most notably one A.M. Bezobrazov, who persuaded Nicholas to ignore the advice of his ministers and instead support those who sought to advance Russia's economic and political interests in the Far East.[91] Officials in the MID were particularly indignant about the power and influence supposedly wielded by Bezobrazov over foreign policy, although some of them believed that Lamsdorff should have worked harder to assert his views with the Tsar.

While such a judgement was certainly too simplistic, not least because the Foreign Minister did threaten to resign on a number of occasions over the issue of policy in the Far East,[92] the personalised structure of decision-making in St Petersburg undoubtedly helped to create a climate in which an individual who commanded the support of the Emperor could carry a great deal of weight, even when advocating policies opposed by the responsible minister. Bezobrazov attended many of the critical meetings at which policy in the Far East was decided, both in St Petersburg and in the region itself, making it difficult for ministers to ignore the ideas and recommendations of an individual known to command Nicholas's personal support. Witte later recalled that in retrospect 'two currents became clearly distinguishable in our Far-Eastern policy: one, official, represented by the Ministers and moderate in character, the other, secret, inspired by Bezobrazov and led by the Emperor himself'.[93] Bezobrazov was even on occasion given confidential instructions by the Tsar which were not made known to Lamsdorff and his staff – a clear recipe for chaos and confusion in the management and implementation of foreign policy.

The eclipse of the MID was most starkly illustrated in the second half of 1903, when Nicholas established a new post of Governor-General of the Far East, which gave its holder considerable if ill-defined powers to manage the execution of foreign policy in the region. The change was made without the knowledge of the Ministries of War, Foreign Affairs or Finance.[94] The new Governor-General was in addition given the right to report to the Tsar direct, rather than through the formal ministerial structure. The dismissal of Sergei Witte in August 1903 also played an important role in weakening the authority of the formal ministerial bureaucracy. Witte's enormous energy had made him the most influential of all ministers, despite the fact that his brusque manner often offended Nicholas. The Minister of Finance had cooperated closely with Lamsdorff on matters of foreign policy over the previous few years, on occasion providing the political 'weight' and determination that the Foreign Minister himself lacked. As a result, the Finance Minister's departure almost certainly weakened the position of the MID, despite the fact that the Ministry of Finance was itself a potential institutional rival to the Foreign Ministry. Witte's successor lacked both

The Russian Ministry of Foreign Affairs 159

the energy and dexterity of his predecessor, and the administrative apparatus of the Ministry of Finance in the Far East quickly began to wither and lose its earlier potency. The man appointed to the new post of Governor-General, Admiral E.I. Alexeev, had for some time been considered, at least by Witte and Lamsdorff, as a sympathiser with the forward policies advocated by Bezobrazov (although the influence of Bezobrazov himself was on the wane by the second half of 1903). In the autumn of 1903, the responsibility for supervising the critical negotiations with Japan to resolve the tensions between St Petersburg and Tokyo over developments in the Far East was moved from the Ministry of Foreign Affairs in St Petersburg to Alexeev's headquarters in the region. While Lamsdorff appears to have supported this move, presumably hoping that it would expedite discussions and reduce the burgeoning tension with Tokyo, the decision effectively reduced still further the power of the MID to supervise a critical area of Russian foreign policy. The 'chain of command and flow of diplomatic and other governmental channels remained confused until the outbreak of the Russo-Japanese War' several months later.[95] The representative from the Foreign Ministry posted to Alexeev's headquarters seems to have 'gone native', still further constraining the influence of the Foreign Ministry over the negotiations.[96] The problems were compounded by the fact that Baron Rosen, the diplomat responsible for conducting many of the face-to-face negotiations with the Japanese in Tokyo, was suspicious of *both* Lamsdorff and Alexeev, illustrating once again the extent of divisions within the MID and the difficulties faced by foreign ministers in asserting their will over subordinates based many thousands of miles away.[97] Alexeev's ignorance of diplomatic procedures, combined with his instinctive support for an assertive Russian policy in the Far East, inevitably made the negotiations with the Japanese very difficult. Despite the fact that Russian demands appeared to moderate in the final weeks of 1903, the change was neither large enough nor swift enough to allay Japanese fears, with the result that war broke out at the start of 1904. The bureaucratic fragmentation and rivalry inherent in the tsarist system of government on the eve of the 1905 Revolution created tensions and suspicions that prevented any individual or ministry from being 'in control' of Russian policy in the Far East, while the institutional machinery simply did not exist to establish effective coordination between the interested parties. Political and administrative chaos led to the adoption of policies that proved, in time, to have disastrous consequences for the Tsarist Empire.

160   *Diplomacy Before the Russian Revolution*

Case-Study 2   Izvol'skii and the Anglo–Russian Rapprochement, 1906–7

It has been seen that the launch of the Constitutional Experiment changed the political and administrative environment within which the tsarist Foreign Ministry operated. At the same time, however, while old patterns of behaviour were modified by the development of new institutions and values, the legacy of the past prevented a smooth transition to any stable form of constitutional government. In the years between 1906 and the outbreak of the First World War in 1914, the Russian political and administrative system was in a state of almost permanent evolution.

While the Fundamental Laws published early in 1906 nominally preserved the autocratic powers of the Tsar, they also created new institutions designed to operate with a degree of freedom from imperial control.[98] The revised Council of Ministers was intended by its architects to act as a kind of *ersatz* Cabinet, an institution in which members could collectively discuss important questions of policy. The new Duma was given some limited powers to scrutinise the activities of ministers although, as subsequent events were to show, the deputies lacked any effective means to assert their will. The status of the MID in this new order was profoundly ambiguous. The Ministry's existing internal structure was effectively confirmed, with some minor changes, by means of the 1906 statute discussed earlier. The conduct of foreign affairs was formally deemed to belong to a category of 'excluded' business which meant that, unlike many areas of domestic policy, it could not usually be discussed by the Council of Ministers. In practice, however, the language of the relevant statute was ambiguous, setting down a number of circumstances under which this constraint could be set aside.[99] The Tsar also retained important constitutional powers in the field of foreign affairs, particularly in cases where the ministers were unable to agree about an appropriate course of action. While the new institutions and procedures were intended to establish a more orderly and coordinated system of government, numerous ambiguities remained concerning the management of foreign affairs. The role of the MID in the making of Russian foreign policy remained uncertain and subject to a myriad of personal and political pressures.

Izvol'skii was appointed Foreign Minister in 1906, in part because the Tsar was (uncharacteristically) shrewd enough to recognise that he would cope more effectively than Lamsdorff in the new political and administrative environment. Izvol'skii was inclined to boast about his liberal instincts and his support for the new political order. While he subsequently claimed, rather unconvincingly, that he never wanted to be Foreign Minister,[100] he repeatedly emphasised his readiness to cooperate both with his fellow ministers and with the Duma in conducting Russia's foreign relations. At the same time, however, Izvol'skii came to office with a strong desire to be the driving force behind Russian foreign policy, and believed that the post of Foreign Minister could be used to give its holder powers both over the formal apparatus of diplomacy and the policy making process.[101] While the British Embassy in St Petersburg initially fretted about his supposedly germanophile tendencies,[102] Izvol'skii quickly showed himself ready to push forward the tentative moves towards an Anglo-Russian *entente* that had been made over the previous few years, in the hope that agreement over Asian questions would allow his country to focus its energies on European ones. The problems encountered by the new Foreign Minister in pursuing his chosen policy in 1906-7 were both similar to, and different from, the difficulties faced by Lamsdorff when he dealt with Russia's affairs in the Far East in 1903. Lamsdorff was confronted by a formidable array of individuals and departments anxious to influence Russia's policy towards China and Korea. Izvol'skii also encountered considerable criticism when he sought to promote the agreement with Britain, but the pattern of opposition varied in the two cases, due at least in part to the political and administrative changes that had taken place in the interim. Lamsdorff and his ministerial allies were unable to promote the cause of a cautious policy in the Far East during 1903, largely because the Tsar gave his support to the advocates of a more assertive policy. By contrast, Nicholas was, rhetorically at least, a proponent of the Anglo-Russian rapprochement. And, in any case, the constitutional and political upheavals of 1905-6 had changed the role of the Tsar in the conduct of foreign affairs. It was perhaps for this reason, more than any other, that Izvol'skii was eventually able to establish the bureaucratic and political coalition needed to bring about the agreement with Britain despite its unpopularity in many quarters.

Given the ambiguities inherent in the new constitutional settlement, Izvol'skii could not rely on his position as Foreign Minister to provide him with sufficient authority to lay down the course of Russian foreign policy. It is clear in retrospect, however, that Izvol'skii was more influential during his first year than at any later period of his time in office. The constitutional changes of 1905-6 had set at least some limits on the power of the Tsar while, more importantly, Nicholas's temporary retreat into a private world of family and friends made him less accessible as a patron to those disgruntled with the activities of particular ministers.[103] At the same time, the attention of the Council of Ministers was dominated throughout most of 1906 and 1907 by the domestic condition of the Tsarist Empire: the continuing urban and rural unrest, the decision to prorogue the first and second Dumas, the need to promote land reform, and so forth. It was only when a degree of tranquillity returned to Russia in the final months of 1907 that ministers were able to take a more sustained interest in foreign policy.[104] Nevertheless, while Izvol'skii enjoyed considerable influence over the making of Russian foreign policy during 1906 and 1907, there were still very real constraints on his power. Since the move towards a rapprochement with England ran counter to the instincts of many important figures in Russia, ranging from a number of the grand dukes through to senior members of the tsarist officer corps, the new Foreign Minister had to work hard to win allies and marginalise opponents in order to promote his chosen policy. Starting the talks with Nicolson in the summer of 1906 was in some ways the most straightforward part of the process of negotiating an *entente*. One of the reasons that the negotiations were so protracted was, quite simply, that Izvol'skii had to fight a series of bruising battles with ministers and officials in St Petersburg before he was able to make the kind of proposals that could serve as a basis for agreement with London.[105]

From the moment he took office, Izvol'skii behaved less like a traditional Russian Foreign Minister than most of his predecessors, seeing himself primarily as a member of a new 'Cabinet' (the Council of Ministers) responsible for the general course of government policy rather than as the chief bureaucrat in his Ministry. The Foreign Minister could not rely on the automatic support of his staff at the MID, not least because his trenchant views about the need for institutional reform and changes in personnel alienated many of them.[106] At least some senior officials were also doubtful about the wisdom of placing a rapprochement with Britain at the heart of Russian foreign policy. While it is certainly too simple to divide officials at the MID according to whether they favoured a pro-German or pro-British orientation in Russian foreign policy,[107] a number of them shared the instinctive distrust of Britain that was characteristic of a sizeable section of the tsarist political elite. The First (formerly Asiatic) Department, in particular, was home to a number of officials whose psychology had been forged by the notion that Britain was Russia's natural enemy. Since the Ministry was, as has already been seen, a highly fragmented organisation, in which the formal hierarchy was easily undermined by intrigue, the Foreign Minister had to struggle to overcome what seems to have been a fairly systematic campaign of obstruction against his chosen policy. Izvol'skii subsequently told Georges Louis, who served as French Ambassador in St Petersburg after the departure of Maurice Bompard in 1908, that he had encountered great opposition inside the MID when negotiating the Anglo–Russian *entente*, apparently from officials who felt that the Minister was too ready to make concessions on matters which they considered to be vital to Russia's national interests. Izvol'skii also faced opposition to his policies from some diplomats posted abroad, a particular problem since his authority was at its weakest when dealing with men hundreds or even thousands of miles from the Russian capital.[108] The veteran ambassador at Constantinople, Zinov'ev, was among the most sceptical in his attitude towards a possible Anglo–Russian convention, fearing that it could damage Russia's interests in Persia. In August 1906 he wrote a lengthy memorandum suggesting that Russia should attempt to subordinate 'Persia to our state power', although without actually seizing any territory or removing the appearance of formal independence, precisely the kind of creeping hegemony which so concerned the British.[109] Zinov'ev presumably hoped that his memorandum would encourage Nicholas to put pressure on the Foreign Minister to take a tougher line in his dealings with Nicolson. In reality, however, Foreign Ministry officials in St Petersburg and diplomats at missions abroad were in a weaker position than in previous years when seeking to oppose the policy of their Minister. In the past, they had been able to persuade friends and allies at Court to use their influence to oppose any decisions with which they disagreed, but in the confusion of 1906 and 1907 it was harder for them to pursue this strategy. The change in the institutional and political 'rules of the game' meant that it was no longer so easy for dissenting MID officials and diplomats to find ways of bypassing the foreign minister in order to promote their chosen policy.

While Izvol'skii had to struggle to overcome obstruction inside the MID, his biggest challenge was promoting the cause of the Anglo–Russian convention beyond his Ministry. The strongest opposition was inevitably found among the military, where many senior officers expressed concern about the defence of Russia's strategic interests in the sensitive lands to the north and west of India. The Council of Ministers does not appear to have served as an important collective focus for discussion about foreign affairs during much of 1906 and 1907, although it did become the setting for some determined last minute opposition to the Anglo–Russian convention in the days before it was finally signed. Occasional set-piece conferences brought together the ministers and officials most affected by the negotiations with Britain (a pattern that resembled the *ad hoc* conferences convened in 1903 to discuss Russian policy in the Far East). Between these conferences, Izvol'skii engaged in a strenuous round of letter-writing and private meetings in an effort to persuade sceptics to offer him their support.[110] The strongest card which the Foreign Minister had in his dealings with other senior civilian officials and soldiers was the absence of any viable alternative to making an agreement with Britain over central Asia: he argued, with good cause, that the recent domestic turmoil had left Russia too poor and too weak to risk any major confrontation with such a formidable adversary.[111] While this argument did not cut much ice with the more 'die-hard' members of the General Staff, who were convinced that Russia's possession of large forces close to British India should be used to win leverage in the diplomatic negotiations, it did win a sympathetic hearing among a majority of Izvol'skii's fellow ministers.

There is no space here to review the lengthy battles that Izvol'skii had to wage in the final months of 1906 and the first few months of 1907. The head of the General Staff, General F.F. Palitsyn, worked assiduously to limit the concessions that the Foreign Minister was authorised to make. While Palitsyn sometimes agreed to Izvol'skii's proposals at formal meetings, he waged a private campaign to have them overturned,[112] encouraging influential figures at Court to persuade the Tsar to overrule his Foreign Minister. The tension was particularly acute when the future of Persia was under discussion, since Palitsyn was determined that Russia should have a larger sphere of influence in the country than considered practical by Izvol'skii, who was more attuned to British sensitivities on the matter. It was not, however, only senior military men who sought to slow down the agreement. Even ministers who were genuinely in favour of an agreement, such as the Minister of Trade D.A. Filosofov, had numerous minor concerns about some of the financial details of the agreement. The slowness of Izvol'skii in responding to British proposals – something which was the despair of Nicolson at the British Embassy – was in large part explained by the need for the Foreign Minister to win support in his own capital. Izvol'skii was effectively compelled to conduct two sets of talks in order to secure the Anglo–Russian agreement. The negotiations with Nicolson were in many ways less fraught than the ones he had to conduct with senior ministers and officials on his own side. The juggling act which the Foreign Minister had to perform was a difficult one: he had a good idea of the kinds of proposals and counter-proposals that would be acceptable to the British, which meant that he had to work hard to build a domestic coalition willing to authorise an agreement on such terms. The strategies available to the Foreign Minister when trying to do this were, however, limited. The fluidity of the Russian political system in the wake of the 1905 Revolution made it difficult for Izvol'skii to identify which individuals were likely to support him and which were not. As a result, he was not even certain of winning the approval of his colleagues for the agreement he had negotiated just days before it was due to be initialled.[113] In the end, his success in securing support for a convention with Britain probably reflected the fact that its opponents were even more disoriented than its supporters, and less adept at developing strategies to help them to pursue their cause in the new political environment.

Case-Study 3   The MID in the years before 1914

Izvol'skii's influence on Russian foreign policy started to wane in the months following the establishment of the Anglo–Russian convention. As Stolypin established a pivotal place for himself at the heart of the Russian government, he began to interpret his role as Chairman of the Council of Ministers in an increasingly interventionist manner. The return of a degree of domestic calm also provided ministers with greater opportunities than before to take a more measured interest in general questions of policy. In the words of one distinguished scholar of the period, Stolypin and his eventual successor, V.N. Kokovtsov, joined the Emperor and the Foreign Minister 'as junior members of the triumvirate which ultimately determined questions of foreign policy'.[114] More recent research has shown the depth of the divisions that developed between Stolypin and Izvol'skii about foreign policy, particularly during the crisis over the Austrian annexation of Bosnia–Hercegovina in the autumn of 1908, and suggests that the Chairman of the Council of Ministers became rather more than a 'junior partner' in the policy making process. In a Council of Ministers meeting at the beginning of 1908, both Stolypin and Kokovtsov strongly urged that 'All matters of state importance should be maturely considered in the milieu of the Council of Ministers', in order to avoid a repetition of the chaos of 1904–5 when 'defeat in the Far East [was] provoked in part by the fact that there had been no unity in the milieu of state actors'.[115] The struggle for control over the policy making process was in turn intimately bound up with a disagreement over policy itself. Izvol'skii believed that he could reach an agreement with Aehrenthal in Vienna under which Russia would accept the annexation of the two provinces by Austria in return for support on the question of Russian access to the straits. Stolypin was by contrast far more sceptical about the possibility and value of such a deal. The Foreign Minister certainly kept the Council of Ministers in the dark about his activities whenever possible during the course of 1908, failing to consult his colleagues in any detail prior to his crucial negotiations with Aehrenthal at Buchlau in the autumn.[116] Stolypin and Kokovtsov predictably reacted with fury when they found out that they had been bypassed, angrily recording their 'extreme chagrin...[that they] had found out so late about a matter of such immense historical significance'.[117] The Chairman of the Council of Ministers launched a bitter attack on Izvol'skii, taking the whole matter to the Tsar, with the result that within a few weeks the Council had effectively managed to assert itself in such a way as to limit sharply the Foreign Minister's autonomy during his remaining time in power. During the final stages of the annexationist crisis, Izvol'skii took much more care to keep the Council informed of all his actions.[118]

It was not only the Council of Ministers that served as a potential check on Izvol'skii's freedom to assert himself as the principal architect of Russia's foreign policy during 1908. When Izvol'skii was first appointed Foreign Minister in 1906, he quickly signalled his readiness to cooperate with deputies in the newly-convened Duma on questions of foreign affairs, a testimony to the liberal instincts about which the Foreign Minister was so fond of boasting. The first two Dumas were in practice too preoccupied with domestic policy to pay much attention to events beyond Russia's borders, but the election of a third Duma on a restricted franchise in the second half of 1907 signalled the emergence of an institution whose members were determined to impose some effective check on ministers. Izvol'skii continued to indicate that he was willing to operate within the spirit of the new constitutional arrangements, giving interviews to selected journalists and establishing a special Press Bureau to manage the MID's relations with newspapers and members of the Duma.[119] In the course of 1908, however, the Foreign Minister increasingly fell foul of some of the more articulate members of the Duma, despite his best efforts to establish his liberal credentials in the public mind. During a debate that took place in February 1908 on the role and organisation of the MID, one of the leading members of the Octobrist Party, A.I. Guchkov, proposed a reduction in the budget appropriation for the Tokyo Embassy – a gesture calculated to emphasise the Duma's (constitutionally questionable) right to be involved in discussion of foreign affairs. In the following months, as already noted, Izvol'skii became less willing than before to speak openly about his policies, particularly on the vexed question of Bosnia–Hercegovina, frankly telling a journalist from *Novoe Vremia* that he intended to keep his own counsel on the subject. The furore that followed this announcement in the press resembled many of the attacks made on the old diplomacy in Britain during the same period. *Rech'* carried several articles condemning Izvol'skii for his reluctance to talk openly about his programme, and attacked the Foreign Minister's Balkan policy as a source of possible disaster in the months ahead. *Novoe Vremia* followed suit, calling for greater openness and public debate about foreign affairs.[120] In the next few weeks, numerous public meetings were held in Moscow and St Petersburg on the subject of the international crisis. Luminaries of the liberal movement such as Paul Miliukov spoke on such topics as the 'Position in the Balkans' and 'Bosnia–Hercegovina under Austrian rule'. In December 1908, a further debate in the Duma on foreign affairs signalled that many deputies were more determined than ever to assert themselves in the international arena, although by now Stolypin and other senior ministers were themselves anxious to restrain such hopes, doubtless because they were reluctant to accept any constraints on their own burgeoning role in the foreign policy making process. While the Foreign Minister had succeeded in maximising his autonomy against a range of counterveiling pressures during his first year in office, the growing assertiveness of other individuals and institutions in the course of 1908 made it impossible for him to continue to enjoy such a degree of authority over the policy making process.

The Foreign Ministry which Sergei Sazonov inherited from Izvol'skii in 1910 bore a striking similarity to the one which Izvol'skii had himself inherited from Lamsdorff in 1906, despite the attempts at reform set in motion by the Gubastov Commission. The MID lacked a well-defined institutional architecture, while the operation of the formal structure was frequently undermined by conflicts of personality and disagreements over policy. At the same time, the influence of the MID in the wider political arena was conditioned by patterns of political change over which its senior members had little control. The nature of the decision-making process in St Petersburg during the critical years before the outbreak of war in 1914 was therefore governed both by a struggle between competing institutions and individuals, as well as by the dictates of an increasingly unpredictable international environment. Sazonov's ability to thrive in such a turbulent world was in part dependent on his own administrative and political prowess, but he was never in a position to ensure that the MID was the undisputed location for authoritative decisions about policy.

Sazonov took office well-prepared for his new role. Educated at the Imperial *Lycée*, he had held senior diplomatic positions at such major embassies as London, as well as serving for some time as Izvol'skii's deputy in St Petersburg. As a result, he had both a good knowledge of the complexities of international politics and a familiarity with the bureaucratic and political intricacies of the policy making process in the capital. The new Foreign Minister shared Izvol'skii's belief that his country's major focus should be on European affairs rather than on central Asia or the Far East. He was considerably influenced by the ideas of the liberal slavophile, Prince G.N. Trubetskoi, who wrote copiously on foreign affairs before rejoining the Foreign Ministry in 1912. Trubetskoi was strongly convinced that the major threat both to international peace and Russia's security came from Germany, and was as a result staunchly committed to the French alliance and the *entente* with Britain, believing that only a combination of these three powers could provide a suitable counterweight to Berlin.[121] He was also a determined advocate of the importance of demonstrating Russia's determination to resist the expansion of Austrian influence in the Balkans.

Trubetskoi's ideas were largely formulated during the years before he rejoined the MID at Sazonov's invitation in 1912, with the result that they were articulated in a far more coherent fashion than those of most of his colleagues. Sazonov himself did not agree with Trubetskoi on all questions, responding instead in an essentially *ad hoc* manner to the pressure of changing circumstances. Nevertheless, fear of Germany and suspicion of Austrian intentions in the Balkans were pronounced features in the Foreign Minister's mental map of the European political scene. They were not, however, shared by all his compatriots. In the last few years before 1914, discussion about Russia's foreign policy became a central theme in domestic political debate, a striking testimony to the increasingly open political environment which emerged in the wake of the 1905 Revolution. It is as ever tempting to reduce the complicated and often inarticulate debate over Russian foreign policy during these years to a simple argument about 'orientation', but in practice the policies favoured by particular individuals and insititutions frequently shifted over time and in response to changing circumstance. Nevertheless, the noisy discussion about foreign policy in pre-war Russia was in large part a result of deep-seated disagreements about fundamental principles and values, a conflict which helped to fuel the contours of the complex political and bureaucratic struggle that determined the role of the MID in the policy making process during the years immediately before 1914.

A good deal has been written about the impact of panslav sentiment on Russian foreign policy during Sazonov's tenure as Foreign Minister.

There is certainly something beguiling about the argument that the rise in panslavism in Russia fuelled the fatal conflict with Austria in the Balkans that eventually exploded into war. In reality, however, it is always hard to identify in a concrete manner how Russian foreign policy was actually affected by some nebulous sense of solidarity with nations such as the Serbs or the Bulgarians.[122] The plight of Orthodox Christians under Turkish rule had certainly attracted sympathy in Russian society for many centuries, while the status of the Slavic populations in the Hapsburg Empire had been a focus of interest for the slavophile movement since the middle of the nineteenth century. Even so, while influential journalists such as Mikhail Katkov had assiduously attempted to fan the flames of panslavism in the late nineteenth century, it was generally frowned upon in official circles, where there was a widespread recognition that it could come into conflict with the principle of dynastic legitimacy. The establishment of the Duma and a free press after 1905 certainly provided new forums where panslav sentiment could be articulated, which in turn created additional sources of pressure on the MID and other important individual and institutional actors involved in the foreign policy making process. Nor is there any doubt that a number of individuals who were in a position to exercise considerable influence on the Tsar were instinctively receptive to panslav ideals – ideals which also struck an echo among a large section of the tsarist officer corps. Nevertheless, it is always difficult to separate the somewhat inchoate influence of panslavism on policy from that of a more traditional Russian nationalism which, whether in its traditional–conservative or liberal–imperialist guise, was always a powerful sentiment among the various elites of late imperial Russia.

The problem of distinguishing between panslavism and conventional nationalism is particularly problematic when looking at the currents of debate *within* the MID itself. While the diffuse anti-Austrian sentiment that became more and more powerful in the Foreign Ministry following the débacle of 1908–9 appears on the surface to echo the growing popularity of panslav sentiment in the wider society, it can also be interpreted as little more than an expression of a traditional nationalist desire to defend and promote the interests of the Tsarist Empire. Once Izvol'skii and Sazonov attempted to move the focus of Russian foreign policy westwards, conflict was always most likely to break out in the Balkans, where both the Hapsburg and Romanov empires could legitimately claim to have vital interests. Nowhere is the confusion clearer than in the case of Hartwig, who became Minister in Belgrade in 1909 following his tempestuous years in Tehran. His determined support for the Serbian cause undoubtedly played an important role in destabilising the situation in the Balkans, since he gave the government in Belgrade the impression that they could rely on Russian diplomatic support in any future conflict in the region. Hartwig's detestation of Austria has often been interpreted as a manifestation of a powerful panslav instinct. In reality, however, during his earlier years as Minister in Tehran and Director of the First (Asiatic) Department in St Petersburg, his main concern had been with Russia's situation in central Asia (most notably *vis à vis* Britain). The most striking theme in Hartwig's career was in reality his fervent defence of Russian state interests in whatever sphere for which he happened to be responsible. None of this is to deny that he was willing on occasion to exploit the rhetoric of panslavism, but it does call into doubt whether such a sentiment should be understood as the key to his outlook and behaviour. What is certain, however, is that the Minister in Belgrade was able to use both his connections at Court and his geographical remoteness from St Petersburg to pursue a more overtly pro-Serbian policy than Sazonov, or indeed most other Russian diplomats in the Balkans, were willing to countenance. He also assiduously cultivated close contacts with *Novoe Vremia*, which became for a time the standard-bearer of panslav and anti-Austrian sentiment, allowing him to exercise considerable influence on a wider public opinion.[123] The perennial divisions within the Foreign Ministry continued to create tensions and uncertainties under Sazonov just at they had under his predecessor.

While Sazonov himself was certainly no rabid panslav, he was instinctively suspicious of the growing closeness between Vienna and Berlin, which in turn made him a strong proponent of the need to build good relations with Paris and London. An instinctive germanophilism had, by contrast, long been a hallmark of many members of the tsarist bureaucratic elite. Count Witte had for years favoured improved relations with Berlin, believing that an alliance with Germany and France provided the best guarantee of Russia's security and prosperity, but his influence on policy was very limited following his dismissal as Chairman of the Council of Ministers in 1906. In the five years before the outbreak of war in 1914, pro-German sentiment began to fade steadily among large sections of the tsarist elite, fuelled less by any widespread enthusiasm for the alliance with France and the *entente* with Britain than by resentment against Berlin's strong diplomatic support for the government in Vienna over events in the Balkans. Nevertheless, even on the eve of war, newspapers such as *Grazhdanin* continued to run articles calling for closer relations with Berlin. In February 1914, the

Minister of the Interior, P.N. Durnovo, wrote a celebrated memorandum for the Tsar warning against the danger of a 'profoundly undesirable' war with Germany, which he feared would lead to major domestic disorder.[124] Such sentiments also continued to strike an echo among at least some senior members of the Foreign Ministry. While it is difficult to classify individual officials and diplomats according to their preferred international orientation, Sazonov always had to reckon with at least some subordinates who were pro-German in their instincts. By itself, of course, this was not necessarily a problem; similar divisions could probably be found in all the major European diplomatic establishments during the period. Nevertheless, the fragmented organisational structure of the MID always raised the prospect that any individual official or diplomat who disagreed with the Foreign Minister might seek to bypass the formal hierarchy and ignore instructions, in exactly the same way that Hartwig was inclined to do during his years in Belgrade.

Sazonov did of course have considerable resources which he could call on when trying to assert his own authority both within and beyond his Ministry. He was, as already noted, an intelligent individual with good experience both of the diplomatic world and the bureaucratic milieu of St Petersburg. The Foreign Minister was more successful than his predecessor at winning the support of officials in the central Ministry, although he still had a difficult time ensuring that diplomats in post abroad carried out their instructions properly. Sazonov was also willing to devolve authority within the Ministry to those who dealt with issues that were peripheral to the main political issues of the day, allowing him to focus his attention on the most important questions. He was, for example, ready to allow the head of the Far Eastern Section enormous freedom to determine Russian policy in the region, since it was no longer deemed to be of such vital concern for Russia's national security and economic welfare. Beyond the Ministry, Sazonov was helped in his early days in office by his close relationship with Stolypin – the two men were brothers-in-law – which helped to prevent the eruption of many of the tensions and suspicions that undermined Izvol'skii's position in 1908. Sazonov's relationship with the Emperor was also surprisingly good. Some of the Foreign Minister's contemporaries even believed that the Foreign Ministry acquired its greatest prestige and independence in the years before 1914. One senior diplomat wrote in his memoirs that following Stolypin's assassination in 1911, foreign policy 'remained solely within the province of the Foreign Office. Sazonoff... was henceforth entirely under the influence of his own environment, and all his decisions were arrived at in select committees of a few collaborators'.[125] In reality, of course, the complex constellation of pressures identified above always placed real constraints on the MID's freedom of action. Senior officials had to be cognisant of the likely reaction of other officials, newspaper editors, army officers, Duma representatives and the Court when considering any particular course of action. In the critical year before the outbreak of war, several high-level conferences were summoned in St Petersburg to discuss foreign policy, which were attended by a large number of ministers and generals.[126] While such conferences might have helped to promote greater coordination at the heart of the Russian government, they inevitably provided a forum which allowed those outside the MID to have an input into decisions about foreign policy. The Russian Foreign Ministry was a major actor in the foreign policy making process in the years between the resignation of Izvol'skii and the start of hostilities in 1914; it was never the dominant one.

The previous pages have shown that there were both continuities and changes in the organisation and operation of the Russian Ministry of Foreign Affairs during the years before 1914. The internal structure of the Ministry went through a number of modifications, while much larger changes took place in the fabric of the political and administrative system in which it was embedded. At the same time, however, the influence of the Ministry on policy, along with that of particular officials within it, always depended on the outcome of a complex series of political and bureaucratic conflicts. Changes in the organisation of the Ministry and the character of the Russian constitution simply provided a shifting backdrop to a continuous struggle for the power and authority to determine the country's foreign policy. The previous pages have also shown how difficult it is to locate the Russian diplomatic establishment within the critical paradigm of old diplomacy constructed by writers and politicians across the continent during the early years of the twentieth century. As was the case in Britain, members of the Russian Foreign Ministry were drawn disproportionately from among those boasting good social connections and a privileged educational background. There is also no doubt that a distressingly large proportion of those who made a career in the Foreign Ministry were neither intellectually talented nor particularly dedicated to their work. At the same time, however, tsarist Russia produced many diplomats and officials who were as well-versed in the complexities of international affairs as any of those who inhabited the *Quai d'Orsay* or the Foreign Office. The organisation and operation of the Russian diplomatic establishment, like its British counterpart, changed considerably in the years before 1914 in response to a whole set of political and administrative pressures.

NOTES

1. The best 'political' biography of Nicholas II is Dominic Lieven, *Nicholas II: Tsar of All the Russias*.
2. The most comprehensive account of the political changes after 1906 can be found in Geoffrey Hosking, *The Russian Constitutional Experiment*.
3. For a useful review of the changing pattern of foreign policy making in Russia during the years before 1914, see David Maclaren McDonald, *United Government and Foreign Policy in Russia, 1900–1914*.
4. Andrew D. Kalmykow (Kalmykov) *Memoirs of a Russian Diplomat*, p. 18.
5. The best argument along these lines can be found in I.V. Bestuzhev, *Bor'ba v Rossii po voprosom vneshnei politiki, 1906–1910*.
6. *Novoe Vremia*, 20 August 1907.
7. *Rech'*, 23 June 1907 (old style).
8. *Novoe Vremia*, 20 January 1908.
9. *Novoe Vremia*, 13 May 1909.
10. *Novoe Vremia*, 13 May 1909.
11. Baron M. de Taube, *La politique Russe d'avant guerre et la fin de l'empire des tsars*, pp. 92–3.
12. For details, see Iu.Ia. Solov'ev, *Vospominaniia diplomata*, pp. 206–18.
13. On the Gubastov reforms, see G.H. Bolsover, 'Izvolsky and Reform of the Russian Ministry of Foreign Affairs', *Slavonic and East European Review*, 63, 1 (1985), pp. 21–40.
14. For a history of the MID, see *Ocherk istorii ministerstva inostrannykh del*; a brief history in English can be found in Teddy J. Ulrichs, 'The Tsarist and Soviet Ministry of Foreign Affairs', in Zara Steiner (ed.), *The Times Survey of Foreign Ministries*, pp. 513–38.
15. *The Memoirs of Dmitrii I. Abrikossow*, pp. 92–3.
16. *Novoe Vremia*, 13 May 1909.
17. Baron R.R. Rosen, *Forty Years of Diplomacy*, Vol. 1, p. 65.
18. Reforms made to the First Department by Izvol'skii, which effectively split it into three parts, may have made officials there more responsive to the Minister, but they did little by themselves to resolve the problems of overlap and duplication.
19. See, for example, *Sobranie tsirkularov ministerstva inostrannykh del po departamentu lichnogo sostava i khoziaistvennykh del 1840–1908*, p. 209.
20. See, for example, *Novoe Vremia*, 20 August 1907; 7 July 1909 (reacting to proposals for reform).

174   Diplomacy Before the Russian Revolution

21. Rosen, *Forty Years*, Vol. 1, p. 18.
22. P.S. Botkin, *Kartinki diplomaticheskoi zhizni*, p. 19ff.
23. Botkin, *Kartinki*, p. 21.
24. See Max Weber, *The Theory of Social and Economic Organisation*, pp. 329–41.
25. Helen Dittmer, *The Russian Foreign Ministry Under Nicholas II, 1894–1914*, pp. 158–9.
26. For a somewhat different view, emphasising the importance of the 'seniority principle' in promotions, see Dittmer, *The Russian Foreign Ministry under Nicholas II, 1894–1914, passim*.
27. Kalmykov, *Memoirs*, p. 20.
28. Solov'ev, *Vospominaniia*, p. 27; for a somewhat more positive view of Kapnist, see Kalmykov, *Memoirs*, p. 27.
29. 'Iz dnevnika V.N. Lamzdorfa', *Voprosy istorii*, 6 (1977), pp. 110–12.
30. Kalmykov, *Memoirs*, p. 139.
31. Botkin, *Kartinki*, pp. 28–9.
32. Abrikossov, *Revelations*, p. 3.
33. Nicholas de Basily, *Memoirs*, p. 3.
34. Kalmykov, *Memoirs*, p. 13.
35. For a useful description of the range of people in the MID, see Botkin, *Kartinki*, p. 28.
36. *Svod rasporiazhenii ministerstva inostrannykh del*, pp. 1–5.
37. A useful comparison of the various recruitment mechanisms for the major European diplomatic establishments can be found in *BPP, 1912–13*, 58 (cd 6100, cd 6268).
38. Abrikossov, *Revelations*, p. 80.
39. On the curriculum of the *Lycée*, see D.C.B. Lieven, *Russia and the Origins of the First World War*, pp. 83–9. A good deal of useful information about the *Lycée* can also be found in Chapter 2 of Dittmer, *Foreign Ministry*.
40. Abrikossov, *Revelations*, p. 85.
41. Botkin, *Kartinki*, p. 28.
42. Kalmykov, *Memoirs*, p. 13.
43. There was some division among MID officials about Lamsdorff's understanding of international politics. For a strong criticism of Lamsdorff, see Rosen, *Forty Years* Vol. 1, pp. 174–5; for a predictably more positive view, see A. Savinsky, *Recollections*, *passim*.
44. Kalmykov, *Memoirs*, p. 23.
45. For Taube's career at the MID, see Taube, *La politique Russe*.
46. Useful information can be found on this topic in Dittmer, *Foreign Ministry*, esp. Chapter 3.
47. The Madrid Embassy was opened in 1896; the Washington D.C. Embassy in 1898.
48. The following information is compiled from the *Ezhegodnik ministerstva inostrannykh del* (various dates); also from *Spisok vysshim chinam*.
49. *Rech'*, 23 June 1907 (old style).
50. *Ocherk istorii MID*, pp. 205–6.
51. *Novoe Vremia*, 13 May 1909.
52. Abrikossov, *Revelations*, p. 99.

The Russian Ministry of Foreign Affairs 175

53. *Ocherk istorii MID* (appendices).
54. Abrikossov, *Revelations*, p. 98; Rosen, *Forty Years*, Vol. 1, p. 103.
55. See, for example, Alexandre Meyendorff (ed.), *Correspondance diplomatique de Baron de Staal*, Vol. 2, Staal to Murav'ev, 3 March 1897; Staal to Murav'ev, 23 November 1897.
56. Abrikossov, *Revelations*, p. 101.
57. Abrikossov, *Revelations*, p. 106.
58. Staal, *Correspondance*, Vol. 2, Staal to Murav'ev, 20 December 1899.
59. Constantin Nabokoff (Konstantin Nabokov), *Ordeal of a Diplomat*, p. 56.
60. 'Sekretnaia zapiska I.A. Zinov'eva ot 25 avgusta', *Krasnyi arkhiv* 69–70 (1935), pp. 5–18.
61. *Novoe Vremia*, 19 March 1908, 13 May 1909.
62. *Svod rasporiazhenii ministerstva inostrannykh del*, p. 7.
63. Figures compiled from the *Ezhegodnik MID* for 1894.
64. *Sbornik konsul'skikh donesenii (1898)* (various reports).
65. Nabokov, *Ordeal of a Diplomat*, p. 18.
66. Nabokov, *Ordeal of a Diplomat*, p. 20.
67. Firuz Kazemzadeh, *Russia and Britain in Persia, 1864–1914*, p. 412.
68. Kazemzadeh, *Russia, Britain and Persia*, pp. 419–20.
69. 'Tsirkulary departamenta lichnogo sostava i khoziaistvennykh del ministerstva inostrannykh del', in *Izvestiia ministerstva inostrannykh del*, Book 3 (1913), p. 137ff.
70. *Izv. MID*, Book 4 (1913), pp. 93–110.
71. See *Kratkii obzor donesenii imperatorskikh rossiiskikh konsul'skikh predstavitelei za granitsei*.
72. Kalmykov, *Memoirs*, p. 140.
73. Abrikossov, *Revelations*, p. 85.
74. A. Savinsky, *Recollections of a Russian Diplomat*, p. 15.
75. Bestuzhev, *Bor'ba*, p. 129.
76. Maurice Bompard, *Mon ambassade en Russie (1903–1908)*, p. 4.
77. *Memoirs of Alexander Iswolski*, pp. 266–7.
78. For a broadly positive view of Lobanov-Rostovskii from one of his staff, see Rosen, *Forty Years*, Vol. 1, pp. 103–5. For a somewhat hagiographic portrait, see V. Teplov, *Kniaz' Aleksei Borisovich Lobanov-Rostovskii*.
79. For two views of Kapnist, see footnote 28.
80. Solov'ev, *Vospominaniia*, p. 27.
81. Sazonov, *Fateful Years*, p. 21.
82. *Ezhegodnik MID* (1894), p. 152.
83. A. Nekludoff, *Diplomatic Reminiscences Before and During the World War, 1911–1917*, p. 2.
84. Bestuzhev, *Bor'ba*, pp. 132–3.
85. See Zinov'ev, *Sekretnaia zapiska*.
86. Kazemzadeh, *Russia and Britain in Persia*, p. 481.
87. The most accessible account of the origins of the Russo–Japanese War can be found in Ian Nish, *The Origins of the Russo-Japanese War*. Other valuable accounts include Andrew Malozemoff, *Russian Far Eastern Policy 1881–1904*; useful material about the foreign policy making process in Russia during the period can be found in McDonald, *United Government*, pp. 31–75.

176   Diplomacy Before the Russian Revolution

88. Rosen, *Forty Years*, Vol. 1, p. 190.
89. FO 800/141, Hardinge to Lansdowne, 6 December 1904.
90. Witte's own recollections of this period are usefully set down in *The Memoirs of Count Witte*.
91. See, for example, Savinsky, *Recollections*, p. 42ff.
92. Savinsky, *Recollections*, p. 45ff.
93. Witte, *Memoirs*, p. 119.
94. Witte, *Memoirs*, p. 123.
95. Malozemoff, *Russian Far Eastern Policy*, p. 224.
96. The views of the MID official attached to Alexeev's HQ, E.A. Planson, can be found in his diary published in *Krasnyi Arkhiv*, 41–42 (1930), pp. 148–204.
97. Rosen, *Forty Years*, Vol. 1, p. 218.
98. The text and a detailed analysis of the new constitution is contained in Marc Szeftel, *The Russian Constitution of April 23, 1906*.
99. M.F. Florinskii, 'Sovet ministrov i ministerstvo inostrannykh del v 1907–1914 gg', in *Vestnik Leningradskogo Universiteta. Ser. istoriia, iazyk, literatura*, 2 (1978), pp. 35–6.
100. *Memoirs of Iswolsky*, pp. 38–9.
101. Bestuzhev, *Bor'ba*, pp. 128–9.
102. FO 800/72, Spring Rice to Grey, 24 May 1906.
103. For a rather different view of Nicholas's role in the year leading up to the Anglo–Russian *entente* from the one offered here, emphasising in particular the Tsar's role in approving Izvol'skii's plans, see A.V. Ignat'ev, *Vneshniaia politika Rossii v 1905–1907gg*, esp. pp. 131–8 and 181–95. Ignat'ev does seem to acknowledge, however, that Nicholas played little role in the day-to-day aspect of the negotiations.
104. For further details on the growing involvement of the chairman of the Council of Ministers in the conduct of foreign affairs, see David Maclaren McDonald, 'A.P. Izvol'skii and Russian Foreign Policy Under "United Government"', in Robert B. McKean (ed.), *New Perspectives in Modern Russian History*, pp. 174–202.
105. For a somewhat different view, stressing the high level of elite support for Izvol'skii's position on Anglo–Russian relations, see McDonald, *United Government*, pp. 108–111.
106. For a somewhat different view, see Savinsky, *Recollections*, pp. 136–7.
107. For useful comments on this theme, see Bestuzhev, *Bor'ba*, p. 137.
108. For Izvol'skii's attempts to win the support of key ambassadors abroad, see Bestuzhev, *Bor'ba*, p. 129.
109. Zinov'ev, *Sekretnaia zapiska*, p. 13.
110. Bestuzhev, *Bor'ba*, p. 137–8.
111. See, for example, the account of a Special Meeting about the negotiations over Afghanistan held on 14 April 1907, published in *Krasnyi Arkhiv*, 69–70 (1935), pp. 25–32, esp. p. 26.
112. *Krasnyi Arkhiv* 69–70 (1935), pp. 19–25; Bestuzhev, *Bor'ba*, p. 139 ff.
113. On the tensions during the final days leading up to the signing of the agreement, see 'Zhurnal zasedaniia osobogo soveshchaniia 11 avgusta 1907g o zakliuchenii s Anglieiu soglasheniia po voprosu ob Afganistane', *Krasnyi Arkhiv*, 69–70 (1935), pp. 32–9.

The Russian Ministry of Foreign Affairs 177

114. Lieven, *Russia and the Origins of the First World War*, p. 60.
115. McDonald, 'A.P. Izvol'skii', p. 188.
116. Lieven, *Origins*, p. 60.
117. McDonald, 'A.P Izvol'skii', p. 174.
118. Kokovtsov, *Out of My Past*, pp. 216–17.
119. See Solov'ev, *Vospominaniia diplomata*, pp. 206–18.
120. Bestuzhev, *Bor'ba*, pp. 101–2.
121. The remainder of this paragraph is taken from Lieven, *Origins*, pp. 95–101.
122. A useful general history of panslavism can be found in Hans Kohn, *Panslavism: Its History and Ideology*.
123. Nekludoff, *Diplomatic Reminiscences*, p. 48.
124. 'Durnovo's Advice to the Tsar in February 1914', in George Vernadsky (ed.), *A Source Book for Russian History from Early Times to 1917*, Vol. 3, pp. 793–8.
125. Nekludoff, *Diplomatic Reminiscences*, p. 33.
126. For reports of some of these meetings, see Friedrich Stieve, *Isvolsky and the World War*, pp. 219–46.

6 The British and Russian Diplomatic Establishments 1914–17

The organisation and operation of the British and Russian diplomatic establishments changed considerably during the First World War, a period that proved to be a critical phase in the disintegration of the old diplomacy. The conduct of the war became a major concern for governments and publics alike, making it even harder than before for national diplomatic establishments to claim a central role in the formulation and execution of policy. At the same time, the enormous impact of military developments on the international arena increased the influence of the military on the foreign policy making process. The institutions and procedures associated with the organisation of international life before 1914 could not survive this barrage of changes unscathed, something that was particularly striking in the context of the Anglo–Russian relationship.

The development of alliance politics exercised a profound impact on the relationship between Britain and Russia, since the dictates of war created a much greater density of official contacts between the two countries than had existed in peace time. New forums and mechanisms had to be devised for promoting cooperation across a range of areas, including military strategy, the production of war materials, and the implementation of financial arrangments to pay for the war. Politicians and bureaucrats from the two countries met far more regularly than in pre-war years in an effort to resolve the numerous problems that could undermine military success. This increase in the flow of personnel between London and Petrograd provided a direct challenge to the authority of the British and Russian diplomatic establishments. Diplomats found that they were no longer necessarily the main conduit for transmitting information about the local political scene back to their respective governments, while officials serving in the two central ministries had to adapt to a situation in which bureaucrats in other ministries might well have opportunities to acquire information or to develop insights that were denied to the foreign affairs 'professionals'. Officials working in the formal institutions of international diplomacy could attempt to establish their status as the principal agents responsible for *coordinating* the relationship between London and Petrograd, but the complexity and fluidity of alliance politics made it difficult for them to secure such a role. Other factors also increased the momentum for change to the traditional pattern of international diplomacy. In Britain, the emergence of such organisations as the Union of Democratic Control increased the rhetorical barrage directed against traditional diplomatic institutions and practices, a rhetoric that was seen in a previous chapter to have spilled over into the political mainstream. In Russia, the rise of the revolutionary left helped to foster the growth of anti-establishment feeling. While the 'defencist' left supported the war against the central powers, its principal representatives were keen to emphasise that they were not simply uncritically endorsing the war aims of the tsarist government; the internationalist left went further, condemning the whole war as a struggle for imperial dominance which was of no concern to the working class across Europe. In the Duma, liberal members of the Progressive Block kept up a chorus of criticism against the government which damaged the prestige of all ministers. The war created a whole kaleidoscope of political and administrative pressures to which members of the British and Russian diplomatic establishments were forced to respond.

THE EMBASSIES

The size of the official Russian presence in London expanded enormously during the First World War, an increase that created a crisis at the Embassy in Mayfair, which was not big enough to cope with the influx. By the start of 1917, around 500 Russian soldiers and sailors were serving in Britain. Some of them spent their time liaising with the British government on purely strategic matters, but a considerable number were responsible for the difficult task of obtaining extra supplies of munitions to deal with the 'shell crisis' which dogged the Russian armies more or less from the start of the war. Since the British were desperate to promote the effectiveness of the tsarist military on the battlefield, in order to prevent German units from being transferred to the Western Front, the government in London was willing to go to considerable lengths to provide St Petrograd with the financial and material wherewithal to keep its armies in the field. Senior officials from the Russian Ministry of Finance frequently visited London to discuss the provision of loans to allow Russia to buy extra munitions on the international market. The Minister of Finance himself, P.L. Bark, came to Britain to conduct in person some of the negotiations which led up to the Treasury Agreement of September 1915, which provided Russia with the money needed to pay for extra supplies of munitions. Organising these visits created a great deal of extra work for staff at the Russian Embassy in London, on top of their existing duties, which added to the strain under which they operated throughout the war years.

The eclectic nature of the official Russian presence in London naturally had an impact on the operation of the Embassy. New committees were set up to facilitate Anglo–Russian cooperation, particularly on the vexed question of the purchase of war material for use on the Eastern Front.[1] Senior staff at the Embassy, including the commercial secretary M.V. Rutkovskii and the military attaché Lieutenant-General N.S. Ermolov, served on the *Commission Internationale de Ravitaillment*, which was responsible for harmonising the purchase and supply of war material between the allied governments. A separate Russian Government Committee was established at the start of 1915, under the chairmanship of General Timchenko-Ruban, which was responsible for bringing greater order to Russia's purchase of munitions in Britain. Despite these initiatives, however, the situation remained chaotic, and in June 1915 the Secretary of State for War, Lord Kitchener, established a new Russian Purchasing Committee staffed by both British and Russian members. Senior tsarist army officers such as Admiral A.I. Rusin also continued to visit London from time to time in an effort to streamline the purchase of war material. A majority of those who staffed these various committees and commissions were not regular members of the Russian Embassy in London, while those who were often found it difficult to find the time to carry out all their new duties. In any case, the Embassy staff most involved in the various initiatives to bring order to the purchase of munitions were seldom career diplomats. Rutkovskii as Commercial Secretary was by background a member of the Ministry of Trade, while the first loyalty of the military and naval attachés was to the Russian Ministry of War in Petrograd rather than to the ambassador in London. Many members of such bodies as the Russian Government Committee had good links with senior officials and ministers back in Petrograd, which in turn fostered the development of new direct channels of communication outside the formal diplomatic structure, eclipsing the Embassy still further in a critical sphere of Anglo–Russian relations. While there was no well-defined and deliberate challenge to the authority of the Russian Embassy in London, the diplomats who worked there certainly faced a degree of marginalisation in the new institutional and administrative environment.

Count Benckendorff was not by instinct inclined to adapt himself to the new pattern of alliance politics, with its characteristic emphasis on technical and financial questions. He had never been fond of dealing with mundane administrative matters of any kind even before the outbreak of war, preferring to delegate them whenever possible to his subordinates. He did play a part in the Russian government's repeated attempts to raise money on the London capital markets during the war years, using his extensive contacts among the British establishment to smooth the process along, and sharply criticising the Finance Ministry in Petrograd for its hesitation in accepting the terms of a loan offered by Barings Bank.[2] Benckendorff seldom participated in negotiations over details, however, leaving them either to Rutkovskii or to senior officials from the Ministry of Finance who periodically travelled from Petrograd to London for the purpose. Nor was he very involved in the attempts that were made to bring order to Russia's purchase of munitions in the west.[3] While Benckendorff was from the start of the war concerned about the confusion surrounding the purchase of armaments,[4] he showed little sustained interest in the work of the committees which were established in London to resolve the problem. He dutifully reported back to Sazonov the details of conversations he had on the subject with ministers such as Lloyd George and Kitchener,[5] but he seldom spent much time trying to grapple with the difficulties himself. The Ambassador preferred to focus his energies on more conventional 'diplomatic' questions, such as the war aims of the allies and the bitter struggle between combattant governments for the support of the various neutral countries, which took place during the early years of the war. He continued to provide Sazonov with the benefit of his advice on a whole range of international problems, even though it seems certain that the Foreign Minister did not always want it![6] Nor does Sazonov seem to have consulted very much with Benckendorff on such important questions as Russia's claim to Constantinople and the Straits, put forward in March 1915, even though it clearly had a critical impact on the Anglo–Russian relationship. The two men also differed sharply about such matters as the commitments that should be made to Italy in return for that country's entry into the war on the side of the Triple Alliance.[7] As a result of these developments, the influence of Benckendorff and his Embassy on the deliberations of policy makers in Petrograd declined markedly in the years after 1914. The changing texture of the bilateral relationship between London and Petrograd shifted the focus of attention away from the traditional agenda of 'high politics' with which Benckendorff was most comfortable, moving it towards technical and financial questions that were beyond the competence of most diplomats.

The British Embassy in Petrograd faced many of the same problems as its Russian counterpart in London. The size of the official British presence in the Russian capital expanded enormously during the war years.[8] New organisations were established such as the Anglo–Russian Press Bureau, headed by the novelist Hugh Walpole, which was charged among other tasks with persuading the Russian public that Britain was providing its ally with all possible military and financial assistance.[9] The British Intelligence Mission to Russia, led during 1916–17 by the Conservative MP Samuel Hoare, was set up to liaise with the Russian authorities about the collection of secret intelligence material on the state of German and Austrian military forces.[10] A senior British General, Sir John Hanbury-Williams, was appointed as British military representative at the Russian military headquarters (the *stavka*), while Admiral Richard Phillimore was also sent to the *stavka* as British naval representative. The result of these changes was to set in place outside the formal diplomatic structure numerous new points of contact in Russia between British representatives and the Russian authorities, with the result that it became harder than before for the Ambassador and his staff to act as the principal conduit between the British and Russian governments.

Buchanan waged a strong campaign to defend the influence of his Embassy in this new environment, but it was not an easy task. The number of professional diplomats posted to Petrograd did not increase significantly during the war, and it was not possible for them to conduct in person all the specialist technical and financial questions at issue between the British and Russian governments. Buchanan was more willing to deal with the 'nuts and bolts' questions of alliance politics than Benckendorff in London, perhaps because he recognised that the Embassy would become more isolated than ever if it did not reorient its focus in this way. The Ambassador was himself directly involved in discussions about the supply of munitions and finance to Russia, particularly when these became vexed enough to command the attention of the Russian Foreign Minister or other senior members of the Russian diplomatic establishment. He also attempted to assert the Embassy's role as the primary institution coordinating the activities of the official British presence in Petrograd, although he was constantly infuriated by the failure of at least some military and civilian representatives to keep him informed about their activities. Buchanan's sensitivities on this matter were well-known in London. The organisation of the Intelligence Mission was overhauled in 1915 in such a way as to make its personnel appear more accountable to the Military Attaché at the Embassy (although the reform was in reality largely cosmetic), while Admiral Phillimore at the *stavka* was instructed to keep Buchanan abreast of all his dealings with senior Russian officials. Nevertheless, the Foreign Office archives for the period are full of bad-tempered notes from Buchanan complaining about the cavalier way in which he was treated by British military personnel of various ranks. While the Ambassador's frustrations were understandable, the increase in the density and complexity of the Anglo–Russian relationship meant that many issues simply could not be accommodated within the framework of conventional diplomacy.

Buchanan was most concerned about protecting his authority on directly political matters, but given the high political salience of such seemingly arcane technical questions as the supply of munitions he found it difficult to achieve his objective. He was particularly perturbed that British civilian officials and soldiers who were not under his direct control might send back to London misleading information about the political situation in Russia, forcing him to spend much of his time countering incorrect 'political gossip'.[11] The Ambassador was also doubtless concerned about defending his Embassy's status as the principal source of authoritative information and advice on Russian affairs. His concerns may, ironically, have been misplaced. Since the British Foreign Office itself lost a great deal of autonomy and influence during the war years,[12] the influence of the dispatches and letters sent there by the Ambassador in Russia was questionable. While Buchanan's reports were routinely read by members of the Cabinet and circulated to officials in interested departments, the diplomatic establishment's loss of status and power during the war meant that its members' views were by no means necessarily of primary importance in determining the development of policy.

Even though Buchanan disliked the way in which the central role of professional diplomats in the Anglo–Russian dialogue was challenged during the war years, he was ready to change the way he went about his own work in Petrograd. The British Foreign Office and Diplomatic Service had for generations insisted that their members did not interfere in the internal affairs of the other great powers. While this diplomatic convention was not always followed, Buchanan himself was by instinct strongly disinclined to play any overt political role in Russian politics; he was even reluctant to acknowledge the cheers of the crowd outside the British Embassy on the day that Britain declared war against the central powers. Nevertheless, as the scale of the defeats on the battlefield triggered growing protests in Russia against the ministers appointed by the Tsar, the Ambassador intervened directly in an effort to persuade Nicholas to appoint men more likely to command public support and unite the population behind the war effort, despite the risks attendant on such a blatant attempt to influence the course of domestic policy. In the autumn of 1915, he sought the permission of the Foreign Office in London to speak to the Tsar about the growing domestic unrest, permission which was quickly forthcoming from Grey and Nicolson, who both had faith in the Ambassador's instinctive caution and tact. The attempt was in the event almost abandoned, apparently following advice from Sazonov, who feared that it might alienate Nicholas altogether and make him even less willing to consider reform. Nevertheless, Buchanan persisted in his plan and at the start of November he had an audience with the Tsar at which he warned him about the dangers of failing to respond to public demand for 'a thorough reform of... a corrupt and inefficient bureaucracy'.[13] The Ambassador was realistic enough to recognise that his words were unlikely to have much effect, but he doggedly persisted in his efforts throughout the next 16 months, at times arousing great irritation in Court circles from individuals who resented his repeated attempts to prompt the appointment of liberal ministers.[14] Just a few weeks before Nicholas's abdication, Buchanan was still vainly warning Nicholas about the danger of 'revolution and disaster' if he did not respond quickly to the public desire for change.[15]

Buchanan believed that direct appeals to Nicholas represented the most effective way of encouraging the Tsar to appoint more moderate ministers capable of winning the trust of large sections of the population, but his view was not shared by many other British officials in Russia, particularly those who did not belong to the regular diplomatic service. Samuel Hoare criticised the Ambassador for his reluctance to have dealings with liberal politicians who were critical of the tsarist government, which he believed made it harder for the Embassy to exercise influence in such a turbulent political landscape.[16] Such a charge was not in fact altogether fair. Buchanan was certainly reluctant to establish close relations with some of the shriller critics of the regime, but he did encourage the journalist Harold Williams, who was married to a leading activist in the Cadet Party, to keep the Embassy informed about the attitudes which prevailed in liberal circles on important political questions. Bruce Lockhart, who served at the Consulate in Moscow, also established excellent links with members of the reform movement and provided the Embassy with detailed accounts of their activities.[17] And, by the second half of 1915, the Ambassador himself regularly spoke frankly with the handful of ministers in whose discretion he trusted.[18] The very nature of alliance politics made the domestic stability of the Tsarist Empire a subject of legitimate concern to British diplomats in a way that would have been inconceivable in more peaceful times.

The arrival of the Milner Mission in Petrograd at the start of 1917, charged with establishing closer coordination between Britain and Russia on supply matters, symbolised the pressures experienced by the Embassy during the war years.[19] Milner himself was a member of the Cabinet, and although he had not been the first choice to lead the Mission, his appointment was indicative of the extent to which issues of supply had acquired enormous political import. The appointment of Sir Henry Wilson to the Mission reflected the growing importance of military men in conducting the Anglo–Russian relationship. While Buchanan himself spent a good deal of time preparing the ground for the Mission's arrival, many of the Embassy staff bitterly resented the extent to which they were effectively bypassed by Milner and his colleagues. The Ambassador and his staff knew perfectly well that the endless discussions between Russian officials and its guests over questions of supply were virtually pointless given the parlous state of the tsarist government. While Milner's ignorance of the local political situation was not so great as sometimes claimed,[20] the whole ethos of the Mission, designed as it was to reduce the bilateral relationship between London and Petrograd to a series of financial and material transactions, was profoundly inappropriate at a time of social and political upheaval. The loss of a broad diplomatic perspective which the Embassy alone could supply made it harder for London to make sense of the changes taking place in Russia.

THE CENTRAL MINISTRIES

The changing texture of the bilateral relationship between London and Petrograd also had enormous consequences for the operation of the British Foreign Office and the Russian Foreign Ministry. The Foreign Office in London went through considerable organisational upheavals in the first few months of the war, designed to allow it to operate more effectively in the new international environment. During the July Crisis of 1914, a three-shift ciphering system was introduced to help keep up with the number of incoming documents; throughout the rest of the war, the level of correspondence remained at a much higher level than in previous years.[21] A special War Department was set up, based on the old Western Department, while a new semi-autonomous Department of Blockade was established to deal with trade issues. A new Contraband Department was also established. Extra staff had to be appointed to deal with the work; rooms were sub-divided and divided again in order to provide sufficient accommodation for them all. When Charles Hardinge returned as Permanent Secretary in 1916, he barely recognised the institution he had left just six years earlier.[22] Nevertheless, despite this impressive increase in size and activity, the influence of the Foreign Office on policy declined sharply during the war years.

While Sir Edward Grey made a great effort to establish a central policy role for the Foreign Office in the years before 1914, he was quick to recognise that the outbreak of war would have a fundamental impact on the pattern of foreign policy making. The Foreign Secretary realised that military criteria would increasingly govern decisions about the development of Britain's international relations, giving military men and departments such as the War Office much greater influence than before. In his memoirs he recalled, perhaps a little ruefully, that:

> There has been a tendency to judge diplomacy in war by the same standards as diplomacy in peace; to make insufficient allowance for the fact that in war words count only so far as they are backed by force and victories.[23]

Grey was also quick to accept the formal and informal shifts in the pattern of decision-making that took place after the start of the war, even though they effectively reined in the autonomy of his Department. The Foreign Secretary sat in the new War Council, and its successor the Dardanelles Committee, but the minutes suggest that he did not play a commanding role in either body.[24] This was in part because the proceedings were often dominated by the service ministers and military men who could comment with some authority on events taking place on the battlefield. Nevertheless, other civilian ministers, most notably Lloyd George, were not backward at commenting on strategic issues about which they had no great expertise. Nor was Grey's willingness to accept a comparatively passive role the only 'personal' factor tending to rein in the influence of the Foreign Office on the policy making process. Sir Arthur Nicolson, who had replaced Hardinge as Permanent Secretary in 1910, never possessed his predecessor's determination to set his stamp on British policy; by 1914 he was increasingly weary and willing to confine himself 'to relieving Sir Edward Grey of the routine work' of the Foreign Office.[25] In any case, the relationship between Grey and Nicolson was never as close as the one that developed between Grey and Hardinge a few years earlier. The Grey–Hardinge axis which had proved so critical in forging increased Foreign Office autonomy during the period leading up to the Anglo–Russian *entente* was already a thing of the past when war broke out, and was not restored even when Hardinge himself returned as Permanent Secretary in 1916.[26]

Grey himself was not particularly at ease with the changing pattern of international relations during the war, something which became evident in the way he dealt with the Anglo–Russian relationship after 1914. The Foreign Secretary never really became closely involved in detailed matters relating to the supply of financial and material assistance to the Tsarist Empire even though, as has been seen, these increasingly formed the substance of the bilateral relationship between London and Petrograd. During the first few months of the war, before the establishment of the Ministry of Munitions, the War Office was the most important department in London dealing with the supply of war material to Russia; it was Lord Kitchener who played the critical role in the first half of 1915 in establishing new forums and procedures to overcome the chaotic situation which existed at the time.[27] The high-handed behaviour of the Secretary of State for War was of course one of the principal sources of tension in the British Cabinet during the early stages of the war. Even senior officials at the *Commission Internationale de Ravitaillment* felt that officials at the War Office did not keep them abreast of the supply situation, at least as far as Russia was concerned, making it impossible for them to serve as a focus for bringing order to Russia's purchase of war material.[28] Indeed, senior members of the Commission and the Foreign Office on occasion cooperated closely in an effort to gather and exchange information which the War Office appeared unwilling to provide. Grey himself seemed to take little interest in these issues, although copies of the more important documents on the subject were routinely sent to him; nor did Arthur Nicolson, who had little talent at dealing with such administrative problems. Lord Kitchener at the War Office did sometimes send his communications to the Russian military authorities about supply matters via Grey and Buchanan, but he also used British representatives at the *stavka* for the purpose, which made it difficult for the Foreign Office to keep abreast of developments. As a result, a whole host of critical transactions between Britain and Russia took place outside the purview of the Foreign Office. The establishment of the Ministry of Munitions in 1915 changed the pattern somewhat, since its operating structure and ethos put rather more emphasis on cooperation with other ministries. Nevertheless, the involvement of a wide range of individuals and departments in decisions about the supply of munitions and loans to Russia continued to place limits on the Foreign Office's ability to serve as a gatekeeper controlling the flows of information that informed the policy making process.

Grey continued to focus on the traditional concerns of diplomacy after the outbreak of war; indeed, the war-time reorganisation of the Foreign Office was to some extent predicated on a decision to allow him to keep to a minimum the amount of attention he gave to such matters as trade and commerce.[29] The Foreign Secretary's contributions to the War Council and its successors were mostly confined to the offer of advice about the likely reaction of foreign governments to a particular course of action. During the early stages of the war, Grey worked hard to convince other members of the War Council about the importance of preserving good relations with Petrograd, if necessary by making concessions on matters of dispute. In March 1915, he called for a positive response to a note from Sazonov demanding that Russia should be given control of Constantinople and access to the Straits after the end of hostilities; the Foreign Secretary apparently believed that failure to meet Russia's demands would weaken Sazonov's position and damage the long-term prospects for Anglo–Russian cooperation.[30] Grey's lengthiest contributions to discussions in the War Council and its successors were usually about the situation in south-east Europe, presumably because the existence of a cluster of neutral countries in this area during the early months of the war meant that conventional diplomatic methods still had considerable relevance in the struggle for power and influence in the region. The Foreign Secretary was certainly much readier than in 1906–7 to keep his colleagues posted on developments, reading *verbatim* lengthy telegrams which had arrived at the Foreign Office. Discussion of foreign policy questions, including relations with Petrograd, was therefore far more genuinely collective than in the period leading up to the 1907 Anglo–Russian *entente* reviewed in an earlier chapter.[31]

The role of the Foreign Ministry in Petrograd was also greatly affected by the outbreak of war in the summer of 1914. There were many reservations about the prospect of war with Germany and Austria among at least some senior tsarist bureaucrats. The Minister of the Interior, Peter Durnovo, wrote a celebrated memorandum early in 1914 warning that such a development was not in Russia's interests and might create a social and economic crisis severe enough to undermine domestic order.[32] These concerns were echoed by many members of the Court, although the personal commitment of the Emperor to the war never wavered down to the time of his abdication in March 1917. There were also some divisions inside the MID itself, although once war had broken out these normally took the form of disagreements about diplomatic strategy. It was seen in the previous chapter that Sergei Sazonov was reasonably successful at asserting himself inside the Foreign Ministry following his appointment in 1910, although its fragmented organisational structure always placed limits on the extent of his authority. Senior diplomats in post during the war, such as Savinskii in Sofia, made little secret of their disagreement with Sazonov about critical areas of policy.[33] Even Benckendorff in London disagreed strongly with some aspects of Sazonov's policy during the first year of the war. A similar pattern was observable in the central Ministry in Petrograd itself, where the Foreign Minister could not assume that his instructions would always be carried out without demur. While the Foreign Minister was widely identified by his contemporaries as the architect of Russia's foreign policy,[34] his friends and critics alike did not always understand the very real limits on his freedom to make decisions.

Sazonov, like Grey, was not instinctively very interested in many of the new questions that formed the substance of Anglo–Russian relations after 1914. While he had considerable dealings with Buchanan over the 'shells crisis', his Ministry was not directly involved in many of the exchanges that took place between British and Russian representatives about such topics. Indeed, so chaotic was the organisation of Russian armaments production and purchase that even successive ministers of war found it difficult to keep track of the process. The failure of the tsarist state to put in place appropriate mechanisms for ensuring the provision of its armies in the field became the defining issue around which moderate opposition to the regime crystallised, particularly after the early summer of 1915. The establishment of the *zemgor* by urban and rural councils across Russia symbolised the growing gulf between state and society which eventually exploded in the spring of 1917. Sazonov's liberal profile on domestic issues meant, however, that he escaped much of the popular wrath that was directed at other ministers for Russia's defeats in the early stages of the conflict with Germany and Austria. In Britain, popular anger over slaughter on the battlefield was directly channelled into a wide-ranging debate about the origins of the war and the failure of professional diplomats to avert it. In Russia, by contrast, the failure to supply the armies on the Eastern Front focused attention on the administrative shortcomings of the Russian government *in toto*, rather than the failings of the Foreign Ministry alone.

The pattern of foreign policy making predictably fluctuated between the outbreak of war and Sazonov's dismissal some two years later. A variety of institutions and individuals were able to exercise an influence on the process at any one time,[35] something that can be seen in the first few months of 1915 during the period leading up to Russia's formal demand for control of Constantinople. In his memoirs, Sazonov argued that he started negotiations with the British and the French about this issue 'on my personal responsibility... I told nothing of my intentions to my colleagues in the Council of Ministers [since] there was no one among them with whom one could profitably discuss questions of foreign policy'. He also noted that he had not informed the Tsar since he did not want Nicholas's reputation to be affected by any failure in the negotiations.[36] In reality, Sazonov did not have as much autonomy in setting the contours of policy as he subsequently implied. Although the Foreign Minister was from the beginning committed to establishing Russian access to the Straits as one of his country's chief war aims, he refused to accept that the acquisition of Constantinople would necessarily be in the country's interests. However, pressure from liberal deputies in the Duma and conservative elements in the army and at Court forced him to include a demand for the city in the note he sent to the British government on 4 March 1915, starkly illustrating the potential impact of both public opinion and the opinion of key elite groups on the Foreign Minister.[37] Sazonov also found it difficult to encourage the generals at the *stavka* to conduct operations in a way that would increase Russia's diplomatic leverage, noting in his memoirs that there was 'no arguing with the General Staff on questions of strategy'.[38] In January 1915, when the Foreign Minister was anxious to see troops dispatched to the south so as to ensure that Russian forces played a part in any seizure of the Straits from Turkish control, senior generals refused to make troops available for the task, despite Sazonov's claim that it would strengthen his international bargaining position.[39] Sazonov, like Grey, had more influence on the policy making process when dealing with neutral countries, since relations with their governments were still largely conducted within a conventional diplomatic framework. As was the case in Britain, the role of the Foreign Minister and his officials at any one time was governed by changing patterns of political and administrative relationships.

While Sazonov was less interested in domestic policy than Izvol'skii, he too accepted that the new constitutional arrangements set up in 1906, most notably the establishment of a reformed Council of Ministers, made him a member of an *ersatz* Cabinet that had a degree of collective responsibility for the course of public policy.[40] The Foreign Minister was regarded by diplomats at the British Embassy as an instinctive 'liberal' on matters of domestic policy; in reality, Sazonov's views were driven less by any clear ideological principles than by a diffuse commitment to furthering political and administrative changes that would promote greater efficiency and secure popular support for the war. The Foreign Minister was less than complimentary about most of those who served on the Council of Ministers with him between 1914 and 1916. He did not believe that any of them were well-versed in international affairs. He was a particularly fierce critic of V.A. Sukhomlinov, who served as Minister of War during the early stages of the conflict, and refused to consult with him on most important decisions – something which undoubtedly added to the confusion at the heart of government. Sazonov played a key role in the attempt to persuade Nicholas to dismiss some of his more incompetent colleagues, including Sukhomlinov, in the summer of 1915, but by September the Tsar was once again signalling his belief that success on the battlefield could best be secured through strengthening imperial rule rather than entering into a dialogue with the more moderate elements in Russian society. The Foreign Minister's own dismissal in the summer of the following year came about in large part because of his views on domestic issues. Sazonov's argument that greater independence should be given to the Polish provinces in the Tsarist Empire aroused considerable anger in Court circles, although the Foreign Minister had for some time been falling out of favour with the Tsar and his immediate entourage; rumours of his dismissal had periodically swept through Petrograd during the previous few months. Neither of the two men who served as foreign minister between Sazonov's dismissal and the March Revolution, B.V. Stürmer and N.N. Pokrovskii, were by background members of the tsarist diplomatic establishment, symbolising the growing eclipse of the MID and, in the case of Stürmer, the growing (if much debated) influence of the 'dark forces' surrounding Nicholas. Pokrovskii managed to win a fair amount of respect at the British Embassy, but Stürmer was heartily loathed by diplomats there, in large part because he was believed to favour the establishment of a separate peace with Germany. Stürmer in fact only spent a few hours a day at the Foreign Ministry,[41] which might have allowed other officials there to increase their influence on policy, but by the summer of 1916 the situation was too chaotic for any individual or ministry to set a stamp on a policy making process that was becoming ever more confused and fragmented. During his six years in office, Sazonov had worked hard to maximise his independence from both the Council of Ministers and the Tsar. While this on occasion helped to give him a considerable degree of leverage and authority, it also meant that his political position was never very certain in the febrile world of late tsarist politics.

THE ABDICATION OF NICHOLAS II AND ITS AFTERMATH

The abdication of Nicholas II in March 1917 had enormous ramifications both for Russian diplomacy in general and the country's relationship with Britain in particular. Most members of the new Provisional Government which emerged in the wake of the abdication were broadly committed to the war aims articulated by their predecessors. The new Foreign Minister, Paul Miliukov, who had for years been one of the most persistent critics of Nicholas and his ministers, saw no reason to believe that revolution at home should lead to changes abroad.[42] He made few alterations either to the organisation of the Russian diplomatic establishment or to the declared objectives of Russian foreign policy, recalling in his memoirs that he 'valued the existing machine from the point of view of technique and tradition'.[43] A number of diplomats and Foreign Ministry officials refused to serve the new government, which damaged the quality of the reports and advice available to Miliukov, but they were the exception rather than the rule. The new Foreign Minister was strongly committed to the agreement secured by Sazonov early in 1915 with the British and French governments about the future of Constantinople and the Straits. While Miliukov was ready to conduct diplomacy in a more open manner than his predecessors, he was not by instinct critical of many of the practices and institutions associated with the old diplomacy. It was largely for this reason that he rapidly became something of a *bête noire* for members of the Petrograd Soviet, where a majority of members were committed to renouncing the war aims of the old tsarist government in favour of a peace based on the principle of 'no annexations'. The whole question of war aims and diplomacy quickly became one of the defining sources of tension between the Provisional Government and the Soviet. Miliukov's commitment to a set of war aims inherited from the tsarist Government was in reality shared by most of his colleagues, but by the spring of 1917 the struggle for the control of foreign policy became a critical issue in Russian politics that eventually cost Miliukov his job.

The Foreign Minister made little secret that he believed a foreign policy based on the principle of 'no annexations' was neither viable nor desirable, particularly given Russia's interests in obtaining control of Constantinople and the Straits. His position became very difficult in April when the Provisional Government, with some reluctance, agreed to endorse the demands made by the Soviet for a peace which renounced the 'forcible occupation of foreign territories'. The same proclamation also committed Russia, however, to all the 'obligations assumed towards our allies' – a position that appeared to be in direct contravention of the commitment to 'no annexations'. In a covering note which Miliukov sent to the allies with the original proclamation, he chose to emphasise the sections committing Russia to the agreements previously made by the tsarist Government, creating a public furore that soon forced his resignation.[44] His successor, Mikhail Tereschenko, had no previous experience in either domestic or foreign affairs. A strong admirer of Kerenskii, the radical Minister of Justice who eventually took over from Prince Lvov as Prime Minister in July, Tereschenko in practice favoured policies that were similar to those supported by Miliukov during his weeks in office; he was, though, more skilled than his predecessor at winning the confidence of the Soviet. Nevertheless, the complexities of the political and military situation meant that no foreign minister could hope to exercise a dominant role in shaping foreign policy and determining the pattern of Russia's international relations.

Suspicion of the traditional pattern of diplomacy was a defining feature of the political *credo* of most deputies in the Soviet. Secret diplomacy was condemned in an article in the Soviet's newspaper *Izvestiia* as a 'natural offspring of autocracy', while members of the diplomatic establishment were condemned as 'gold-plated gentlemen'.[45] The same paper also called for 'a decisive break with the traditions of the Izvolskiis and the Stürmers in the realm of foreign policy'.[46] The antipathy between leading members of the Soviet and ministers in the Provisional Government was not only reflected in a dispute about war aims; it was also manifested in a fundamental struggle about how foreign policy should be made and executed. Members of the Soviet such as Irakl Tseretelli not only insisted on their right to influence the decisions about foreign policy made by the Provisional Government; they also insisted on their right to be actively involved in the day-to-day business of inter-state relations. It was for this reason that the Soviet played such a critical role in the attempts to bring about unity between the left-wing parties of the various combattant countries, urging the need for socialists across Europe to force their governments to commit themselves to a policy of 'peace without annexations'.[47] The Soviet also played a vital part in the manoeuvres leading up to the controversial Stockholm Conference planned for the summer of 1917. By appealing directly to public opinion in other countries, the Executive Committee of the Soviet helped to undermine the principle that international relations should take place between governments via a well-established set of formal institutions and procedures. The ideology of internationalism could not be contained within the traditional framework of diplomacy. Since the British and French governments showed themselves willing to respond to this new mood by sending to Petrograd representatives believed to have the right socialist credentials to thrive in the radical political environment found in the Russian capital, rather than the more traditional skills associated with members of their respective diplomatic establishments, they effectively gave an added impetus to the radical challenge to conventional diplomacy. When combined with the array of other challenges to the 'old diplomacy' which developed following the outbreak of war, the domestic upheavals in Russia played an important part in tearing apart the values and practices of international life that existed before 1914.

The Russian Embassy in London was also affected by the events taking place in Petrograd in 1917. Benckendorff died from pneumonia a few weeks before the abdication of Nicholas II, and the Provisional Government never appointed a successor, in large part because of disagreements about who should fill the post. Konstantin Nabokov, who had first arrived at the Embassy in the last weeks of 1915, took charge there following the death of the Ambassador. The *Chargé d'Affaires* and most of the diplomats who worked under him were happy to take orders from the new Provisional Government, although many of the military men in London were convinced monarchists who were unwilling to accept the new order of things, a sentiment which naturally created tension among the various official Russian representatives in Britain. Nabokov wrote in his memoirs that the position of the Embassy took on 'an entirely different character'[48] after the March Revolution, prompted in large part by the pressure of events rather than by any deep-seated commitment to change the patterns of conventional diplomatic activity. A Commission sent from Petrograd to investigate the organisation of the Embassy received 'van loads of reports and denunciations'[49] from members of the Russian community in London, but only one diplomat was actually suspended (apparently for his alleged relations with the Russian secret police). The Embassy had in previous years studiously avoided having any links with the political emigrés based in Britain, but following the March Revolution its staff quickly became involved in the process of repatriating erstwhile exiles back to Russia. Nabokov was well aware of the political tensions attendant on this process, warning the Ministry of Foreign Affairs back in Petrograd that the return of Bolshevik emigrés would 'cut the branch upon which you are sitting'.[50] The *Chargé d'Affaires* was, however, repeatedly frustrated by the failure of the MID to respond to his concerns. Miliukov never sent a single private letter to Nabokov during his time as Foreign Minister, leaving Embassy staff feeling isolated and uncertain of how to deal with the problems they faced. When Tereschenko took over, the reports sent to London 'represented the situation [in Petrograd] in brighter colours than were justified by the reality', which did little to ease the Embassy's plight, since it was impossible for staff to gauge the political situation back home.[51] To make matters worse, as the internal disorders in Russia began to undermine the country's military contribution to the war against the central powers, Nabokov found that he was increasingly excluded from important allied meetings taking place in London. The confusion in the Russian capital and the pressures placed on the Embassy by the Russian emigrés in Britain combined to make the situation of Nabokov and his staff extraordinarily difficult.

The March Revolution also transformed the context in which members of the British diplomatic establishment dealt with Russia. The British government moved quickly to recognise the Provisional Government, hoping that it would be more effective than its predecessor at mobilising Russia's resources for the struggle against Austria and Germany, although there was on the whole something decidedly unconvincing about many of the enthusiastic congratulations sent to the new ministers.[52] Nabokov believed that the Foreign Office in London, now headed by Arthur Balfour, following Grey's resignation at the end of 1916, was decidedly sceptical about the changes in Petrograd.[53] He even believed, although without much evidence, that he was himself treated with suspicion by the Foreign Office because he 'rejoiced at the change of regime'. In Petrograd itself, Buchanan made little secret that he believed an eventual restoration of some sort of monarchical regime would represent the best future for Russia,[54] although some of the non-diplomatic representatives, such as Samuel Hoare, were hopeful that the Provisional Government would provide both the political leadership and the administrative reform required to resurrect Russia from the chaos into which it had fallen. The concern expressed by many senior members of the British diplomatic establishment about the March Revolution was not, however, for the most part due to any enthusiastic commitment to the tsarist *ancien regime*; it was, rather, based on an instinctive concern that the Revolution would signify both the growth of domestic radicalism and the export of chaos into the international arena.

The revolution in Russia helped to accelerate changes in the operation and organisation of the British diplomatic establishment that were already underway. The appointment of Lloyd George as Prime Minister a few weeks before the March Revolution undoubtedly had an impact on the foreign policy making process, since his interventionist approach on all matters of foreign policy eclipsed still further the influence of the Foreign Office. The vital role of Russia in the war had for a long time been an article of faith with Lloyd George, who was sceptical about the possibility of achieving a victory on the Western Front alone. Since Russian success on the battlefield was of such importance to the new government in London, its members were ready to contemplate innovations in traditional diplomatic procedures designed to respond to the situation unfolding in Petrograd. In May 1917, Lord Robert Cecil told the War Cabinet that Buchanan was no longer a suitable representative in Petrograd since he was indelibly associated in the public mind with the previous regime. He went on to suggest the need for a new appointee who would be more sympathetic to 'the democratic elements which now predominate in Russia'.[55] The War Cabinet eventually decided to send the Labour politician Arthur Henderson to Petrograd, rather than a professional diplomat, a decision which, not surprisingly, appalled staff at the Petrograd Embassy who were loathe to be bypassed in this way.[56] In the event, Henderson soon realised that he lacked the skills and experience needed to play the role of Britain's representative, and he recommended to London that Buchanan be kept in place. The whole rather ungallant episode showed clearly, however, that the British government was willing to accept the principle that political character rather than professional expertise should on occasion be the criterion used to determine diplomatic appointments.

The British Embassy in Petrograd was itself greatly affected by the March Revolution. The gradual breakdown of order on the streets created growing risks for the staff there, while the rise in prices made it difficult for them to afford even the basic necessities of life. The social rituals of the old diplomacy largely evaporated in the face of high workloads and social disintegration. George Buchanan became more and more interventionist in his dealings with the Provisional Government, on many occasions taking Kerenskii to task for the failure of his ministers to restore order in the towns and discipline in the army.[57] Many other British representatives in Russia, both military and civilian, were even more acid in their comments about the failure of the government to take decisive action to crush the more revolutionary parties. It seems certain that some British soldiers in Russia were involved in the various intrigues which led up to the celebrated attempt by General Kornilov to stage a coup and seize control of Petrograd, although Buchanan himself made it clear that he would not have any dealings with the plotters. In the chaos of 1917, when the British still hoped that the fading might of Russia could be turned against Germany and Austria, the boundary between domestic and international affairs became more blurred than ever. Even George Buchanan, who was by instinct a strong adherent of all the conventions and procedures associated with the old diplomacy, found that he was dragged into a quasi-political and public role that was at odds with all his deepest instincts. The collapse of the tsarist regime unleashed political pressures that oscillated around the globe and challenged conventional patterns of inter-state relations.

The Bolshevik seizure of power in Petrograd on the night of 6–7 November inevitably amplified the challenges to conventional diplomacy brought about by the upheavals that took place in Russia throughout 1917. Just two days later, the new government issued a decree solemnly abolishing secret diplomacy and committing itself 'to conduct all negotiations absolutely openly before the entire people'.[58] Over the next few days, the new Commissar for Foreign Affairs, Leon Trotskii, began the process of publishing the various secret treaties which had been signed by Russia during the war. The Bolshevik government also appealed to the various belligerent governments – and, more significantly, directly to their populations – for immediate peace. In the event, Trotskii's naive hope that he would soon be able to 'shut up shop',[59] as global revolution transformed the structure of the global order, proved to be quite wrong. Lenin's willingness to accept the harsh German terms demanded at Brest–Litovsk during the first few months of 1918, in return for peace, represented a first attempt by the Bolshevik government to come to terms with the durability of the state system. Over the next few decades, the Soviet government continued to promote its interests vigorously within the structures and procedures of the global diplomatic order, while simultaneously using such non-state institutions as the Comintern to further its goals by non-traditional means. The Bolshevik Revolution helped to bring about major changes in the pattern of international life, but it never succeeded as its authors hoped in supplanting the need for formal diplomatic relations between governments.

NOTES

1. Useful material about the attempts by the Russian Government to purchase munitions in Britain during the war can be found in Keith Neilson, *Strategy and Supply, passim*; also see D.S. Babichev, 'Deiatel'nost' russkogo pravitel'stvennogo komiteta v Londone v gody pervoi mirovoi voiny (1914–1917)', *Istoricheskie zapiski*, 57 (1956), pp. 276–92.
2. See, for example, *Mezhdunarodnye otnosheniia v epokhu imperializma*, Ser. 3, Vol. 6, pt. 1, Benckendorff to Sazonov, 23 September 1914; Benckendorff to Sazonov, 27 September 1914.
3. Babichev, 'Deiatel'nost' russkogo komiteta', p. 280.
4. *Mezhdunarodnye otnosheniia*, Ser. 3, Vol. 6, pt. 1, Benckendorff to Sazonov, 3 November 1914.
5. *Mezhdunarodnye otnosheniia*, Ser. 3, Vol. 6, pt. 2, Benckendorff to Sazonov, 24 January 1915.
6. Nabokov, *Ordeal of a Diplomat*, p. 37.
7. *Mezhdunarodnye otnosheniia*, Ser. 3, Vol. 7, pt. 1, Benckendorff to Sazonov, 10 March 1915.
8. S.J.G. Hoare, *The Fourth Seal*, p. 237.
9. On Walpole's time in Russia, including material about the press bureau, see Rupert Hart Davis, *Hugh Walpole: A Biography*, esp. Chapters 10–11.
10. For a useful account, see Keith Neilson, 'Joyrides? Intelligence and Propaganda in Russia, 1914–1917', *Historical Journal*, 24, 4 (1981), pp. 885–906.
11. FO 371/2446/156, Buchanan to Grey, 20 December 1914.
12. For a useful discussion, see Roberta M. Warman, 'The Erosion of Foreign Office Influence in the Making of Foreign Policy', *Historical Journal*, 15, 1 (1972), pp. 133–59.
13. FO 800/75, Buchanan to Foreign Office (Grey), 5 November 1915.
14. Hughes, *Inside the Enigma*, pp. 74–6.
15. Buchanan, *Mission to Russia*, Vol. 2, p. 49.
16. Hoare, *Fourth Seal*, pp. 241–2.
17. On Lockhart's reports from Moscow, see Michael Hughes, 'British Diplomats on the Eve of War and Revolution', *European History Quarterly*, 24, 3 (1994), pp. 341–66 *passim*.
18. See, for example, Buchanan's conversation with Krivoshein, detailed in FO 371/2454/140516, Buchanan to Foreign Office, 28 September 1915.
19. For a useful account of the Milner Mission, see Neilson, *Strategy and Supply*, pp. 225–48; for memoirs of some of the participants, see Lindley Papers, MS 1372/2, p. 28; C.E. Callwell (ed.), *Field Marshal Sir Henry Wilson: His Life and Diaries* Vol. 1, pp. 301–27; Buchanan, *Mission to Russia*, Vol. 2, pp. 52–4.
20. For Lloyd George's criticisms of Milner, see Lloyd George, *War Memoirs*, Vol. 3, p. 1587.
21. John Tilley and Stephen Gaselee, *The Foreign Office*, p. 172.
22. Hardinge, *Old Diplomacy*, pp. 196–7.
23. Grey of Fallodon, *Twenty Five Years, 1892–1916*, Vol. 2, pp. 159–60.
24. The minutes of the War Council can be found in the Public Record Office, class CAB 22. The minutes identify individual ministers by name, making it comparatively easy to develop some idea of the attitudes and opinions of a particular individual.

Diplomatic Establishments 1914–17   199

25. Nicolson, *Lord Carnock*, p. 427.
26. Hardinge, *Old Diplomacy*, p. 196.
27. See, for example, Neilson, *Strategy and Supply*, pp. 43–79 for a discussion of the organisation of British assistance to Russia during the first half of 1915.
28. The remainder of this paragraph is based on documents located in FO 371/2447.
29. Tilley and Gaselee, *Foreign Office*, p. 180.
30. CAB 22/1/13, 3 March 1915.
31. Briton Cooper Busch, *Hardinge of Penshurst*, p. 255.
32. 'Durnovo's Advice to the Tsar', in Vernadsky, *Source Book*, Vol. 3, pp. 793–8.
33. Savinsky, *Recollections*, p. 292 ff.
34. Nekludoff, *Diplomatic Reminiscences*, p. 33.
35. Brief details of some of the formal meetings between MID officials and representatives of other ministries about such topics as policy in the case of the disintegration of Turkey can be found in 'Dnevnik ministerstva inostrannykh del za 1915–1916 gg', *Krasnyi arkhiv*, 31 (1928), pp. 3–50.
36. Sazonov, *Fateful Years*, p. 248.
37. W.W. Gottlieb, *Studies in Secret Diplomacy*, p. 68.
38. Sazonov, *Fateful Years*, p. 252.
39. Gottlieb, *Secret Diplomacy*, pp. 88–9.
40. Sazonov himself later claimed in his memoirs that he had no ability to influence domestic policy, but his own account shows several episodes where he did just that.
41. 'Dnevnik ministerstva inostrannykh del', p. 68.
42. Z.A.B. Zeman, *A Diplomatic History of the First World War*, p. 209.
43. Paul Miliukov, *Political Memoirs, 1905–1917*, p. 427. Details of some of the changes made at the MID can be found in Thomas Riha, *A Russian European: Paul Miliukov in Russian Politics*, p. 295.
44. The documents can be found in Robert Paul Browder and Alexander F. Kerensky, *The Russian Provisional Government, 1917*, Vol. 2, Chapter 19.
45. Gottlieb, *Secret Diplomacy*, p. 111.
46. Riha, *Miliukov*, p. 301.
47. See, for example, the 'Soviet Appeal to the Peoples of All the World', in Browder and Kerensky', Vol. 2, pp. 1077–8.
48. Nabokov, *Ordeal of a Diplomat*, p. 74.
49. Nabokov, *Ordeal of a Diplomat*, p. 91.
50. Nabokov, *Ordeal of a Diplomat*, p. 103.
51. Nabokov, *Ordeal of a Diplomat*, pp. 113–14.
52. Lockhart, *Memoirs of a British Agent*, p. 173.
53. Nabokov, *Ordeal of a Diplomat*, p. 82.
54. FO 371/2998/58189, Buchanan to Foreign Office, 18 March 1917.
55. CAB 23/2, War Cabinet 144, 23 May 1917.
56. FO 800/205, Bruce to Clerk, 26 May 1917; FO 800/205, Knox to DMI, 26 May 1917.
57. See, for example, FO 371/2998/171455, Buchanan to Foreign Office, 31 August 1917.
58. Jane Degras (ed.), *Soviet Documents on Foreign Policy*, Vol. 1, p. 2.
59. Leon Trotsky, *My Life*, p. 355.

Conclusion

Even the most cursory study of inter-war diplomacy suggests that the continuities with the pre-war system were as striking as the changes. The diplomatic structures and mentalities familiar in Europe before 1914 were profoundly affected by the First World War, but they were not destroyed by it. Many of the attitudes and practices which were evident during the negotiation of the Treaty of Locarno in 1925 would not have seemed out of place 20 years earlier. The creation of the League of Nations and the rise of Geneva as a central location for diplomatic discourse did not signal the end of traditional means for managing inter-state conflict; rather they provided a new language and institutional framework in which conventional practices and attitudes continued to flourish. As E.H. Carr argued in *The Twenty Years' Crisis*, many of the problems and uncertainties that plagued Europe in the 1920s and 1930s stemmed from the existence of two competing systems of diplomacy, each of which undermined the logic and coherence of the other.

The previous chapters have suggested that the system of old diplomacy which existed on the eve of the First World War was a more complex phenomenon than has sometimes been recognised by historians and students of international relations. These chapters have also suggested that many of the charges made against its practitioners during the first two decades of the twentieth century were fundamentally unfair. It was seen in Chapter 1 that the term 'old diplomacy' has itself always been a somewhat elusive concept that has meant different things at different times to different people. While it is possible to identify some of the defining features of the diplomatic system that existed in Europe in the early years of the twentieth century, it is difficult to provide a precise characterisation of such an inherently complex phenomenon. Nevertheless, Harold Nicolson was undoubtedly right to argue in his 1953 Chichele lectures that the diplomatic system in place before 1914 was characterised by its eurocentricity and its emphasis on the role of great powers in determining the texture of inter-state relations; he was also right to emphasise that the existence of a sense of 'corporate identity' among pre-war diplomats was one of the defining hallmarks of diplomacy before 1914. Even such an acute commentator as Nicolson could not, however, capture all the most important features of the diplomatic order in Europe on the eve of the First World War in the space of a few lectures, with the consequence that he did not give enough attention to the way in which developments in the international diplomatic sphere were often governed by administrative and political changes taking place at the level of the state. As a result, Nicolson was too inclined to underestimate the 'national' dimension of diplomacy, failing to give enough attention to the way in which the participation of diplomats in the international arena was often determined by domestic considerations. A successful diplomat in pre-1914 Europe had to balance the competing demands of the separate domestic and international arenas in which he was expected to operate, reconciling the demands of his own government with the demands of other states and peoples.

Nicolson was particularly impressed by the *esprit de corps* which he believed united diplomats across Europe before 1914, arguing that a degree of detachment from domestic considerations made it easier for them to broker agreements between their governments. Most critics of the old diplomacy writing in the early years of the twentieth century were, by contrast, staunch proponents of the need to 'renationalise' diplomatic establishments, by making sure that their members were more responsive to domestic pressures. Radical writers in Britain such as E.D. Morel and H.N. Brailsford believed that diplomats and Foreign Office officials should be forced to accept greater public scrutiny of their activities, a conviction that was informed by the two men's belief that public opinion was inherently pacific and would not tolerate the supposedly bellicose behaviour of professional diplomats. More moderate critics who sat on such bodies as the Walrond Committee and the MacDonnell Commission were by contrast anxious to ensure that British consuls and diplomats carried out their duties in a way that corresponded with the interests and wishes of important domestic constituencies. Similar patterns of criticism were discernible in Russia, where radicals on the left of the political spectrum dismissed professional diplomats as servants of a crumbling autocratic state committed to the implementation of imperialist policies, while moderates expressed dismay at the organisational incoherence of the Foreign Ministry and the ineptitude of its staff. The common themes in this international chorus of criticism were that members of national diplomatic establishments had shown themselves to be too detached from the prevailing values and sentiments of the national political and administrative systems to which they belonged, while at the same time demonstrating a lack of the skills and knowledge needed to meet the demands placed upon them by their fellow countrymen.

The case-studies presented in previous chapters have cast doubt on some of these assumptions. It has been seen that members of both the British and Russian diplomatic establishments were seldom able to establish themselves as the supreme arbiters of foreign policy. In Britain, for example, the role of the Foreign Office in policy making towards Russia fluctuated sharply in the 20 years before the 1917 Revolution, in line with a whole constellation of domestic and international circumstances. It is true that the triumvirate of Grey, Hardinge and Nicolson played a pivotal role in formulating policy during the months leading up to the establishment of the Anglo–Russian *entente* in the summer of 1907. It would be quite wrong, however, to imagine that the achievement of a rapprochement with St Petersburg was in some sense a Foreign Office policy imposed by officials there in the face of massive opposition. The logic of a rapprochement with Russia was in reality deep-rooted in the changing structure of the international environment. The Balfour administration had already given serious attention to the whole question in 1903–4, while the domestic crisis in Russia during 1905–6 meant that the government in St Petersburg was always likely to be far more conciliatory and willing to make concessions than in previous years. And, while there was certainly a good deal of anxiety about an agreement with Russia on the left of the political spectrum in Britain, most members of the Campbell-Bannerman Cabinet had no great objection to such a policy. Grey and Hardinge were effective at insulating the negotiations with Russia from wider political pressures, but there is little evidence that the Anglo–Russian convention was foisted on a hesitant cabinet or a reluctant nation. Indeed, while Grey's commitment to a russophile policy did become a standing source of irritation to many on the left of his party in the years leading up to 1914, it was Izvol'skii in Russia who faced the most serious opposition when trying to promote the cause of an Anglo–Russian agreement during 1906–7. Few senior members of the British political establishment were completely opposed to the principle of an agreement with St Petersburg, but numerous leading soldiers and officials in Russia were very hostile indeed to the prospect of such a development. Izvol'skii had to battle with his own officials in the Foreign Ministry as well as with other ministers and members of the General Staff in order to gain support for an agreement. While it would be wrong to suggest that the Russian Foreign Minister only secured the agreement with London in the teeth of unified opposition from other ministers and senior officials, he was certainly faced with much more coherent and determined obstruction than Grey ever encountered. Nevertheless, in Russia as in Britain, the victory of the supporters for an Anglo–Russian agreement in 1906–7 does not really tell us much about the role of the diplomatic establishment in the foreign policy making process *per se*. All it reveals is that the matrix of political and international circumstances was for a brief time such that the advocates of an agreement within the two diplomatic establishments were able to have their way. There is, in short, little real evidence that members of either the British or Russian diplomatic establishments were consistently able to dictate the course of foreign policy in the years before 1914. While skilful individuals could maximise their influence and room for manoeuvre, the policy making process in both countries was too complex and multi-faceted to allow it to be dictated by a single institution or coterie of individuals. Neither the Foreign Office in London nor the Foreign Ministry in St Petersburg were able to establish themselves as the gatekeeper or guardian of foreign policy making.

One other favourite charge made against the old diplomacy was that its practitioners were incompetent, although the nature of their supposed shortcomings varied a good deal according to the perspectives and values of different critics. Radical writers focused much of their attention both before and after 1914 on the failure of diplomats across Europe to manage international tensions and prevent the outbreak of war. Diplomats were on some occasions accused of being instinctively bellicose and committed to a belief that war was an endemic feature of the international system. E.D. Morel argued in *Morocco in Diplomacy* that the growing tension between Britain and Germany in the first decade of the twentieth century was in large part due to the machinations of officials in the British Foreign Office rather than to the baneful effects of German militarism. In *The War of Steel and Gold*, Brailsford attacked the commitment of diplomats across Europe to the principle of the balance of power, arguing that 'Alliances give no security that the stable equilibrium will be maintained'.[1] Francis Neilson argued in his 1915 book on *How Diplomats Make War* that the readiness of members of the British Foreign Office to engage in secret diplomacy in the years before 1914 had played a pivotal role in fostering the kind of international suspicion and mistrust that had subsequently exploded into war.[2] Each of these writers also believed, however, that the bellicose instincts and penchant for secrecy displayed by leading diplomats across Europe were not simply a result of individual or corporate malfeasance, but were rooted instead in the nature of the dominant international and domestic order. Brailsford, for example, argued in *The War of Steel and Gold* that international tension was rooted in an imperialist conflict for markets and resources, rather than a straightforward rivalry between various national governments for power and prestige. Radical critics of the old diplomacy in Russia similarly condemned officials at the Foreign Ministry there for executing an imperial policy that was founded on the principles of war and conquest. The Soviet newspaper *Izvestiia* bitterly attacked the 'behind-the-scenes diplomatic work' that allowed the tsarist government to commit itself to expansionist policies that had made war virtually inevitable.[3] In both Britain and Russia, the failure of diplomats to secure peace was seen as a consequence of flaws in the prevailing diplomatic structures and practices, as well as evidence that professional diplomats were themselves imbued with values and beliefs that made it hard for them to further the cause of international harmony.

The vexed question of the causes of the First World War is of course far beyond the scope of this book, but the previous chapters have certainly cast doubt on the idea that most practitioners of old diplomacy were willing to countenance war as a necessary and even desirable feature of the international order. The members of the British and Russian diplomatic establishments in fact devoted enormous energy in the 20 years before 1914 to avoiding war and pursuing alternative means of managing and resolving international conflict. The failure of many radical writers in the two countries to recognise this was largely due to their uncritical assumption that diplomats formed an integral part of a unified national political elite whose members shared common attitudes on important matters of domestic and international politics. In reality, however, both British and Russian diplomats and foreign ministry officials were often appalled by the more aggressive voices that were so frequently audible in their two countries. It was seen in Chapter 5 that Count V.N. Lamsdorff devoted enormous energy to opposing the elaborate schemes for Russian imperial expansion in the Far East, which won such favour in Court circles early in the twentieth century, precisely because he feared that they might lead to conflict with the other great powers. Izvol'skii's desire to negotiate a convention with Britain in 1906–7 was matched only by his determination to ensure that it did not damage relations between St Petersburg and Berlin. Charles Hardinge's despair over Curzon's attempts to promote British influence beyond the Indian frontier in 1904–5 echoed a wider sentiment among senior officials in the British Foreign Office and Diplomatic Service that imperial adventures which might lead to international complications and conflict with other great powers should whenever possible be avoided. The moderating role of diplomats and Foreign Office officials in both Britain and Russia was never clearer than at times of crisis such as the Dogger Bank affair of 1904, when the ability of members of the two diplomatic establishments to maintain a dialogue between themselves undoubtedly helped to prevent the outbreak of war. Far from reflecting and amplifying the more bellicose sentiments prevalent in their respective countries at the height of the crisis, British and Russian diplomats provided a filtering mechanism which reduced the dangers of international conflict and facilitated instead a search for consensus. They were adept at using various types of formal and informal negotiation to identify strategies that could foster compromise between their respective governments. Writers like Morel and Brailsford sought to limit the autonomy and freedom enjoyed by diplomats, in the belief that the cause of peace would be promoted by subjecting them to closer supervision and control; in reality, however, it does not seem fanciful to suggest that such a change might have increased the chances of international conflict, by making it harder for diplomats from different countries to engage in the kind of informal discussions that helped to identify possible areas of compromise. A diplomat committed to maintaining peace could never of course ignore or discount the sentiments and attitudes prevailing in his own country, but he could carefully exploit the fragments of autonomy which he enjoyed in an effort to resolve international conflict by negotiation rather than war.

Critics of the old diplomacy who came from within the political establishment were usually less concerned with questions of peace than with more mundane considerations of efficiency, although the outbreak of war in 1914 did extend concern about the most effective ways of managing international conflict into the political mainstream. There is little doubt that the organisation of both the British and Russian diplomatic establishments at the end of the nineteenth century left a good deal to be desired; administrative procedures were antiquated and inefficient, while resources were often sparse and ill-deployed. Nevertheless, major administrative reforms did take place in the British Foreign Office between 1903 and 1906, which helped to rationalise the existing administrative structures, while diplomats posted abroad were increasingly required to treat their duties as a full-time occupation rather than as a glorified sinecure. The calibre of recruits to both the Foreign Office and the Diplomatic Service also increased sharply from the late nineteenth century onwards. It is of course difficult to measure anything so nebulous as 'effectiveness' when dealing with diplomacy, but there is ample evidence that a concerted process of administrative modernisation and reform was taking place within the British diplomatic establishment early in the twentieth century, which transformed both the organisation and the culture of the Foreign Office and the Diplomatic Service. The situation was less clear cut in Russia, however, where the central Foreign Ministry in St Petersburg was undoubtedly over-staffed and bureaucratically slothful in comparison with its British counterpart. Nevertheless, major changes did also took place in the organisation of the Russian diplomatic establishment in the years before 1914, inspired in part by the new spirit of constitutional and administrative reform engendered by the partial disintegration of the old autocratic order in 1905–6. The Izvol'skii–Gubastov reforms reviewed in Chapter 5 largely originated within the Foreign Ministry itself, proving that at least some senior officials there were sensitive to the shortcomings of their organisation.

If it is true that many of the charges made against the old diplomacy in the early years of the twentieth century were unfair, the question remains as to why so many intelligent commentators were impelled to make such unjust criticisms of its practitioners. The answer is undoubtedly complex. Professional diplomats were among the most obvious scapegoats for the cataclysm that ripped Europe apart after 1914, given their status as the bureaucratic professionals most directly concerned with the conduct of international affairs. To add to their plight, members of the unholy coalition of politicians, newspaper editors and business people who played such a large part in fanning tension in the pre-war years were by no means willing to acknowledge in retrospect their own part in the fatal process, but were instead quite happy to join in the chorus of complaints against the failings of the old diplomacy. In any case, the foppish top-hatted diplomat of caricature was an easy target both for left-wingers and for populist writers in the mainstream press, especially at a time when undeserved 'privilege' was seen in a growing number of countries as being inimical to the causes of both social justice and national efficiency. Above all, however, diplomats and consuls across Europe were condemned by the simple fact that they were forced to respond with limited resources to competing demands. They were expected both to advance national interests and welfare while simultaneously promoting the cause of peace, even though in reality international conflict was in large part created precisely by competition between states for power and resources. As a result, members of the British and Russian diplomatic establishments quickly became scapegoats at home both for national setbacks in the international economic and political arena as well as for breakdowns in international order – something that is doubtless the fate of diplomats at all times and in all places.

Conclusion 207

Students of diplomatic history have over the past few decades turned away from the study of 'what one clerk said to another clerk', recognising that the texture of international relations is determined by a much wider set of pressures than the wishes of diplomats and even governments. Such a development is to be welcomed, since it reflects the fact that the policy making process is governed by a wide range of pressures. At the same time, however, it is too easy to forget that the pattern of diplomacy has always been profoundly affected by the character of individual diplomats and the organisation of the institutions in which they operate. A proper understanding of the relationship between Britain and Russia in the late nineteenth and early twentieth centuries cannot be understood without reference to a vast number of factors, ranging from history through to economics and culture. It should not be forgotten, though, that in the years before 1914 relations between governments were still to a great extent conducted by a handful of individuals working within a particular set of diplomatic institutions and practices. Understanding the fluid nature of the political and administrative order in which they operated must always form part of any attempt to make sense of the texture of international relations on the eve of the First World War.

NOTES

1. Brailsford, *War of Steel and Gold*, p. 19.
2. Francis Neilson, *How Diplomats Make War*.
3. Browder and Kerensky, *Russian Provisional Government*, Vol. 2, p. 1081.

Select Bibliography

A complete list of the literature and archival material relevant to all the topics touched on in this book would be enormous. The following bibliography therefore only contains published and archival material included in the notes, along with a small number of other works that have been of particular value in preparing the text. The date and place of publication given is the date of the edition used and not necessarily the date of first publication. In cases where publication took place simultaneously in the United Kingdom and abroad, only the place of publication in the United Kingdom is listed.

UNPUBLISHED PAPERS

British Library (Manuscripts Section)

Balfour Papers
Campbell-Bannerman Papers

British Library (Oriental and Indian Division)

Curzon Papers

Cambridge University Library

Hardinge Papers
Wallace Papers
Hoare Papers

Churchill College Archives Centre, Cambridge

Spring Rice Papers

House of Lords Record Office

Lloyd George Papers

Imperial War Museum (Department of Documents)

The Papers of Admiral Sir Richard Phillimore
The Papers of Lieutenant J.R. Parsons

Leeds Russian Archive (Leeds University)

The Papers of Sir Francis Lindley

Public Record Office (Kew)

CAB 2	Minutes of the Committee of Imperial Defence
CAB 22	War Council and Successors: Minutes
CAB 37	Papers circulated to Cabinet
CAB 41	Prime Minister's Letters to Monarch
FO 65	General Correspondence before 1906 (Russia)
FO 181	Commercial Correspondence
FO 366	Chief Clerk's Department
FO 369	Foreign Office Consular Department: General Correspondence from 1906
FO 371	Foreign Office Political Department: General Correspondence from 1906
FO 447	Embassy and Consular Archives Russia: Moscow Correspondence 1857–1950
FO 800	Balfour Papers Bertie Papers Curzon Papers Grey Papers Lansdowne Papers Nicolson Papers Spring Rice Papers
HD 3	Permanent Under-Secretary's Department: Correspondence and Papers
WORK 10	Public Buildings Overseas

Royal Archives

Edward VII Papers

PUBLISHED DOCUMENTS AND OFFICIAL PUBLICATIONS

British Parliamentary Papers.
British Documents on the Origins of the War, G.P. Gooch and Harold Temperley (eds), 11 Vols (London 1927–38).
Documents Diplomatiques Francais, 2nd series (Paris, 1930–5).
The Foreign Office List (1894–1918).
General Instructions for His Majesty's Consular Officers (London, 1907).

Iswolsky, Alexandre, *Au service de la Russie: correspondance diplomatique, 1906–1911*, 2 vols (Paris, 1937–9).
Krasnyi arkhiv:
'Anglo-russkaia konventsiia 1907g i razdel Afganistana', 13 (1925).
'Anglo-russkoe sopernichestvo v Persii v 1890–1906 gg', 56 (1933).
'Dnevnik ministerstva inostrannykh del za 1915–1916 gg', 31 (1928).
'K istorii anglo-russkogo soglasheniia 1907 g', 69 (1935).
Mezhdunarodnye otnosheniia v epokhu imperializma, 2nd and 3rd series (Moscow, 1931–40)
Ministerstvo inostrannykh del:
Ezhegodnik ministerstva inostrannykh del (St Petersburg, 1894–1917).
Izvestiia ministerstva inostrannykh del (St Petersburg, 1913).
Ocherk istorii ministerstva inostrannykh del, 1802–1902 (St Petersburg, 1902).
Sbornik konsul'skikh donesenii (St Petersburg, 1898–9).
Sobranie tsirkularov ministerstva inostrannykh del po departamentu lichnogo sostava i khoziaistvennykh del 1840–1908 (St Petersburg, 1908).
Svod rasporiazhenii ministerstva inostrannykh del po departamentu lichnogo sostava i khoziaistvennykh del (St Petersburg, 1912).
Ministerstvo torgovli i promyshlennosti, *Kratkii obzor donesenii imperatorskikh rossiiskikh konsul'skikh predstavitelei za granitsei, postupivshikh v otdel torgovli ministerstva torgovli i promyshlennosti za vremia s 1 ianvaria po 31 dekabria 1915 goda* (St Petersburg, 1916).
The Russian Provisional Government, 1917: Documents, Robert Paul Browder and Alexander Kerensky (eds) 3 vols (Stanford, 1961).
Spisok vysshim chinam gosudarstvennogo, gubernskogo i eparkhial'nogo uprav lenii (St Petersburg, 1910).
Soviet Documents on Foreign Policy, Jane Degras (ed.) 3 vols (London, 1951–3).
Staal, Baron de, *Correspondance diplomatique de Baron de Staal*, Alexandre Meyendorff (ed.) 2 vols (Paris, 1929).
Stenograficheskii otchot gosudarstvennoi dumy (St Petersburg, 1906–14).

NEWSPAPERS AND JOURNALS

Daily Mail
Daily Telegraph
Golos Moskvy
Grazhdanin
Manchester Guardian
The Nation
Novoe Vremia
Rech'
The Times

MEMOIRS, DIARIES AND CONTEMPORARY WRITINGS

Abrikossow (Abrikossov), D.I, *The Revelations of a Russian Diplomat. The Memoirs of Dmitrii I. Abrikossow*, ed. George Alexander Lensen (Seattle, 1964).

Select Bibliography

Angell, Norman, *The Foundations of International Polity* (London, 1914).
Baring, Maurice, *The Puppet Show of Memory* (London, 1987).
De Basily, N., *Memoirs* (Stanford, 1973).
Benckendorff, Count Constantine, *Half a Life: Reminiscences of a Russian Gentleman* (London, 1954).
Beresford, Colonel C.E. de la Poer, 'Kundschaftsdientse', *National Review*, 56 (1910–11), pp. 954–64.
Bompard, Maurice, *Mon Ambassade en Russie, 1903–1908* (Paris, 1937).
Botkin, P.S., *Kartinki diplomaticheskoi zhizni* (Paris, 1930).
Brailsford, Henry Noel, *The War of Steel and Gold* (London, 1914).
Bruce, H.J., *Silken Dalliance* (London, 1947).
Buchanan, Sir George, *My Mission to Russia and Other Diplomatic Memoirs*, 2 vols (London, 1923).
Callwell, Major-General Sir C.E., *Field Marshall Sir Henry Wilson, Bart, GCB, DSO: His Life and Diaries*, 2 vols (London, 1927).
Chamberlain, Sir Austen, *The Life and Letters of the Right Honourable Sir Austen Chamberlain*, ed. Sir Charles Petrie, 2 vols (London, 1939–40).
Curzon, George N., *Russia in Central Asia in 1889 and the Anglo-Russian Question* (London, 1967).
Fletcher, Giles, 'Of the Russe Commonwealth', in *Russia at the Close of the Sixteenth Century* (London, 1856).
Gerhardi, William, *Memoirs of a Polyglot* (London, 1931).
Gregory, J.D., *On the Edge of Diplomacy: Rambles and Reflections, 1902–28* (London, 1929).
Grey of Fallodon, *Twenty Five Years, 1892–1916*, 2 vols (London, 1925).
Haldane, Richard Burdon, *An Autobiography* (London, 1929).
Hanbury-Williams, Sir John, *The Emperor Nicholas II as I knew him* (London, 1922).
Hardinge of Penshurst, *Old Diplomacy* (London, 1947).
Harris, James (First Earl of Malmesbury), *Diaries and Correspondence*, 2 vols (London, 1844).
Henderson, Nevile, *Water Under the Bridges* (London, 1945).
Hoare, S.J.G, *The Fourth Seal: End of the Russian Chapter* (London, 1930).
Hobhouse, Charles, *Inside Asquith's Cabinet: From the Diary of Charles Hobhouse*, ed. Edward David (London, 1977).
House, Colonel, *The Intimate Papers of Colonel House*, 2 vols (London, 1926).
Izvol'skii, A.P., *The Memoirs of Alexander Iswolski* (London, 1920).
Kalmykow (Kalmykov), Andrew D., *Memoirs of a Russian Diplomat. Outposts of the Empire* (Yale, 1971).
Knox, Sir Alfred, *With the Russian Army, 1914–1917*, 2 vols (London, 1921).
Kokovtsov, V.N., *Out of My Past* (Stanford, 1935).
Kuropatkin, A.N., *The Russian Army and the Japanese War*, 2 vols (London, 1909).
Lamsdorff, Count V.N., *Dnevnik V.N. Lamzdorfa* (Moscow, 1926).
Lamsdorff, Count V.N., 'Iz dnevnika Lamzdorfa', *Voprosy istorii*, 6 (1977), pp. 98–115.
Lloyd George, David, *War Memoirs*, 5 vols (London, 1933–6).
Lockhart, R.H. Bruce, *Memoirs of a Secret Agent* (London, 1937).
Louis, Georges, *Les Carnets de Georges Louis*, 2 vols (Paris, 1926).

Low, Sidney, 'The Foreign Office Autocracy', *Fortnightly Review*, January 1912, pp. 1–10.
Morel, E.D., *Morocco in Diplomacy* (London, 1912).
Morel, E.D., *Truth and the War* (London, 1916).
Morley, John, *Recollections*, 2 vols (London, 1917).
Nabokoff, Constantin, (Nabokov, Konstantin), *The Ordeal of a Diplomat* (London, 1921).
Nekludoff, A.V., *Diplomatic Reminiscences Before and During the World War, 1911–1917* (London, 1920).
Nicholas II, Emperor, *Dnevnik imperatora Nikolaia II, 1890–1906* (Berlin, 1923)
Nicholas II, Emperor, *Letters of the Tsar to the Tsaritsa, 1914–1917* (New York, 1929).
Nicholas II, Emperor, *Journal intimé de Nicholas II* (Paris, 1925).
Onslow, Earl of, *Sixty Three Years* (London, 1944).
Pares, Bernard, *My Russian Memoirs* (London, 1931).
Paléologue, Maurice, *An Ambassador's Memoirs*, 3 vols (London, 1923–5).
Planson, E.A., 'V stabe adm. E.I. Alekseeva', *Krasnyi arkhiv*, vols.41–42 (1930), pp. 148–204.
Ponsonby, Arthur, *Democracy and the Control of Foreign Affairs* (London, 1912).
Ponsonby, Arthur, *Democracy and Diplomacy* (London, 1915).
Rennell Rodd, Sir James, *Social and Diplomatic Memoirs*, 3 vols (London, 1922–5).
Rosen, Baron R.R., *Forty Years in Diplomacy*, 2 vols (London, 1922).
Savinsky, A., *Recollections of a Russian Diplomat* (London, 1927).
von Schoen, Wilhelm Eduard, *The Memoirs of an Ambassador* (London, 1922).
Selborne, Earl of, *The Crisis of British Power: The Imperial and Naval Papers of the Second Earl of Selborne*, ed. D. George Boyce (London, 1994).
Solov'ev, Iu.Ia., *Vospominaniia diplomata* (Moscow, 1959).
Spring Rice, Cecil, *The Letters and Friendships of Sir Cecil Spring Rice*, ed. Stephen Gwynn, 2 vols (London, 1929).
Taube, Baron M, *La politique russe d'avant-guerre* (Paris, 1928).
Tcharykow, N.V., *Glimpses of High Politics* (London, 1931).
Trotsky, Leon, *My Life* (London, 1984).
Trubetskoi, Prince E.N., *Vospominaniia* (Sofia, 1922).
Victoria, *The Letters of Queen Victoria*, ed. George Earle Buckle, 3 vols (London 1932).
Walters, H.H., *Secret and Confidential: The Memoirs of a Military Attaché* (London, 1926).
Witte, Sergei, *The Memoirs of Count Witte* (London, 1921).
Zinov'ev, I.A., *Rossiia, Angliia i Persiia* (St Petersburg, 1913).

SECONDARY WORKS

Ambrosius, Lloyd C., *Woodrow Wilson and the American Diplomatic Tradition: The Treaty Fight in Perspective* (Cambridge, 1988).
Anderson, M.S., *The Rise of Modern Diplomacy, 1450–1919* (London, 1993).
Andrew, Christopher, *Secret Service: The Making of the British Intelligence Community* (London, 1985).

Select Bibliography 213

Babichev, D.S., 'Deiatel'nost russkogo pravitel'stvennogo komiteta v Londone v gody pervoi mirvoi voiny (1914–1917)', *Istoricheskie zapiski*, 57 (1956), pp. 276–92.
Beloff, Max, *Lucien Wolf and the Russian Entente, 1907–1914* (London, 1951).
Bendiner, Elmer, *A Time for Angels: The Tragicomic History of the League of Nations* (London, 1975).
Bestuzhev, I.V., *Bor'ba v Rossii po voprosom vneshnei politiki, 1906–1910* (Moscow, 1961).
Bolsover, G.H., 'Izvolsky and Reform of the Ministry of Foreign Affairs', *The Slavonic and East European Review*, 63, 1 (1985), pp. 21–40.
Brook-Shepherd, *Uncle of Europe: The Social and Diplomatic Life of Edward VII* (London, 1975).
Busch, Briton Cooper, *Hardinge of Penshurst: A Study in the Old Diplomacy* (Hamden, Connecticut, 1980).
Carr, E.H., *The Twenty Years Crisis* (London, 1995).
Cecil, Lamar, *The German Diplomatic Service, 1871–1914* (Princeton, 1976).
Chapman A., and Greenaway, J.R., *The Dynamics of Administrative Reform* (London, 1980).
Chickering, Roger, *Imperial Germany and a World Without War: The Peace Movement and German Society, 1892–1914* (Princeton, 1975).
Churchill, Rogers Platt, *The Anglo-Russian Convention of 1907* (Cedar Rapids, 1939).
Cline, Catherine Ann, 'E.D. Morel and the Crusade against the Foreign Office', *Journal of Modern History*, 39, 2 (1967), pp. 126–37.
Cline, Catherine Ann, 'E.D. Morel: From the Congo to the Rhine', in A.J. Anthony Morris (ed.), *Edwardian Radicalism, 1900–1914* (London, 1974), pp. 234–45.
Cline, Catherine Ann, *E.D. Morel, 1873–1924: The Strategies of Protest* (Belfast 1980).
Cromwell, Valerie and Steiner, Zara, 'The Foreign Office before 1914: A Study in Resistance', in Gillian Sutherland (ed.), *Studies in the Growth of Nineteenth-Century Government* (London, 1972), pp. 167–94.
Crowe, Sibyl and Corp, Edward, *Our Ablest Public Servant: Sir Eyre Crowe GCB, GCMG, KCB, KCMG, 1864–1925* (Braunton, 1993).
Davies, Dido, *William Gerhardie: A Biography* (Oxford, 1990).
Dilks, David, *Curzon in India*, 2 vols (London, 1969).
Dugdale, Blanche E.C., *Arthur James Balfour*, 2 vols (London, 1936).
Feldman, Eliyahu, 'British Diplomats and British Diplomacy and the 1905 Pogroms in Russia', *The Slavonic and East European Review*, 64, 4 (1987), pp. 579–608.
Fleming, Peter, *Bayonets to Lhasa* (London, 1961).
Florinskii, M.F., 'Sovet ministrov i ministerstva inostrannykh del v 1907–1914gg', *Vestnik Leningradskogo universiteta*, 1 (1978), pp. 35–9.
Fraser, Peter, *Joseph Chamberlain: Radicalism and Empire, 1868–1914* (London, 1966).
Friedberg, Aaron L., *The Weary Titan: Britain and the Experience of Relative Decline, 1895–1905* (Princeton, 1988).
Geyer, Dietrich, *Russian Imperialism. The Interaction of Domestic and Foreign Policy* (Leamington Spa, 1987).

Select Bibliography

Germany on the Brain (London, 1915).
Gilmour, David, *Curzon* (London, 1994).
Gooch, G.P., *Before the War: Studies in Diplomacy*, 2 vols (New York, 1938).
Gottlieb, W.W., *Studies in Secret Diplomacy During the First World War* (London, 1957).
Grainger, J.H., *Patriotisms: Britain, 1900–1939* (London, 1986).
Grenville, J.A.S., *Lord Salisbury and Foreign Policy at the Close of the Nineteenth Century* (London, 1970).
Guttsman, W.L., *The British Political Elite* (London, 1963).
Hale, Oron James, *Publicity and Diplomacy* (London, 1940).
Hamilton, Keith, *Bertie of Thame: Edwardian Ambassador* (London, 1990).
Hamilton, Keith and Langhorne, Richard, *The Practice of Diplomacy* (London, 1995).
Hankey, Lord, *Diplomacy by Conference: A Study in Public Affairs, 1920–1946* (London, 1946).
Hart Davis, Rupert, *Hugh Walpole: A Biography* (London, 1952).
Heinrichs, Waldo H., 'Bureaucracy and Professionalism in the Development of American Career Diplomacy', in John Braeman, Robert H. Brebner and David Brody (eds), *Twentieth Century American Foreign Policy* (Columbus, 1971), pp. 119–206.
Hinsley, F.H. (ed.), *British Foreign Policy Under Sir Edward Grey* (Cambridge, 1977).
The History of the Times: The Twentieth Century Test, 1884–1912 (London, 1947).
Hopkirk, Peter, *The Great Game* (Oxford, 1990).
Horn, D.B., *Great Britain and Europe in the Eighteenth Century* (Oxford, 1967).
Hosking, Geoffrey, *The Russian Constitutional Experiment: Government and Duma, 1907–1914* (Cambridge, 1973).
Howard, Christopher, *Splendid Isolation* (London, 1967).
Howe, M.A. de Wolfe, *George von Lengerke Meyer: His Life and Public Services* (New York, 1919).
Hughes, Michael, 'British Diplomats in Russia on the Eve of War and Revolution', *European History Quarterly*, 24, 3 (1994), pp. 341–66.
Hughes, Michael, 'Diplomacy or Drudgery?: British Consuls in Russia in the Early Twentieth Century', *Diplomacy and Statecraft*, 6, 1 (1995), pp. 176–95.
Hughes, Michael, *Inside the Enigma: British Officials in Russia, 1900–1939* (London, 1997).
Hynes, Samuel, *The Edwardian Turn of Mind* (Princeton, 1968).
Ignat'ev, A.V., *Russko-angliiskie otnosheniia nakanune Oktiabr'skoi revoliutsii* (Moscow, 1966).
Ignat'ev, A.V., *Vneshniaia politika Rossii v 1905–1907gg* (Moscow, 1986).
Jones, Raymond A., *The British Diplomatic Service, 1815–1914* (Gerrards Cross, 1983).
Jones, Ray, *The Nineteenth Century Foreign Office: An Administrative History* (London, 1971).
Judd, Denis, *Balfour and the British Empire: A Study in Imperial Revolution, 1874–1932* (London, 1968).
Judd, Denis, *Radical Joe: A Life of Joseph Chamberlain* (Cardiff, 1993).
Kazemzadeh, Firuz, *Russia and Britain in Persia, 1864–1914* (New Haven, 1968).

Kennedy, Paul, *The Realities behind Diplomacy: Background Influences on British External Policy, 1865–1980* (London, 1981).
Kohn, Hans, *Panslavism: Its History and Ideology* (New York, 1960).
Koss, Stephen E., *John Morley at the India Office, 1905–1910* (London, 1969).
Larner, Christina, 'The Amalgamation of the Diplomatic Service with the Foreign Office', *Journal of Contemporary History*, 7, 1–2 (1972), pp. 107–26.
Lauren, Paul Gordon, *Diplomats and Bureaucrats: The First Institutional Responses to Twentieth-Century Diplomacy in France and Germany* (Stanford, 1976).
Lee, Sir Sidney, *King Edward VII: A Biography*, 2 vols (London, 1925–7).
Leventhal, F.M., 'H.N. Brailsford and the Search for a New International Order', in A.J.A. Morris (ed.), *Edwardian Radicalism 1900–1914* (London, 1974), pp. 202–17.
Liddell Hart, Basil, *History of the First World War* (London, 1970).
Lieven, Dominic, *Nicholas II: Emperor of all the Russias* (London, 1993).
Lieven, D.C.B., *Russia and the Origins of the First World War* (London, 1983).
Link, Arthur S., *Wilson the Diplomatist: A Look at his Major Foreign Policies* (Baltimore, 1957).
Lockhart, Robin Bruce, *Reilly: Ace of Spies* (London, 1983).
Mahajan, Sneh, 'The Defence of India and the End of Isolation. A Study in the Foreign Policy of the Conservative Government, 1900–1905', *Journal of Imperial and Commonwealth History*, 10, 2 (1982), pp. 168–193.
Matthew, H.C.G., *The Liberal Imperialists: Ideas and Politics of a Post-Gladstonian Elite* (Oxford, 1973).
Mattox, Henry C., *The Twilight of Amateur Diplomacy* (Kent, Ohio, 1989).
Mayer, Arno, *Political Origins of the New Diplomacy, 1917–1918* (New Haven, 1959).
Mayers, David, *The Ambassadors and America's Soviet Policy* (New York, 1995).
McDonald, David Maclaren, *United Government and Foreign Policy in Russia, 1900–1914* (Cambridge, Mass., 1992).
McDonald, David Maclaren, 'A.P. Izvol'skii and Russian Foreign Policy under 'United Government', in Robert B. McKean (ed.), *New Perspectives in Modern Russian History* (Basingstoke, 1992).
Minto, Mary, Countess of, *India, Minto and Morley, 1905–1910* (London, 1934).
Monger, George, *The End of Isolation: Britain's Foreign Policy, 1900–1907* (London, 1963).
Morgenthau, Hans, 'The Permanent Values in the Old Diplomacy', in Stephen D. Kertesz and M.A. Fitzsimmons (eds), *Diplomacy in a Changing World* (Notre Dame, 1959).
Morris, A.J.A., *Edwardian Radicalism, 1900–1914* (London, 1974).
Morris, A.J. Anthony, *Radicalism against the War, 1906–1914* (Totowa, New Jersey, 1972).
Murray, John A., 'Foreign Policy Debated. Sir Edward Grey and his Critics, 1911–1912', in Lillian Parker Wallace and William C. Askew (eds), *Power, Public Opinion and Diplomacy* (Durham, N.C., 1959), pp. 140–71.
Neilson, Francis, *How Diplomats Make War* (New York, 1916).
Neilson, Keith, *Britain and the Last Tsar* (Oxford, 1995).
Neilson, Keith. 'Joyrides? Intelligence and Propaganda in Russia, 1914–1917', *Historical Journal*, 24, 4 (1981), pp. 885–906.

Neilson, Keith, *Strategy and Supply: The Anglo-Russian Alliance, 1914–1917* (London, 1984).
Newton, Lord, *Lord Lansdowne: A Biography* (London, 1929).
Nicolson, Harold, *The Evolution of Diplomatic Method* (London, 1953).
Nicolson, Harold, *Sir Arthur Nicolson, Bart, First Lord Carnock: A Study in the Old Diplomacy* (London, 1971).
Nightingale, Robert T., *The Personnel of the British Foreign Office, 1851–1929*, Fabian Society Tract, no. 232 (London, 1930).
Nish, Ian, *The Origins of the Russo-Japanese War* (London, 1985).
O'Day, Alan, *The Edwardian Age: Conflict and Stability, 1900–1914* (London, 1979).
D'Ombrain, Nicholas, *War Machinery and High Policy: Defence Administration in Peacetime Britain, 1902–1914* (Oxford, 1973).
Perkin, Harold, *The Rise of Professional Society* (London, 1989).
Platt, D.C.M., *The Cinderella Service: British Consuls since 1825* (London, 1971).
Robbins, Keith, *Sir Edward Grey: A Biography of Lord Grey of Fallodon* (London, 1971).
Ronaldshay, Earl of (Dundas), *The Life of Lord Curzon*, 3 vols (London, 1928).
Ross, Stephen, *Asquith* (London, 1976).
Satow, Sir Ernest, *A Guide to Diplomatic Practice*, 2 vols (London 1922).
Schulzinger, Robert D., *The Making of the Diplomatic Mind* (Middletown, 1975).
Searle, G.R., *The Quest for National Efficiency: A Study in British Politics and British Political Thought, 1899–1914* (Oxford, 1971).
Silberman, Bernard S., *The Cages of Reason* (Chicago, 1993).
Steiner, Zara, 'Elitism and Foreign Policy: the Foreign Office before the Great War', in B.J.C. Mckercher and D.J. Moss (eds), *Shadow and Substance in British Foreign Policy, 1895–1939* (Edmonton, 1984), pp. 19–55.
Steiner, Zara, 'Grey, Hardinge and the Foreign Office, 1906–1910', *The Historical Journal*, 10, 4 (1967), pp. 415–439.
Steiner, Zara, *The Foreign Office and Foreign Policy, 1898–1914* (Cambridge, 1969).
Steiner, Zara, 'The Last Years of the Old Foreign Office, 1898–1905', *Historical Journal*, 6, 1, (1963), pp. 59–90.
Stieve, Friedrich, *Isvolsky and the World War* (London, 1926).
Swanick, H.M., *Builders of Peace* (London, 1924).
Szeftel, Marc, *The Russian Constitution of April 23, 1906* (Brussels, 1976).
Taylor, A.J.P., *The Struggle for Mastery in Europe, 1848–1918* (Oxford, 1954).
Taylor, Philip, 'Publicity and Diplomacy: The Impact of the First World War upon Foreign Office Attitudes Towards the Press', in David Dilks (ed.), *Retreat from Power* (London, 1981), Vol. 1, pp. 42–63.
Teplov, V., *Kniaz Aleksei Borisovich Lobanov-Rostovskii* (St Petersburg, 1897).
Tilley, Sir John and Gaselee, Stephen, *The Foreign Office* (London, 1933).
Ulrichs, Teddy, 'The Tsarist and Soviet Ministry of Foreign Affairs', in Zara Steiner (ed.), *Foreign Ministries of the World* (London, 1982), pp. 513–38.
Verrier, Anthony, *Francis Younghusband and the Great Game* (London, 1991).
Warman, Roberta M., 'The Erosion of Foreign Office Influence in the Making of Foreign Policy', *Historical Journal*, 15, 1 (1972), pp. 133–59.

Weber, Max, *The Theory of Social and Economic Organisation*, ed. Talcott Parsons (New York, 1964).
Wight, Martin, 'The Balance of Power', in Herbert Butterfield and Martin White (eds), *Diplomatic Investigations: Essays in the Theory of International Politics* (London, 1966).
Wilson, John, *A Life of Sir Henry Campbell-Bannerman* (London, 1973).
Wolpert, Stanley A., *Morley and India, 1906–1910* (Berkeley, 1967).
Zeman, Z.A.B., *A Diplomatic History of the First World War* (London, 1971).
Zaionchkovskii, A.M., *Podgotovka Rossii k imperialisticheskoi voine* (Moscow, 1926).

DISSERTATIONS

Corp, E.T., *The Transformation of the Foreign Office, 1900–1907* (University of Kent doctoral thesis, 1977).
Dittmer, Helen, *The Russian Foreign Ministry Under Nicholas II: 1894–1914* (University of Chicago doctoral thesis, 1977).

Index

Abrikossov, Dmitri, 134–6, 143
d'Aehrenthal, Count, A., 75, 165–6
Alexander II (Tsar), 62
Alexander III (Tsar), 87, 124, 131, 136
Alexeev, Admiral, E.I., 158–9
Algeciras Conference, 86
Angell, Norman, 5
Anglo-Jewish Society, 48
Anglo-Russian Press Bureau, 182
Ardingly College, 102
Asquith, Herbert Henry, 34, 42

Bagge, Picton, 23
Balfour, Arthur, 30–2, 34–5, 37–41, 54, 84, 195, 202
Barings Bank, 181
Bark, P.L., 180
de Basily, Nicholas, 134
Bayley, Charles, 101, 103, 105
Belostock (1906 pogrom in), 47–8
Benckendorff, Count, A.K., 37, 39, 50, 53, 79, 81, 84–5, 140–5, 153, 181–2, 189–90
Berchtold, Count, 75
Beresford, Colonel C.E. de la Poer, 76
Berthelot, Philippe, 7, 9, 130
Bertie, Francis, 21, 27, 33
Bezobrazov, A.M., 157–9
Birmingham Chamber of Commerce (submission to Board of Trade Inquiry into the workings of the consular services)
Björko, Treaty of (1905), 152,
Bloody Sunday (January 1905), 89
Board of Trade (Great Britain), 44, 97–8, 119
Board of Trade Journal, 106–7
Boer War, 6, 37
Bompard, Maurice, 74–6, 163
Bosanquet, Vivian, 103
Botkin, P.S., 136
Brailsford, H.N., 5–6, 9, 150, 201, 203, 205

Brest-Litovsk, Treaty of (1918), 197
Bright, John, 4
British Intelligence Mission in Russia, 182
Bruce, H.J., 26
Brunner (Russian consul in Newcastle-on-Tyne), 146
Buchanan, Sir George, 12–13, 65–67, 69–70, 77, 88, 90, 92, 112, 119, 182–5, 187, 189, 195–7
Buxton, Noel, 56

Cambridge University, 22, 67
Campbell-Bannerman, Sir Henry, 34–5, 41, 44, 46, 50, 202
Carr, E.H., 200
Catherine the Great, 62
Cecil, Lord Robert, 9, 196
Chamberlain, Austen, 38
Chamberlain, Joseph, 31
Chancellor, Richard, 1
Chirol, Valentine, 46, 52, 55, 87
Clarendon Commission, 23
Comintern, 197
Commission Internationale de Ravitaillment, 180, 187
Committee of Imperial Defence (CID), 31–2, 35, 44
consuls (British)
 background of officials, 102
 commercial role, 106–8
 criticism of, 97–8
 lack of resources, 100–1
 organisation of consular representation in Russia, 98–9, 102–4
 pastoral role, 104–6
 political reporting role, 108–12
 reform proposals, 97–8, 118–20
 role in collection of secret intelligence, 112–8

218

Index

consuls (Russian)
  concern about quality of officials, 149
  duties, 145
  in Britain, 146–7
  in India, 147–8
  in Persia, 148–9
  status and role within Foreign Ministry, 131,
Cooke, Charles, 113–4
Cranley, Viscount, 67
Crowe, Eyre, 27, 130
Curzon, Lord George, N., 31, 40–1, 43, 54, 204

Daily Telegraph, 47–8, 52, 77
Delcassé, Théophile, 74
Dillon, E.J., 52, 77
Dogger Bank Incident, 17, 80–5, 89, 205
Dreyfus affair, 7
Durnovo, P.N., 171, 188

Edward VII, King, 3, 31–2, 35, 37–8, 44, 82, 141
embassies, British Embassy in St Petersburg
  activities of military attachés, 76–7
  involvement of staff in social life of city, 72–3
  negotiating role, 78–86
  relations with Court, 69–70
  relations with other foreign representatives, 73–6
  relations with Russian Foreign Ministry, 70–2
  reporting role, 86–92
  social and professional background of staff, 64–68
embassies, Russian Embassy in London
  influence on Russian foreign policy, 144–5
  operation and organisation, 141–4
  tenure of staff, 140–1
Ermolov, General, N.S., 180

Erskine, Robert, 101
Eton College, 22, 102

Filosofov, D.A., 164
Foreign Ministry (France, *Quai d'Orsay*), 7–8, 130, 173
Foreign Ministry (Germany, *Wilhelmstrasse*), 10
Foreign Ministry (Russia)
  bureaucratic ethos, 132–3
  calibre of officials, 133–4, 136–8
  criticism of in press and Duma, 126–9
  organisation, 130–2
  organisational reforms (Gubastov reforms), 129–30
  review of role in policy making, 150–4
  role in policy making before Russo-Japanese war, 155–59
  role in policy making before Anglo-Russian convention, 160–5
  role in policy making before 1914, 165–72
  social and educational background of officials, 134–6
Foreign Office (Great Britain)
  attempts by senior officials to limit influence of Cabinet on policy towards Russia, 42–45; to limit influence of public opinion on policy towards Russia, 45–50
  criticism of, 5–7, 9–10
  influence on policy towards Russia during Balfour government, 36–41; during Campbell-Bannerman government, 41–55
  organisational reforms (1903–6), 27–30
  review of role in policy making, 29–36

Foreign Office (Great Britain) – (*continued*)
  role of senior officials in negotiations for Anglo-Russian entente (1907), 50–54, 79–80
  size, 20–1
  social and educational background of officials, 21–5

Giers, N.K., 70, 136, 152
Goethe, 4
Golitsyn, Prince P.A., 133
Golos Moskvy, 128
Goremykin, I.L., 91
Gorst, Sir Eldon, 45
Goschen, Sir William, 66
Government of India, 40–42
Grazhdanin, 170
Great Game, 2, 17, 112, 147, 149
Gregory, J.D., 23–4
Grey, Sir Edward, 5–6, 26, 30, 34–6, 41–56, 63, 80, 144, 184, 186–90, 195, 202
Grove, Montgomery, 101–11, 117, 119
Gubastov, K.A., 129–30, 153, 167, 206
Guchkov, A.I., 166

Haldane, Richard, 34, 44, 56
Hanbury-Williams, General Sir John, 182
Hardinge, Sir Arthur, 40
Hardinge, Sir Charles, 25–27, 29–30, 33–40, 42–51, 53–56, 63, 65–70, 74, 76, 80–5, 88–90, 92, 108–10, 112, 130, 156, 186–7, 202, 204
Harrow School, 102
Hartwig, N.G., 71, 136, 140, 153–4, 169–71
Henderson, Arthur, 196
Hoare, Samuel, 182, 184, 195
Hobhouse, L.T., 56,
Hodgson, Robert, 100
Home Office (Great Britain), 27
Howard, Sir Henry, 66

India Office, 31, 43–4, 51, 54
Ivan the Terrible, 1
Izvestiia, 193, 204
Izvol'skii, A.P., 8, 47, 49–53, 71, 74–5, 79–80, 129, 133, 136, 138, 143–4, 151, 155, 160–69, 172, 190, 193, 202, 204, 206

Kalmykov, A.D., 131, 133–4, 150
Kapnist, D.A., 133, 138, 153
Katkov, Mikhail, 169,
Kerenskii, Alexander, 193, 196
Kitchener, Lord (Earl Horatio Herbert), 180–1, 187
Knollys, Lord, 81, 84, 89
Kokovtsov, V.N., 165–6
Kornilov, General, L.G., 197
Kuropatkin, General Alexander, 156–7

Lamsdorff, Count, V.N., 47, 71, 74, 81–4, 129, 132–3, 137–8, 152, 155–61, 167, 204
Lansdowne, Lord, 22, 27–8, 30–35, 37–40, 48, 81–5, 97
Lascelles, Sir Frank, 65–6, 69, 87–8
League of Nations, 4, 12, 200
Lenin, 197
Leslie, E.H.J., 23
Lessar, P.M., 137–8
Lindley, Francis, 66–7
Liverpool University, 78, 118
Lloyd George, David, 9, 34, 181, 186, 196
Lobanov-Rostovskii, Prince A.B., 136, 152
Locarno, Treaty of (1925), 200
Lockhart, Robert Bruce, 101–2, 107, 112, 184
Louis, Georges, 74, 163
Low, Sidney, 10–11
Lvov, Prince G.E., 193
Lycée, Imperial Alexander, 135–7, 167

MacDonald, Ramsay, 9, 48
Malecka, Kate, 105
Manchester Guardian, 56
Marlborough College, 102

Martens, F.F., 138
Maxwell, F.P., 25, 45
Meyer, George, 76
MID, see Foreign Ministry (Russia)
Miliukov, Paul, 167, 192, 195
Milner Mission to Russia
 (1917), 185
Ministry of Finance (Russia), 150,
 152, 156, 158–9, 179, 181
Ministry of Munitions (Great
 Britain), 187
Ministry of Trade and Industry
 (Russia), 149, 180
Ministry of War (Russia), 150, 156,
 158, 180
Minto, Lord, 43
Morel, E.D., 5–6, 9–10, 150, 201,
 203, 205
Morley, John, 42–44, 51, 54
Murav'ev, M.N., 70, 144, 152
Murray, Alexander, 101–2,
 104, 107–9

Nabokov, Konstantin, 131, 144,
 147–8, 194–5
The Nation, 56
National Efficiency Movement, 24
National Review, 55
Neilson, Francis, 203
Nicholas II, Tsar, 10, 49–50, 54,
 69–70, 72–3, 84–5, 87–8, 90,
 111, 124–6, 132, 140, 151,
 155, 157–8, 160–1, 163–4,
 166, 169, 171, 184,
 189–92, 194
Nicolson, Sir Arthur, 36, 42–5, 47,
 49–54, 56, 64–6, 68–9,
 74–5, 77, 79–80, 88, 91–2,
 162–4, 184, 186–7, 202
Nicolson, Harold, 13–15, 79, 200–1
Norman, Herman, 25, 45
Northcote-Trevelyan
 Report, 26–7
Novoe Vremia, 11, 127–8, 131,
 150, 166–7, 170

O'Beirne, Hugh, 66–7, 91
O'Conor, Sir Nicholas, 65–6, 69, 79
October Manifesto, 77, 111

Orlov, Prince N.A., 141
Oxford University, 22, 67

Paléologue, Maurice, 74
Palitsyn, General F.F., 164
Pares, Bernard, 77–8, 118–20
Peter the Great, 62, 134
Pichon, Stephen, 7
Phillimore, Admiral
 Sir Richard, 182–3
Plehve, V.K., 88
Pokhitinov, I.F., 149
Poklevskii-Kozell, S.A., 51, 79,
 142–4, 153
Pokotilov, 138
Pokrovskii, N.N., 191
Ponsonby, Arthur, 56
Portsmouth, Treaty of (1905), 74

Rasputin, 88
Rech', 11, 128, 139, 150, 167
Reilly, Sidney, 113
Rennell Rodd, Sir James, 12–13, 26
Ripon, Lord, 44
Rosen, Baron, A.A., 131, 155, 159
Rothschild, Lord Nathaniel, 48
Royal Commission on Reform
 of the Civil Service (the
 MacDonnell Commission),
 6, 64, 97, 201
Rozhdestvenskii,
 Admiral, Z.P., 82–3
Rusin, Admiral, A.I., 180
Russo-Japanese War, 30, 32, 34,
 37–9, 70, 81, 89, 154–59
Russian Freedom Society, 48
Russian Government
 Committee, 180
Russian Purchasing
 Committee, 180
Russo-Chinese Bank, 156
Rutkovskii, M.V., 180–1

Salisbury, Lord, 26–7, 30, 33, 45
Samuel, Stuart, M.P., 48
Sanderson, Sir Thomas, 26–27, 29,
 33–35, 89, 115, 117
Satow, Sir Ernest, 14
Savinskii, A., 189

Sazonov, S.D., 71, 136, 138, 143, 152–3, 167–71, 181, 184, 188–92
von Schoen, W.E., 74–5
Scoones's Academy, 23, 64
Scott, Sir Charles, 38, 65–6, 69, 74, 88–9, 114
Selborne, Lord, 31, 39
Sheffield Chamber of Commerce (submission to Board of Trade Inquiry into the workings of the consular services), 97
Shishkin, N.P., 153
Smith, Captain Aubrey, 76
Smith, Charles, 102–4, 106, 111, 117–8
Speyer, A.N., 154
Spring Rice, Cecil, 45, 51, 56, 66–7, 88–90, 101, 110, 154
de Staal, Baron, G.G., 140–4, 153
Steiner, Zara, 21
Stevens, Patrick, 103, 107, 110, 114–8, 120
Stockholm Conference, 193–4
Stolypin, Peter, 72, 78, 91–2, 165–7, 171
Stürmer, B.V., 191, 193
Sukhomlinov, General, V.A., 191
Sykes, Percy, 148

Taube, Baron, M., 138
Tereschenko, Mikhail, 193, 195
Timchenko-Ruban, General, 180
The Times, 9, 46, 48, 52, 55, 77–8
Treasury (Great Britain), 28, 31, 38, 44
Trotskii, Leon, 197,

Trubetskoi, Prince G.N., 138, 168
Tseretelli, Irakl, 193
Tyrrell, William, 45, 56

Ungern-Sternberg, Baron, 147
Union of Democratic Control, 4, 179

Versailles Peace Conference, 4, 12
Villiers, Francis, 28

Wakefield Chamber of Commerce (submission to Board of Trade Inquiry into the workings of the consular services), 97
Wallace, Sir Donald Mackenzie, 77, 78, 91
Walpole, Hugh, 182
Walrond Committee (1902–3), 6, 97, 201
War Office (Great Britain) 31, 113, 115, 187
Wilhelm II, Kaiser, 10, 152
Williams, Harold, 184
Wilson, Sir Henry, 185
Wilson, President Woodrow, 3, 9, 12
Witte, Sergei, 47–8, 72, 77, 150, 156–8, 170
Wolf, Lucien, 46
Woodhouse, Arthur, 103, 108–9, 119–20

Younghusband affair (1903–4), 41

Zinov'ev, I.A., 163